CHANGING
LIFE
PATTERNS

EXPANDED EDITION

CHANGING LIFE PATTERNS

Adult Development in Spiritual Direction

ELIZABETH LIEBERT, S.N.J.M.

St. Louis, Missouri

Excerpts from Jane Loevinger, *Ego Development: Conceptions and Theories* (San Francisco: Jossey-Bass, 1976) are quoted with permission.

Excerpts from Elizabeth Liebert, "Eyes to See and Ears to Hear," *Pastoral Psychology* 34 (Summer 1989) are quoted with permission.

Excerpts are reprinted by permission of the publisher from THE EVOLVING SELF by Robert Kegan, Cambridge, Mass.: Harvard University Press, Copyright © 1982 by the President and Fellows of Harvard College.

Material adapted from Steven S. Ivy, *The Structured-Developmental Theories of James Fowler and Robert Kegan as Resources for Pastoral Assessment* (Ph.D. diss., Southern Baptist Theological Seminary, 1985), is used with permission of the author.

Cover design: Elizabeth Wright
Cover photograph: © Photo disk

This book is printed on acid-free, recycled paper.

Visit Chalice Press on the World Wide Web at
www.chalicepress.com

10 9 8 7 6 5 4 3 2 1   00 01 02 03 04

Library of Congress Cataloging–in–Publication Data

Pending

Printed in the United States of America

Contents

Preface to the Second Edition

Having a book published begins a unique kind of conversation. One's thinking is now open to anyone who chooses to read the book. Potential dialogue partners increase geometrically. The critics and friends of one's own choosing, whose comments and criticisms, trenchant though they may be, have been delivered personally are now joined by other reviewers, and the strengths and weaknesses of one's thinking, the validity and usefulness of one's conclusion appear in public. One becomes, in a strange kind of way, an observer to the fate of one's own creation, which, from the time it is turned in to the publisher, becomes frozen in the language and thought patterns of that moment. The book says what it says, and tomorrow it will say the same thing, even though someone else has just raised an interesting point.

A second edition becomes a welcome opportunity to say "Wait, there's more!" All the developmentalists upon whom the first edition was based (except Jane Loevinger, who, even then, was retired) have continued to expand their notions of development. The persons we followed through the first edition, Roger, Tom, Mary Beth and Katherine, continued to live in more or less developmentally helpful environments and to make more or less useful developmental moves. Eastminster Presbyterian Church called an interim pastor and now finds itself and its Kitchen Ministry six years into the tenure of a subsequent pastor and pushed to its limits by "the end of welfare as we know it." And the audience of the book opened to include students in pastoral ministry and spiritual direction programs, not just working pastors and spiritual directors.

The exigencies of publishing do not permit me to start at the beginning and rewrite the entire manuscript. I have, however, added a new chapter, in which I suggest the direction of the recent work in the structural theories of development, particularly those developmentalists upon whom the first edition was based, noting the significance for the tasks of spiritual direction and spiritual guidance. Tom, Mary Beth, Roger and Katherine make a brief appearance at Eastminster Presbyterian Church. Finally, I have added a bibliography of the most significant works employed in this volume, providing a tool to facilitate further work in the primary sources themselves.

Special thanks to Jon L. Berquist of Chalice Press for the opportunity of this second edition. His prompt and cheerful replies to all my questions made the work of this revision delightful. Thanks too to Lewis Rambo and Jeanne Stevenson Moessner, both of whom kept me writing about development in the intervening years since the first edition. Thanks to those who have used *Changing Life Patterns* and whose comments have unfailingly encouraged me to "try to get it even clearer." And finally, thanks to my students and spiritual directees, who, by simply living and learning, keep my thoughts about both human development and spiritual direction based in reality.

Introduction

Four persons and one church congregation appear within these pages. Mary Beth, Roger, Tom and Katherine differ significantly from each other and, as individuals, differ even more noticeably from Eastminster Presbyterian Church. Yet each, individuals and congregation alike, participates in the process of spiritual guidance.

The current renaissance in spiritual guidance evolves in dialogue with contemporary insights into human persons and cultures. This work seeks to extend and clarify one aspect of that dialogue, the relationship between adult development and spiritual guidance. It introduces the structural theories of human development and examines how these theories might impact spiritual direction with particular individuals, illustrated by Mary Beth, Roger, Tom and Katherine. Finally, it extends this developmental perspective into issues of spiritual guidance within a congregational setting, exemplified by Eastminster Presbyterian Church.

Spiritual guidance, as I will use the term, refers to all the pastoral responses which have been called "care of souls" or "cure of souls" since the time of Gregory the Great in the sixth century, insofar as these pastoral functions raise our awareness of God's call and our appropriate responses. Spiritual direction particularizes spiritual guidance to each person's unique experiences, life circumstances, decisions and yearnings. Furthermore, spiritual direction always involves an explicit covenant to sensitize persons to God and encourage them to deepen this relationship in all its ramifications. Thus, spiritual direction is a more specific, individualized form of spiritual guidance.

Since spiritual direction most frequently occurs in long-term, one-to-one situations, it provides a somewhat more manageable context for examining the rich developmental contingencies occurring in all forms of spiritual guidance. Attending to individual spiritual direction allows these developmental dynamics to appear more straightforwardly and helps to cultivate a developmental ear. Only after considering at some length the developmental issues in spiritual direction will this developmental perspective be extended to the vastly more complex developmental dynamics involved in the congregation as a whole.

Although this work focuses largely on spiritual direction, I do not wish to produce another general discussion of this ministry. Rather, I stand just slightly outside this process and look at it through contemporary research on how human beings change over

1

time. I bring a developmental perspective to bear on spiritual guidance processes, and ask what difference such a perspective makes
to spiritual direction and then, somewhat more briefly, to spiritual
guidance in a group setting.

The developmental perspective pursued in these pages addresses the human person's potential for seeing, hearing, naming,
celebrating and acting within which all spiritual guidance occurs. It
examines the human side of the divine-human relationship,
namely, our capacities to receive grace and to cocreate with God. It
probes possibilities and limitations in how we human beings structure our world into a coherent whole. It dwells particularly on how
we understand ourselves in relation to the environment and to persons, including our own selves and God. It examines how these
self-interpretations can change over time and, equally useful for
our purposes, why these self-perceptions might not change much at
all. Then it pursues the question: "What difference does all this
make for spiritual guidance?"

Our task involves uncovering various frames of reference,
various "logics" about how the world works, various "hermeneu-
tics," if you will, with which people put the world together. These
largely unconscious or preconscious assumptions about the organization of the world are not left behind when a person meets with a
spiritual director or other minister. Such notions include the following: how "big" one's God is; where one locates God; what responsibility one assumes in relationship to this God; how one
frames moral issues and moral responsibility; how one understands
one's vocation; and how much ability one has to focus on and to
name experiences and feelings. All these factors will significantly
influence the processes of spiritual direction and congregational
spiritual guidance. Thus, communication and empathy may increase as spiritual guides understand the seeker from within that
person's own frame of reference. Accurate empathy is as appropriate and important within spiritual guidance as within other
helping relationships.

It is equally important to know the limits of this developmental perspective. It cannot provide the goal of spiritual guidance,
namely, responding as individuals and as a community ever more
fully to the God who calls. It cannot provide the contents of spiritual guidance; these come to us through the faith of the believing
community, its experience and its centuries of reflection on its
texts, traditions, worship and service. It cannot provide the desire
to grow to maturity in Christ; the Holy Spirit freely gifts us with

this grace. It can, however, provide us with valuable insights about how humans develop and provide many clues about encouraging that process within spiritual direction and congregational spiritual guidance.

The discussion unfolds as follows. The first two chapters introduce the images and assumptions that lie behind my treatments of spiritual direction and human development. The first will serve as an introduction to spiritual direction for persons less acquainted with that term. For those familiar with the dynamics and terminology of spiritual direction, this chapter will locate my perspective within the range of understandings about spiritual direction current today.

The second chapter, the images and assumptions about human development, departs from the tone one might expect in a work in which psychological theory plays a major role. It begins by appropriating a familiar modern fable for my own purposes. My gratitude goes to Antoine de Saint Exupéry for creating the Little Prince —my apologies to him for borrowing this wonderful character for my own purposes. Saint Exupéry is not responsible for the new planet which I have the Little Prince visit on his journeys. Following the fable, I will introduce the assumptions underlying the structural paradigm for development upon which the subsequent treatment rests.

In the third chapter, we will meet Roger, Tom, Mary Beth and Katherine, who will help concretize the unfolding developmental theory. As composites of real people who have formally requested spiritual direction, they will serve as "ideal types," illustrating in rather pure form some of the developmental contingencies underlying the practice of spiritual guidance.

In the fourth chapter, we will resume our reflection on Mary Beth as we explore the theory of change which underlies the structural developmental perspective. Since spiritual guides are in some way concerned with spiritual development, how might that spiritual development be related to general human development? How do people change? How should ministers and spiritual directors be involved in that change process? A nuanced understanding of developmental change must ground all developmentally oriented responses, whether one is a pastor, parent, educator or spiritual director. The subject of the fourth chapter, the possibilities and limits of change, may therefore be far more important than the descriptions of the stages themselves.

The developmental continuum, gleaned from major structural

developmental theories, forms the heart of chapters five, six and seven. A chapter will be devoted to each of the three stages at which most adults cluster, and which I call the Conformist, the Conscientious and the Interindividual stages. In each case, we will examine the transition which precedes the stage, the characteristics of the stage itself, and typical issues which might arise in spiritual direction. Each chapter concludes by following either Roger, Tom or Katherine as they continue in spiritual direction.

In the final two chapters, we will broaden our focus from individual spiritual direction to spiritual guidance in the congregational context. We will examine how developmental dynamics underpin some of the formational processes which occur in every congregation. We hope to learn how to see and act in a developmentally informed way with groups as well as individuals.

This book is addressed to all those whose ministry includes facilitating the spiritual growth of others. Some will understand themselves by the traditional title of spiritual director. Others will understand themselves as ministers or spiritual guides to congregations or to other groups of Christians. Still others will simply see themselves as co-pilgrims, who have been asked by others to walk with them into their sacred places. I include pastors among the readers of this book—though they will be included within the terms minister or spiritual guide—because I assume that their primary responsibility includes the spiritual guidance of the congregation as a whole as well as its individual members. Much as pastoral counselors might immerse themselves for a time in depth-oriented psychotherapy as a way to grasp the underlying dynamics of all human interactions, pastors do well to study the dynamics of spiritual direction for clues about their task of congregational spiritual guidance.

Each group of readers may choose to use this book differently. Those who have little previous acquaintance with the structural theories of human development will find in chapters two and four the essential elements of this perspective. Pastors and others in general ministry settings may find the material in chapters five through seven more specialized than their situation usually requires, and may wish to read chapters eight and nine before these three. On the other hand, spiritual directors may find that the concluding chapters encourage them to think more systemically than their usual one-to-one situation and to grapple with the implications developmental theories pose for group spiritual direction and for a larger congregational context.

Any author writes from within a particular social location. Being clear about mine will also alert readers to my starting points, biases and limitations. I am a white, American, middle-class, Roman Catholic sister whose academic training was concentrated on religion and personality sciences. Although I borrow freely from clinical theory and language, my primary identity is that of spiritual guide, not of counselor, and I employ psychological theory and clinical techniques in service of this basic identity.

As a spiritual director, I find myself most at home in the tradition which originated with Ignatius of Loyola, the sixteenth-century founder of the Society of Jesus, especially as it has been reclaimed and reinterpreted in recent years.[1] This tradition balances both reason with feeling, and contemplation with action. It encourages a variety of prayer forms and offers experientially based, functional rules for discernment. It also insists that spiritual exercises address the capacities and graces of the individual seeker and that the director not come between the seeker and God. As I listen to a spiritual direction conversation, I frequently return to the concepts and dynamics which Ignatius articulated from his experience, although I do filter his perceptions and understandings through my own experiences as a woman who lives in the twentieth-century United States.

As a Roman Catholic who teaches spiritual guidance and spiritual direction to largely Protestant constituencies in seminary and graduate school, I have come to recognize subtle differences in perception, language and theological worldview characterizing those who approach spiritual direction from within Roman or Anglo-Catholic theological and ecclesial perspectives, and those who approach spiritual guidance from the Protestant pastoral care and counseling perspectives. Since I envision both kinds of readers, I have sought to make my language and approach as inclusive as possible of both perspectives and experiences. I do expect, however, that each group will occasionally be puzzled by why I included one point and omitted another, or why I expressed myself this way and not that.

My experience as a woman working with other women in parish and higher education settings and within my own religious congregation convinces me that women's voices and experiences have been underrepresented in personality sciences and in the spiritual tradition passed down to us. I have sought to bring a balance by specifically including research which focuses on their experience. I believe that in so doing, our understanding of human dynamics, men's as well as women's, will become clearer.

I cannot claim to represent women or men from other cultural and socioeconomic backgrounds, though of course I hope that they also will recognize themselves in these pages. No theory or model can encompass the vast topics of human development or spiritual guidance. I offer this developmental perspective as one particular lens, hoping that it will contribute to understanding the process which Paul called coming to "the measure of the full stature of Christ" (Eph 4:13).[2]

I. Images and Assumptions about Spiritual Direction

"What is spiritual direction anyhow? I hear the term, but I don't have any idea how spiritual direction would be much different from pastoral counseling."

"How do I find a spiritual director, and once I find one, what do I do then?"

"I'm preparing for ministry. Should I be preparing to do spiritual direction?"

"John Wesley is my touchstone when it comes to spiritual guidance. What can developmental psychology add over and above the wisdom he models?"

Such questions are common in my present context, a Protestant seminary which is beginning to address the spiritual dimension of theological education from within an ecumenical consortium. These questions, and others like them, make it amply clear that no single understanding currently exists about the nature and context of spiritual direction. I, too, have assumptions which may not be universally shared by other spiritual directors. What, then, do I mean when I speak of spiritual direction? Answering this question requires that we proceed on several levels. We will look first at spiritual direction as a mode of acting involving distinctive ways of seeing, hearing, responding, naming, celebrating and choosing; this section concludes with a definition of spiritual direction. Second, we will explore various elements of this definition, addressing some of the theological and psychological assumptions which undergird this perspective. Next, we will clarify the goal of spiritual direction, distinguishing it from the goal of counseling, pastoral or otherwise. Finally, we will examine the relationship between psychology and theology as it appears in this work and as it impacts the spiritual director's task.

Images of Spiritual Direction

Spiritual direction elicits from both the spiritual director and the seeker particular modes of seeing, hearing, naming, responding, celebrating and acting. Illuminating these qualities sets the context for a more formal description of spiritual direction.

Spiritual direction involves *noticing*. It encourages seeker and director alike to become sensitized to signs of God's activity in the frequently mundane flow of life. Spiritual direction develops the eyes to see God's activity in all its subtle grandeur.

Spiritual direction involves *hearing*. It develops an active listening which encourages, receives, honors and ultimately sets free the language of the soul, the hunger of the heart, the desires of the spirit, the integrity of the whole person.

Spiritual direction involves *responding*, to the seeker, to God's work with the seeker, and to the imperative for action which God's presence invariably sets in motion. God's initiative always elicits a response, but not in any sense a predetermined one. Such seeing and hearing provoke questions: What ought I to do? Where ought I to go? Who am I to be?

Spiritual direction involves *naming*, giving voice to the experience of God in one's own life and in that of others. Without language to express what is happening, this spiritual reality so easily remains submerged, half-grasped, largely private, even incommunicable. Naming brings to life, gives substance, creates the possibility of a shared reality and response. The Christian tradition reveals that we recognize and respond to God from within relationships, within a community of faith. Spiritual direction is a small community of faith, which is set within a community of faith ultimately as large as the Christian community itself, indeed as large as the community of all seekers, past and present.

Spiritual direction involves *celebrating*. After awe, humility, and speechlessness, comes worship. Liturgy, literally "the work of the people," becomes the first work of spiritual direction as we, director and seeker alike, respond to God's presence with prayer or simple ritual.

Ultimately, spiritual direction concerns *acting*. To be a Christian requires the active and deep love of God, self, others, earth. As Christians, we recognize that we are already saved and set free from the powers of darkness. The full experience of that salvation, however, is yet to be realized in ourselves, our relationships or in the rest of the cosmos. To be a Christian means to live in hope that our actions ultimately do matter in the coming of God's perfect reign. Spiritual direction offers one means among many to keep this vision and action alive when much of the culture actively denies its truth.

Christian spiritual direction, then, is an interpersonal helping relationship, rooted in the church's ministry of pastoral care. In this relationship, one Christian assists another to discover and live out in the context of the Christian community his or her deepest values and life goals in response to God's initiative and the biblical mandate. Let me make this particular choice of language and some underlying assumptions more explicit.

Theological and Psychological Assumptions

For many, the very words "spiritual" and "direction" present immediate problems because of their highly imperative and directive connotations. However, this terminology has long historical precedent, and other terms seem unable to cover the reality conveyed by the classical terminology and introduce ambiguities of their own. Consequently, though I will continue to speak of "spiritual direction," I hope to lessen discomfort with this phrase by assigning particular meanings to each of these words.

As I understand it, "direction" does not mean one person telling another what to do, even after careful seeing, listening, naming and celebrating. The "direction" of spiritual direction refers simply to the seeker's orientation. Thus, "direction" is the goal of this interpersonal relationship, not its means.[1] Spiritual direction facilitates the seeker's process of finding her or his own direction, path, process and integrity in dynamic relationship to the person and call of God.

Nor does "spiritual" connote the ethereal or other-worldly. "Spiritual" points to that intangible reality at the core of personality, its animating life principle, its life-breath as a graced human among other creatures. "Spirit" and "spiritual" are simply words which alert us to look for the deepest dimension of human experience.[2] That dimension is not restricted to what we ordinarily think of as holy. Rather, the spiritual suffuses all actions. It can be uncovered in what is said and not said, in the way one moves and holds oneself, the way one enters into intimate and distant relationships, the way one uses time or spends money. Spiritual direction is a process of uncovering and bringing to conscious awareness this deepest level of reality in which each human being lives.

The word "spiritual" also alerts us to look for the presence and action of the Holy Spirit. A deep strand of the Christian tradition speaks of the Holy Spirit as the animating Person of God: The Holy Spirit is God's active presence on our behalf. The Holy Spirit teaches us the meaning of the life, death and resurrection of Jesus of Nazareth, calling to mind what Jesus said while he was present on earth, bringing understanding about who the Christ is for us today. The Holy Spirit names the indwelling, re-creating presence of God within all of creation, in communities of faith and, particularly and uniquely, within each human heart.[3] Thus, the deepest reality of one's being lies where the Holy Spirit and one's human spirit intersect. In Christian spiritual direction—for we will not concern ourselves with spiritual direction in other religious traditions—the Holy Spirit is the true spiritual director. Any human spiritual director simply helps foster the relationship between the seeker and the Holy Spirit. "Spiritual direction," then, describes the search for the traces of the Holy Spirit in one's own spirit and in the world.

Other assumptions about God ground my perspective. The simplest of them is perhaps the most incredible: God is with us. I believe that God desires to be in relationship with individual humans—indeed, with all creatures. The polar opposite of this statement clarifies the magnitude of the positive assertion. Imagine a God who created at the beginning of time and never again interfered with creation, just watched it, perhaps coolly or perhaps even passionately, but from a distance. This deistic God leaves no need for spiritual companionship.

But the relational God whom I believe dwells in the heart of the cosmos does not exist above us or in any way over and against us. "God's will," a phrase which frequently creeps into conversations about upcoming decisions, does not signify something fixed and immutable and "out there"—something one searches for in order to conform to it. Rather, God wills that, using all the given circumstances, one makes the best, most creative choice possible. God's call flows from one's present response as a discrete moment in the constant dynamic exchange that marks all significant relationships.[4]

Furthermore, God always desires our good, and in every event of our lives, God is present. That means that, at some level, God's sustaining presence will be revealed if we have the patience to wait and the eyes to see. Obviously, one must exercise careful pastoral sensitivity in responding to persons who have just suffered severe loss or trauma. No one can ever say for someone else that their suffering is "God's will." Rather, we must stay with—yes, suffer with—such persons, until *they* can recognize the trace of God's supporting and ultimately consoling presence from within their own experience. The discipline of spiritual direction allows no cheap grace. But it does expect to discover genuine grace.

Studies of perception and motivation indicate that we humans notice what we are looking for and also that we overlook what we don't expect, somehow don't want to see or don't have any criteria for interpreting. Indeed, this book will elaborate such processes of selective perception. The corollary may be equally enlightening: the more we look, the more we will see; the more we see, the more we are moved to look for. This psychological truth points to an underlying spiritual reality as well. Seeing God's action in our lives gives us eyes to see that divine action even more frequently.

This faith perspective provides me with the essential grounding for spiritual direction, as for all spiritual guidance. If we believe that all things are saturated by the Spirit of God, that we are surrounded and buoyed continually by God's presence, we will, in fact, begin to notice the signs that this is so. Effective spiritual guidance helps to bring that saturation to greater consciousness so that we may choose how to respond.

Unfortunately, our culture offers us incredibly little assistance in recognizing and affirming the religious dimension of experience. We live in what Morton Kelsey calls a space-time box, where the "really real" is assumed to be that which can be touched, measured, verified by experiment. We are offered few, if any, categories or safe places to speak about transcendent experiences. Spiritual directors, then, perform an essential function in our culture: who else stands for, and provides a place safe enough for subtle or threatening experiences of the transcendent to be noticed, named and befriended?

God's touch can be as delicate as any dream. We are well aware that if we do not notice and record our dreams, they vanish almost before our waking eyes. Religious experience can be equally fleeting. A spiritual direction relationship provides a place to name and therefore to record the delicate religious experiences that, because of distractions and inner resistances, evaporate almost immediately before our conscious awareness.

In employing spiritual direction as a means to foster the individual's relationship with God, I assume that God works uniquely with each individual through ordinary human processes. Kenneth Leech reminds us how central to the Christian tradition is the assertion that the way to the knowledge of God must go through the way of self-knowledge.[5] Analogically speaking, though God is surely "free" to set aside such patterns, God generally operates within the normal boundaries of human functioning. Thus, psychological understandings of human personality can serve in spiritual direction, just as they serve in pastoral counseling, therapy, education, crisis intervention, social casework and other interpersonal helping relationships. Furthermore, the interaction between spiritual director and seeker will participate in the same kinds of psychological dynamics that mark other interpersonal relationships.

From an ecclesial perspective, I understand spiritual direction to be a particular dimension of pastoral care, and as such, I place it within the scope of the church's mission to heal, sustain, guide, reconcile and nurture its members. It flows from this assertion that, at least ideally, spiritual direction takes place within the context of the Christian community. Spiritual direction is a ministry within the church rather than an office; therefore, spiritual directors may come from the ranks of all baptized Christians, not merely from those ordained. In choosing a particular spiritual guide and entering a spiritual direction relationship, the seeker thereby confers authority on the director. This conferral of authority occurs by virtue of the director's experience, learning and giftedness for this ministry. However, responsibility for all the seeker's choices remains with the seeker, never with the director.

I have described spiritual direction as a helping relationship; let me clarify the ways it is similar to and, perhaps more significantly, different from other helping relationships. In all helping relationships, one person assents to serve another in a particular fashion, and in so doing, agrees to put the other's agenda and goals at the center of their relationship. The person on the helping side of the relationship recognizes that an intrinsic, if temporary, imbalance of power exists and assumes responsibility for ethical use of that power in the other party's best interests. She or he further assumes the responsibility to initiate changes in the relationship when the agreement can no longer be fulfilled: for example, when the helper's own agenda or issues interfere with the agreement; when a more basic relationship, such as marriage, obscures the helper's ability to act unambiguously in favor of the other party; or when the helper's services no longer assist in moving toward an agreed-upon goal. Formal spiritual direction shares all these characteristics of helping relationships.

Some differences also exist between spiritual direction and other helping relationships. Both the spiritual director and the seeker, by virtue of their common baptism, belong to the Christian community as equal members of the body of Christ. Both are therefore committed to responsible discipleship within that context. Two nuances in the relationship follow. First, not only seekers, but also spiritual directors must attend to the integrity with which they respond to God, usually through their own spiritual direction. Second, the Christian community context lessens the degree of separation between spiritual directors and seekers, who all share a common eucharistic table. Spiritual guides and seekers are companion-journeyers in the Christian life.

Finally, most theories of counseling and psychotherapy hold that the relationship between the client and the counselor or therapist functions as the change agent. In spiritual direction, by contrast, the effective change agent is the relationship between the seeker and God, not the relationship between the seeker and the spiritual director. The spiritual director underlines and enhances that primary relationship. This difference reflects both obvious and subtle contrasts in goal and in the means to achieve it.

The Goal of Spiritual Direction

The goal of most helping relationships consists in removing some impediment or solving some problem. These difficulties can be as varied as physical illness, ignorance, crippling psychological dynamics, insufficient interpersonal support systems, and legal or financial difficulties. Once the impediment has been removed or the problem solved, the helping relationship terminates. In spiritual direction, however, the goal is the continually deeper realization of what it means to be a human being who has been created and called by a gracious God, as one who lives in a particular place and time, within a particular web of relationships and commitments. As a consequence, spiritual direction generally continues over time, though the intensity may ebb and flow, and spiritual directors may change as circumstances evolve.

Various theological and spiritual traditions within Christianity have expressed the process of spiritual growth in diverse ways, including "discipleship," "sanctification," "deepening one's relationship with God," and "striving for holiness." However, many of these traditional formulations have also fostered privatized, static, disembodied or otherwise dualistic interpretations of either the goal or the processes of spiritual growth. An adequate formulation of this goal should overcome such dualisms as body/spirit, sacred/profane, thinking/feeling, prayer/action, individual/community, male/female and humankind/other creatures by maintaining a dynamic interplay between these poles. Our "spiritual home" lies in interconnection and interdependence more surely than either autonomy or submission, either extremely differentiated or highly enmeshed relationships, either solitude or community. Paul expressed such a unified vision of reality in terms of the most pointed dualisms of his culture: "There is no longer Jew or Greek, there is no longer slave or free, there is no longer male and female; for all of you are one in Christ Jesus" (Gal 3:28).

A key virtue in such a holistic vision of reality is compassion:

> Compassion and solidarity flow from a vision of the self in which connection is a central motif. To be a self in this vision is not to be a separate and isolated individual, but rather to be widely and deeply related to the world and other selves, being shaped by them and in turn shaping a world. Compassion is the full expression of a world view in which we understand ourselves to be communal individuals, members of the one body Paul describes to the Corinthians.[6]

This compassion and connectedness applies to God as the author of creation, so that Dietrich Bonhoeffer can speak of a powerless and suffering God, and Abraham Heschel can speak of God's pathos.[7] God shares in the world's suffering; God is moved by our pain to work in and through us as we suffer. God continually seeks to liberate us, and calls us to join in the divine struggle against suffering.[8] Understood in this context, God's call is not out of the world or away from relationships, but precisely into the heart of the world, into the heart of relationships in order that both might be transformed.

If Christian spirituality is, as Susanne Johnson claims, our self-transcendent capacity to recognize and participate in God's creative and redemptive activity in all of creation,[9] then spiritual growth facilitates transcending ourselves—not *obliterating* ourselves—as we increasingly recognize and join with God in cocreating the world. Kathleen Fischer reminds us that the New Testament depicts the reign of God[10] as a vision of human wholeness for which we are willing to relinquish everything—possessions, security, even our view of ourselves as holy.[11] We could assert, then, that the goal of spiritual growth is deepening our participation in the reign of God here and now. Herein lies the basis of our relationship with God and with all creation; herein lies intimacy with God which is simultaneously intimacy with ourselves and with the world.

Thus far, we have looked at the divine-human relationship primarily from the perspective of who God is and how God acts toward humans. If we shift our perspective and approach the divine-human relationship from the side of humankind, we come face-to-face with a particularly thorny issue, namely, the relationship between the goal of spiritual growth and "maturity." Are they identical, overlapping, or totally distinct? I have intentionally underscored this issue by speaking of spiritual direction as one Christian assisting another "to live out, in the context of Christian community, his or her deepest values and life goals in response to God's initiative and the biblical mandate." Another language perhaps more frequently used to describe the goal of spiritual direction, that of increasing intimacy or relationship with God, reveals important aspects of the goal of spiritual guidance, but downplays the crucial relationship of psychological and spiritual maturity.

"Maturity" is a slippery concept, its meaning at least partly defined by the underlying anthropology of the discipline or theory in which it occurs. In addition, views of an "ideal" (mature) person relate to the culture's most critical issues, and shift as those parameters shift. Various psychologies promote different images of an "ideal person"; likewise, various biblical authors promote different biblical anthropologies. Therefore, our task is to articulate a vision of spiritual maturity which speaks to the critical spiritual questions of our day, while still flowing directly from the general sense of the biblical tradition. In this task, Christian spirituality and theology provide the primary criteria for describing maturity, but the wisdom and nuances provided by the social sciences must also enter the dialogue.

In our search for an adequate biblical anthropology, we inevitably face the problem of which biblical view of the human person to choose. We could select a single biblical anthropology and treat it as foundational, but in doing so, we may fall again into one of the dualisms which have plagued spirituality over the centuries. The biblical canon allows a variety of anthropologies to coexist side by side, sometimes complementing and sometimes apparently contradicting one another. Perhaps this reality offers a useful clue when searching for an adequate biblical anthropology. No single view of the person will suffice as adequate; the tension between the sometimes opposing views invites us to move away from "either . . . or" to "both . . . and" in order to find an adequate view of the human person today.

If we were to treat this principle of "both . . . and" as a way of searching for a biblical anthropology, how might such a hermeneutical principle function? A variety of views of human nature and behavior appears in the Hebrew scriptures, including the following. The various strands in the book of Genesis describe humans as created in God's image and therefore as good. But all is not in order within either individuals or humankind as a whole: sin has entered the world and we constantly feel its effects in violence, pain, suffering, death, ruptured relationships all through the human community, and between the human community and its earth home. Exodus claims that God sides with the oppressed and the outcast, forming a covenant relationship within which an unlikely rabble of slaves in Egypt eventually understood themselves as a chosen people. Amos and other prophets insist that the liberated are not free to oppress once they possess power: slavery, poverty, illness and dependence are evils which we must strive to overcome within our community and beyond. The Psalms encourage us to express the whole gamut of human yearnings and emotions, not just among ourselves, but to God. Proverbs, on the other hand, encourages us to plan, to live soberly, and to use common sense in our familial and civic relationships. Leviticus prescribes restrictive spheres for sexual expression, while the Song of Songs lavishly portrays the beauties of sexual love in explicitly sexual terms. We could continue with emphases gleaned from other books, making our anthropology more inclusive as we add the particular insight of each book or group of books.

If we move to the gospels, we may expect views of the "ideal person" to cluster around each community's views of Jesus, for disciples attempt to live the spirit of their mentor. Mark's Jesus embarks in the power of the Spirit on an itinerant mission of healing, exorcising and preaching, and widens the bounds of kinship to include all who do the will of God. Finally, Jesus enters into his death, and its meaning becomes his last and greatest parable. In Matthew, Jesus fulfills the law and brings it to completion as its greatest teacher. "You have heard it said," says Matthew's Jesus, "but I say to you. . . ." The result is a simpler, freer law of more radically inclusive love. The gospel of Luke describes Jesus in terms of Isaiah's servant of the Lord, who announces good news to the poor, liberty to captives, recovery of sight to the blind, and a year of favor from the Lord. The Jesus of the fourth gospel invites us to radical belief in his person and teaching as the foundation of Christian community: "As the Father has loved me, so I love you; abide in my love. Love one another as I have loved you." Although the gospels differ in the way they portray Jesus, inclusivity emerges quite clearly as a characteristic vision, reinforced by the dynamic tension which results when all four gospels share a place in the same canon.

The other New Testament authors struggle to understand what it means to live as a disciple of Jesus in concrete communities and cultures. They share no single "ideal person" either. The most prolific among them, Paul, individualizes his instructions to the needs of each community, trying to balance the radical demands of the gospel of Jesus Christ with the cultural exigencies of various churches. Perhaps his most enduringly helpful solution to the ambiguity of their situations—and ours—emerges when he points out contrasting strengths and weaknesses which either foster or hinder spiritual maturity. We recognize one list as the "fruit of the Spirit": love, joy, peace, patience, kindness, generosity, faithfulness, gentleness and self-control (Gal 5:23). Again, it is not one or other of these virtues which we should hold up as the norm, but the increase among all of them *in tandem* by which we can assess our decisions in ambiguous situations. Nor can we treat this list as exhaustive; it is one possible summary of the fruits which accompany growth in the inclusive, radical love characteristic of increasing spiritual maturity.

Thus, attempts to describe an "ideal person" are contingent upon specifying the particularities of a given culture, worldview, and community context. No single normative person proves adequate when we proceed, book by book, through the biblical canon. It is possible, however, to hold various biblical views of the human in tension with one another, seeking to grasp the general in the particular, and attempting to proceed by "both . . . and" rather than "either . . . or" formulations. Our very hermeneutical principle, then, also illumines some characteristics of a potentially normative biblical anthropology: it must be inclusive, non-dualistic, flexible and nuanced.

These characteristics, among others, mark the goal of spiritual growth, but they also point toward a biblical view of "maturity." Joann Wolski Conn concludes her brief review of (primarily New Testament) biblical understandings of spiritual maturity in this way:

> In the biblical vision, spiritual maturity is deep and inclusive love. It is the loving relationship to God and others born of the struggle to discern where and how God is present in the community, in ministry, in suffering, in religious and political dissension and in one's own sinful-

ness. Guidelines which help one "test the spirits" do not eliminate the need, ultimately, to trust one's own sense of vocation in the absence of certitude. Maturity is understood primarily as a matter of relationship. Yet the dimension of self-direction and adult freedom is also present in the language of a call to conversion and to fidelity in spiritual darkness.[12]

At a minimum, then, the goals of spiritual growth and "maturity" share some common characteristics, yet spiritual maturity cannot simply be reduced to psychological maturity.

In fact, with others[13] I will claim that psychological maturity forms the ordinary human foundation upon which adequate spirituality rests. Psychological and spiritual growth typically and ideally proceed as two aspects of the same growth process. Psychological growth creates more potential for spiritual growth; spiritual growth spills over into psychological growth. This claim rests upon the unity of the human person, which cannot be divided into the abstract realms of psychological and spiritual.

The Dialogue between Theology and Psychology

Let us select one moment from the long history of western Christian spirituality, the period just prior to Vatican II, to illustrate another foundational principle upon which an adequate anthropology for contemporary spiritual direction might rest. If we were to survey Roman Catholic spiritual theology between the Council of Trent and Vatican II and the humanistic psychology prevalent among religious professionals in the late 1960's, we might conclude that their views of the "ideal person" are diametrically opposed. The first appears to call for death to self and the second for self-actualization. In keeping with the decision to grant priority to biblical/theological views of the human person, are we then to throw out the psychological view in favor of the theological? Clearly a more nuanced solution is necessary. In our era, we can and indeed must dialogue with the social sciences as we seek to elaborate an adequate anthropology for our task. Furthermore, this dialogue must have the character of mutually critical correlation. That is, all the conversation partners must be allowed to address and critique the others' positions.

In order to illustrate briefly how such a dialogue might proceed, let us return to the somewhat simplistic dichotomy posed above, and suggest some aspects (again overly-simplified) such a mutually critical dialogue might include. Feminist psychological theories compel the theological/spiritual tradition to revise unnuanced understandings of such "spiritual" issues as self-denial, self-abnegation, free will and pride.[14] Self-denial can hardly be a virtue when it fosters the kind of overdependent relationships and dysfunctional systems which breed addictive and abusive behaviors, and which then tend to be passed on to succeeding generations. As we come to realize that whole classes of persons have been encouraged to internalize submissiveness as a virtue, finding themselves increasingly disenfranchised and impoverished, we must question our traditional understandings of self-abnegation. Self-abnegation for whom and for what goal?

Some versions of theological anthropology and of humanistic psychology stand to learn about the power of various determinisms from psychoanalytically-oriented psychologies. Free will, the psychoanalytic perspectives demonstrate, is not as free as it often appears. Insight does not always result in changed behavior, even when the person most hurt is the individual himself or herself. Furthermore, a notoriously frequent gap exists between what we say and what we actually do. Many of the forces which impinge on our freedom are not even conscious. They appear to be "the way things are," and as individuals, families and entire social systems, we live them out tacitly and unquestioningly. As Carol Gilligan clearly demonstrated, studies of women and other groups not "present" during theory-building reveal that human nature is far more complex than many ethical systems take into account.[15]

When appropriately chastened on these points, the spiritual tradition in its turn still challenges unnuanced self-actualization theories and calls them to see that the severed relationships between individuals, societies and the world must be reconnected. Autonomy without interdependence is as bankrupt as are the overly-dependent relationships appropriately critiqued by humanistic psychology.

The developmental theories which undergird this book indicate how slow and often arduous human development can be, and how frequently people find it easier to "settle in" than to evolve. These theories also suggest why some people can't seem to grasp what others see as self-evident, and why they understand quite different things when examining the same event. And, critical for the vision of interconnection and inclusiveness which I am posing, these theories illustrate why such inclusiveness is an elusive goal for many persons. That is, from within their proper scope and methodology, developmental theories reinforce what great spiritual giants also knew: growth in holiness is a long, protracted affair, best approached with patience, simplicity, humor, trust in God, and supportive companionship.

Still, the direction of development posited by these theories echoes the characteristics of a normative anthropology which we sketched above: inclusive, non-dualistic, nuanced, and flexible. As later chapters will elaborate in more detail, structural developmental theories indicate that persons progress from being fully at the mercy of their environment to being able to have some influence and control over it; from being totally self-centered and incapable of differentiating "self" from "not-self" to being able to differentiate and integrate subtle differences among people, events and objects in their environment; and from being incapable of relating to other people to being able to relate deeply, intimately and harmoniously with others.[16] Thus, insofar as the developmental view tends to point toward an end-point shared with our theological/spiritual anthropology, its findings may also help illumine some of the possibilities and pitfalls in the journey.

In focusing on the developmental context of spiritual direction, we will expand our understanding of the dynamic contingencies brought by the individual seeker and the director. We will add to our general understanding of human personality, in the interest of grasping more deeply the mystery and uniqueness of persons participating in spiritual guidance. A developmental perspective acts as an interpretive framework through which we listen, helping us better understand the complexity embedded in each conversation and the relationship as a whole. Whether or not we are conscious of doing so, we filter all active listening through a variety of such interpretive grids. To the extent that we are conscious of their variety, and of what each reveals and conceals, can we advance the art of spiritual guidance.

The developmental theories do more for spiritual directors, therefore, than simply assist in framing empathic responses. These theories also help us articulate the *human* competencies which undergird the progressive realization of spiritual maturity. They act as a conversation partner in the continual process of evaluating both the qualities of spiritual maturity and the progress toward this goal.[17]

These same developmental theories, however, need to be supplemented by a theological/spiritual tradition in order to provide sufficient detail and specificity to be most useful to spiritual guidance. The developmental theories remain relatively mute about what motivates us to change in the face of considerable pressure to the contrary, about appropriate ethical responses in increasingly ambiguous situations, about the specific content that religious traditions offer their adherents in the face of ultimate questions. The developmental perspective I offer here can function as a companion, even a forceful one, but it needs to be placed within a wider theological/spiritual view of the goal of human life and growth.

The theological and biblical assumptions set out in this chapter may appear self-evident to many. But I wish to be clear about this perspective and context, because once launched into the psychological viewpoint, I will proceed primarily from that perspective. Ultimately, the psychological context of spiritual direction must take its meaning from its wider theological context and its goal: responding ever more fully to the God who calls.

II. Images and Assumptions about Development

Erik Erikson employs a vivid image at the beginning of his epoch-making book *Childhood and Society*. He speaks of embarking on a "conceptual itinerary."[1] This journey turned out to be one of the most significant statements about human development in the contemporary era. Gradually, and largely because Erikson saw all of life as developmental, the concept of "adult development" ceased to be a contradiction in terms, and became an exceptionally fruitful field for study.

From Erikson, we absorbed the concepts of life cycle, identity crisis, ages and stages of human development and "cogwheeling of generations," his colorful name for the dynamic relationship between one generation and the next. He introduced us to the interplay among biological time clocks, cultural and social realities and the individual ego, and between psychosexual and psychosocial developmental schedules. We have grown accustomed to looking for the tasks and challenges of each period of the human life cycle. Many are familiar with Erikson's "eight ages of man": infancy (whose crisis centers around trust versus mistrust), early childhood (autonomy versus shame and doubt), play age (initiative versus guilt), school age (industry versus inferiority), adolescence (ego identity versus role confusion), young adulthood (intimacy versus isolation), middle adulthood (generativity versus self-absorption and stagnation), and old age (ego integrity versus despair). Because of Erikson, we see that adulthood is not one long, static period, unbroken by the throes typical of adolescence. Instead, we now recognize that adulthood is characterized by its own advances and retreats, its own crises and challenges.

Erikson's images and schedules of development have so evolved that they form part of the intellectual and cultural heritage of psychologically literate American adults. In fact, the concept of development itself has become almost synonymous with the metaphors and concepts traceable to Erikson. As original and creative as Erikson's developmental vision was, the concept of human development had already been cultivated by his well-known predecessors, Sigmund Freud and Carl Jung. While the views of this trio differed concerning the range and driving force of human development, some shared assumptions about human beings formed the basis of an entire paradigm of human development. Other researchers and writers elaborated these developmental images and concepts, greatly increasing the commerce of this paradigm.[2] Not surprisingly, these developmental concepts and images eventually influenced spiritual direction.[3]

Meanwhile, an additional understanding of development took shape, this time following basic parameters set down by Jean Piaget. It is this second set of images and concepts that I wish to pursue at length in this book. Before introducing these Piaget-based theories, I invite you to suspend your disbelief for a few minutes, and come along on another kind of "conceptual itinerary," which, as we shall see, is also a developmental journey.

A Fable and Commentary

Imagine, if you will, that we have crept between the covers of Antoine de Saint Exupéry's book, *The Little Prince*. The story opens someplace in the middle of the desert, during an aviator's desperate scramble to repair his downed plane before he runs out of drinking water. In the middle of the night, a thousand miles from any habitation, he is awakened by an odd little fellow, asking, "If you please—draw me a sheep!" We join the story at the moment when the aviator realizes that the little person has been to several other planets before he came to earth:

> It took me a long time to learn where he came from. The little prince, who asked me so many questions, never seemed to hear the ones I asked him. It was from words dropped by chance that, little by little, everything was revealed to me. . . .
>
> At that moment, I caught a gleam of light in the impenetrable mystery of his presence; and I demanded abruptly:
> "Do you come from another planet?". . .
>
> I had thus learned a second fact of great importance: this was that the planet that the little prince came from was scarcely any larger than a house! . . .
>
> As each day passed I would learn, in our talk, something about the little prince's planet, his departure from it, his journey. The information would come very slowly, as it might chance to fall from his thoughts. . . .[4]

As we reconstruct the story for our own purposes, let us imagine that our little traveler has visited one more planet, a seventh one, before coming to earth. This planet looks rather like an egg, somewhat fatter on one end than the other. As the little prince described it to me, I have made a drawing of that planet:

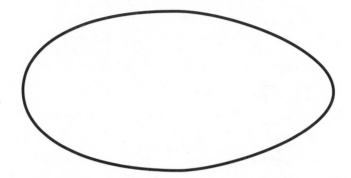

The countries, six of them, are clearly bounded from each other. I learned that each country had a strange name consisting of three letters which were meaningless to me when I first heard them; in order to remember them, I finally resorted to mnemonic devices. So that you can find your way around this planet, let me diagram the countries' boundaries and add their names and my mnemonic devices:

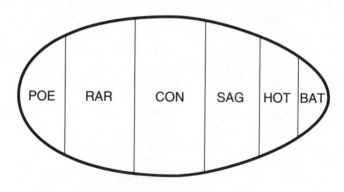

Legend

POE—"Port Of Entry"
RAR—"Rough And Ready"
CON—"Community of Neighbors"
SAG—"Self As Guide"
HOT—"Hold Others Too"
BAT—"Balance All Things"

I also found out that this planet had some rather strange and strict laws. The little prince insisted I had better know what some of them were, just in case I had to travel there. I gathered up everything he said in his circuitous way into the following list.

The first thing a traveler learns is that the only way into the planet is through the country marked POE. Later, in my human attempts to remember the names of the countries, I decided to let POE stand for "Port of Entry," since everybody on this planet must arrive by way of POE.

Then I found out that if I wished to move around on this planet, I had to follow internal rules of travel. I was free to travel wherever I wished on the entire planet if—and only if—I abided by four basic laws of time and space. First, I must make the effort to get to a new country. That didn't sound so bad at first glance, rather obvious, really. Nor did traveling entail much effort initially. Lots of people in POE were on the move, headed for the neighboring country. At least that's what I inferred, since the natives communicated rather poorly. The entire economy seemed set up to accommodate this exodus.

But I soon discovered that some of the other travel restrictions made it increasingly time-consuming and difficult to continue to the farther reaches of the planet. The second rule, I found out, was this: for each country I emigrated to, I was required to stay long enough to learn the local customs, including the language, to explore the whole country pretty extensively, and to settle down for at least some months and take out citizenship. If, after all that time and effort getting acclimatized, I still wanted to pack up and move on to the next country, I was free to do so. Moving on, however, entailed one further sacrifice, which was rule three: I had to give up my citizenship in the country I was just leaving, and agree never to take up permanent residence there again. Returning for even rather extended visits was commonplace, however.

Clearly, many people put out this kind of effort only three or four times in their lives. Then the lure of the unknown ceases to outweigh the comfort of the known. But, just to keep life interesting, there was a fourth rule: in order to decide if I wanted to go to all the trouble and expense of moving to the next country, I could talk to people who had returned on short visits from the neighboring country. If I were sufficiently interested to plan my own scouting excursion, that kind of exploratory foray was quite possible, and even encouraged. So, some few venturesome souls did continue to travel from country to country. Despite the basically positive descriptions of the language, culture and geography of those who ultimately took up residence at the end of this world, the population of the final country, however, was reputed to be quite sparse.

Intrigued by what I had so far learned, I decided to question the little prince about the people in the various countries. Here is a brief summary of what I found out:

POE: This country's inhabitants were poised to relocate, and the country was organized around moving new arrivals to the next country. It was clear that POE wasn't very exciting. With everyone headed on, very little culture existed. Everything seemed quite functional, and eating, drinking, sleeping, and eliminating assumed major significance.

RAR: Everybody agreed that things were a bit more interesting here. More was going on. This country was, however, somewhat rough and uncivilized—and dangerous. The permanent residents seemed almost addicted to the constant excitement, or they found enough like-minded friends, or were making enough money to stay put. So the mnemonic device to remember this country's name came quite easily: "Rough and Ready" would help me remember RAR.

For my part, I decided that it would require just too much energy to keep order at home and in the neighborhood. With no reliable police or fire departments here, and with no consistent discipline in the schools, educating the children and myself would be difficult—even more so while trying to hold a decent job with a company that itself always seemed to be in crisis. The streets of the cities were littered with the casualties of this country's culture—or rather, its lack of it. The next country seemed more civilized and inviting.

Numerous people, it appeared from the little prince's narrative, were relieved to arrive at CON. Compared with RAR, the planned structures and government seemed to have obvious advantages. Rather than function as a law unto themselves, the people here apparently delighted in cooperation. I decided to dub CON "Community of Neighbors." Each community took pride in the organization and order of the neighborhood, agreeing to build similar houses and run their schools based on common values. The citizens spent little energy on organizing the basic laws of living together; clearly everyone expected to join a planned community and fit right in. It was a good place to settle down and raise children, and many people did just that. After some time in CON, the citizens would have explored three countries and learned three languages—quite enough work and movement for the time being.

However, this planet had three more countries. The fourth one, SAG, attracted those people who eventually tired of the planned sameness and group organization in CON. SAG was noted for its self-determining citizens, so I made SAG stand for "Self as Guide." This country seemed set up on a different premise: the people themselves searched out and developed the few laws that the country shared in common, and otherwise, the citizens used their judgment about what was best for themselves. This social vision convinced a goodly number to settle permanently. But eventually, some recognized that doing what's best for themselves and their families, even from the rather enlightened perspective which many SAGites held, still left out other legitimate perspectives, to say nothing of less fortunate citizens. These few people, mostly middle-aged, veteran travelers, prepared to move yet again.

When they arrived at HOT, they soon found out that they were one country short of the end of the world. Glad that they had learned so many languages and cultures, they realized that their horizons should be equally broad. These citizens of HOT considered their minorities important. They spent much energy making sure that all were treated as if they were members of the same human family—an anchoring principle of their society. So, after some pondering, I realized that I could remember their country by the phrase "Hold Others Too."

The HOTites, I noticed, felt somewhat left out of their own planetary community; most other countries thought they were crazy to spend so much energy taking care of others. The sparse population of HOT found it rather difficult to carry out such ambitious social projects. Some of the citizens in HOT showed the strain of trying to keep their social vision, their personal aspirations and their family responsibilities all simultaneously juggled. Most of them learned to approach life with a little bit of humor; otherwise their enormous task would be overwhelming. The citizens in HOT, though, seemed pleased with their choice. As with the citizens of the other countries, they couldn't go back and take up permanent residence. However, a few of them dreamed of an even better country. Some had visited it already and a smaller number had emigrated there. Almost everyone knew about one or two persons who had moved on to the last country. Even though few in number, it seemed these citizens of BAT had made an impact on the world.

The population of this last country at the end of the planet was truly sparse. Only one percent of the planet's population migrated as far as BAT. Many people in the nearby countries looked respectfully to the BATers. But I picked up quickly that the citizens in the first countries thought they were really rather weird, their values too abstract and unattainable for ordinary folks. Since even the little prince had not met many BATers personally, I had to question him closely about what they were really like. I finally decided to remember this final country by "Balance All Things."

The Two Faces of Development

How will this imaginary planet with its rules and peoples help to expand and reinterpret our understanding of development? Let us begin by considering Freud, Jung and Erikson together as one paradigm. Because each of these men linked development in some way to the maturing of the biological organism, we might name this paradigm "maturational development." Since Erikson, most of the maturational developmentalists have investigated the whole life span (or concentrated on one or two particularly rich developmental periods); consequently, a second and equally useful name for the maturational paradigm could be "life-span development."

The maturational theories are tied quite closely to biological age, although they do allow for individual variation in time schedules. Each era brings its particular challenge, which Erikson calls a "crisis," from its original Greek meaning, "decision." A developmental crisis occurs as three dynamics intersect, namely, one's own history and personality, one's biological maturation, and the sociocultural expectations of one's culture. "Good enough" mastery of each era's unique challenge results in the psychic strength necessary to meet the next era's crisis. But inadequate mastery leaves this psychosocial strength at risk as the next task approaches. Again, whether or not one has successfully resolved the crisis of the present or past eras, life continues to bring the subsequent developmental tasks. It is possible, though more difficult, to resolve a psychosocial crisis at a later time. To do so requires that one rework the past unresolved issue in terms of life's present contingencies.

For example, mid-life issues arise at a point when our children tend to become more independent and our parents more dependent, and when our earlier strivings and successes begin to be judged against the realization of the shortness of our remaining years. Whether or not we have dealt with the issues of young adulthood or even of adolescence, mid-life issues eventually appear on the horizon despite attempts to stave them off. Likewise, with or without the experience of adequate parenting or some chances to "practice" for it, the arrival of one's first child forces the issues of intimacy and generativity. The outcome may be particularly problematic when developmental tasks must be handled out of the ordinary sequence, such as when a twelve-year-old becomes a parent before finishing the tasks of childhood, or when a person beginning the adolescent years faces a terminal illness.

A typical list of developmental tasks of adulthood, this one by Robert Havighurst, illumines the expectations that our culture places upon us at various places in the life cycle.

Developmental Tasks of Early Adulthood
1. Selecting a mate and getting married.
2. Learning to live with a marriage partner.
3. Starting a family and rearing children.
4. Getting started on an occupation.
5. Taking on civic responsibility.
6. Finding a congenial social group.

Developmental Tasks of Middle Age
1. Achieving mature social civic responsibility.
2. Assisting teenage children to become responsible and happy adults.
3. Reaching and maintaining satisfactory performance in an occupational career.
4. Accepting and adjusting to the physiological changes of middle age.
5. Adapting to aging parents.
6. Developing adult leisure-time activities.

Developmental Tasks of Late Adulthood
1. Adjusting to decreasing physical strength and health.
2. Adjusting to retirement and reduced income.
3. Adjusting to death of spouse.
4. Establishing satisfactory physical living arrangements.
5. Becoming explicitly affiliated with the late adulthood age group.[5]

For most people, the concept of development usually connotes precisely these kinds of issues and tasks.

The particular contribution which maturational (life-span) theories make to our understanding of personality development occurs by focusing on how we resolve life's inevitable demands. But this developmental paradigm has a limitation too: it has difficulty accounting for the sameness of the individual personality in the face of constant change. Why is it that we don't either disintegrate or metamorphose into different personalities as one developmental crisis after another washes over us? A second developmental paradigm, called structural development, offers a way to deal with this problem.

Another clue also suggests that development may be more complex than the maturational paradigm can explain, though at first the issue does not appear to be linked to development at all. Various persons approach the same developmental tasks in vastly different ways—so different, in fact, that they assign importance to quite dissimilar aspects of their common task. Recall the arrival of a first child, with its ascendant life-span issue of generativity. One person might be preoccupied with survival in a hostile environment of subsidized housing, Aid For Dependent Children, the Welfare system, or staying in school while juggling vastly increased responsibilities with inadequate supports. For her, a good mother "keeps her kids clean and dry and doesn't let them mouth-off." Another person may be primarily concerned with being an ideal parent in the traditional or stereotypical sense characteristic of her socioeconomic, religious or cultural spheres. She might envision a good mother as one "who stays home with her children while they are small because raising a family is the most important thing in any woman's life." A third person may delight in the self-fulfillment and enhanced self-understanding which the presence of this new life has precipitated. She might claim, "a good mother learns lots about life from her own children." Still another person may be preoccupied with a sense of responsibility for and hope that the world's systems can welcome and sustain this new life. For her, a good mother "wants to make life good for other women's daughters and sons"[6] as well as her own. These varying perceptions about mothering constitute qualitatively different contexts to work out generativity. The observant reader might have noticed that they also correlate with the preoccupations of the citizens in four countries from our imaginary planet, RAR, CON, SAG and HOT.

Jean Piaget first provided the conceptual tools to grasp the idea that such differences in worldview could have a developmental basis. Piaget carefully observed how small children approach and solve problems, something most people largely overlook. Eventually he recognized that certain conceptual tools were required to "solve" certain problems, and that these tools were acquired in a predictable order. You may perhaps recall Piaget's description of the progression from sensorimotor thinking in infancy, to preoperational or intuitive thinking in early childhood, to concrete operational thinking around elementary school age, and finally to formal operational thinking during high school years. Each kind of thinking involves a qualitatively more complex logic system, which Piaget called a stage. Successive stages cannot be achieved simply by repeating again and again the earlier set of operations. They can only occur through the application of a whole new principle of logic to the problem.

Let me illustrate from my own experience. As a ninth-grader, I had great difficulty with algebra. Substituting letters where before I had used numbers created a level of abstraction which confounded me. I could do the operations with numbers, but as soon as the letters appeared, I was stymied. Formal operational thinking, the ability to think about the process of thinking, requires one to step outside the literal one-to-one correspondence between a number and an object. But I was reduced to memorizing the ways the operations worked and repeating the pattern every time I wanted to solve a problem. I now recognize that, at fourteen, my ability for formal operational thinking was insufficiently developed to accommodate the level of abstraction algebra required.

Lawrence Kohlberg took Piaget's system and applied it to the development of moral thinking, and in so doing, opened the way for other cognitive structural theories. Soon, the structural pattern broadened from cognitive development into other personality domains. Although they were less restricted to cognitive functions, these new theories still follow, with more or less rigor, the structural pattern traceable to Piaget, namely, structural wholeness, invariant sequence, and generalizability across individuals and cultures.[7]

Of these second-generation Piagetians, two theorists anchor the developmental scheme unfolded in this book. Jane Loevinger's research on ego development provides the skeleton for the stage descriptions, while Robert Kegan's theory of the evolving self augments our understanding of movement and transition.[8] The relationship between the countries on our imaginary planet, the formal stage names used throughout this book, and Loevinger's and Kegan's stage names appear in Table 1. Summaries of Loevinger's stages, "Milestones of Ego Development," and Kegan's stages,

"Balances of Subject and Object as the Common Ground of Several Developmental Theories," appear in Tables 2 and 3. I will explore Kegan's contributions more extensively in subsequent chapters. Here I will concentrate on Loevinger's contributions.

Loevinger's view of the human being provides the flexibility for placing the developmental theory in a wider theological and spiritual context. She understands humans to be active, interacting, partially free to determine their destiny, and changing in the direction of an end or goal, the essence of which she leaves unspecified. Since the normative view of the human person upon which spiritual guidance rests appropriately comes from theology/spirituality, though in dialogue with psychology, the absence of an "ideal person" in Loevinger's theory is not, in itself, crucial for our project as long as the inner direction of development does not contradict goals of spiritual direction. Loevinger holds that development increases flexibility, inclusiveness, differentiation, relationship and reconciliation of dualisms, matching the direction of the biblical anthropology elaborated in the first chapter. Therefore, beliefs about humans which undergird spiritual direction, for example, that humans exercise freedom over at least some areas of life and their destiny transcends this world, are well within the parameters of Loevinger's concept of human nature.

Loevinger defines a stage as a "frame of reference," and ego development as "transformation of motives." These perspectives can potentially undergird an understanding of spiritual discernment. She understands ego not as a part of the mind but as the *process* of meaning-making. For her, ego is formed through the interpenetration of impulse control, interpersonal style, conscious preoccupation and cognitive style. Ego means approximately that to which we refer when we use the word "I"; thus, she calls her stages "I-levels." Loevinger claims that ego development includes moral development and that it provides a more inclusive and powerful framework by which to understand moral development than either Lawrence Kohlberg or James Fowler has described. Her holistic conception of ego fits well with the holistic view of humans prevalent in the contemporary practice of spiritual direction.

Loevinger culled her theory of ego development from a wide variety of sources, past and present, and then refined and corrected it by the empirical data generated from her Washington University Sentence Completion Test.[9] Since Loevinger insisted that all empirical data be accounted for theoretically, the resulting theory does not preempt human "messiness" in order to arrive at a flawlessly logical progression.[10] This fact matches my experience that the real people who come for spiritual direction never fit neatly into stages.

Loevinger frequently claims that "higher stages" are not necessarily "better." In what way can we understand this claim? Certainly "higher stages" are more adequate, in that one has more scope with which to make moral judgments and decisions, more inner resources to call upon in times of stress, greater potential for rich and nuanced relationships. In this sense, later stages are "better" than earlier ones, and we ought to rejoice in stage change precisely because it enhances these potentials. By insisting that "higher is not better," however, Loevinger intends to discourage any tendency to judge others or to attempt to push them on to some "ideal" stage. She wishes to point out that each stage's ascendant strength conceals a corresponding weakness, to which we must also attend. Greater potential also brings greater responsibility, greater ambiguity, and potentially deeper suffering through enhanced awareness.

Furthermore, from the moral and spiritual point of view, "higher" cannot be equated with "holier." Holiness is an intensive quality which flows from the adequacy and appropriateness of one's response given all one's circumstances, including one's stage of development.[11] Children may indeed be holy, though they have not (yet, at least) developed to very "high" stages. One could be holy at any developmental stage, but holiness will be manifested differently at each stage.

A final reason why Loevinger's work is particularly useful for this project concerns her research population. Loevinger and her colleagues did most of the initial test construction and theory building by studying the responses of women and girls. At the time Loevinger was engaged in her large-scale research, such a move was almost unheard of in psychological circles.[12] Besides allowing her to escape the critique which Carol Gilligan later leveled at Kohlberg,[13] Loevinger's predominantly female data base can also help prevent spiritual directors from unconsciously capitulating to the androcentric perspective which permeates much of the spiritual development literature. Male experience, we are learning, is not normative for all.

Loevinger's process of theory building (culling the commonalities out of various literatures on personality development, naming that abstract commonality "ego," and refining and correcting the resulting theory empirically) proves extremely useful for our purposes. First, the resulting concept of "ego" identifies the underlying structure of personality as the process of constituting order and meaning in and around oneself. Since this process also can reveal the ultimate values and goals which comprise the focus of spiritual direction, investigating their transformations will also shed some light on what happens in spiritual direction.

Second, since Loevinger intentionally built her theory eclectically, it is not surprising that her stage descriptions correlate strikingly well with those of a variety of other stage theories.[14] I shall follow her methodological example and assume that developmental theories which have appeared since hers will extend her treatment of ego, while still fitting generally within her broad scheme. And the developmental fare which has appeared in recent years is rich indeed.[15]

Structural Developmental Theories: Commonalities and Processes

Second and third generation structural theorists have nuanced and extended the axioms of stage progression based on Piaget's pioneering work. The following principles, derived from my synthesis of a variety of these theories, describe the structural developmental paradigm and, at the same time, distinguish it from the more prevalent life-span paradigm.

(1) *Structural development highlights the formal ordering principles of personality and the way they function to organize a coherent outlook on the world.* By definition, then, structural theories deal with abstractions, and must resort to a meta-language to describe the *patterns, styles and principles* out of which we act. Maturational theories, on the other hand, tend to describe actions themselves, and therefore can vividly depict familiar and concrete matters. Immediately, one of the reasons why structural developmental theories never appear on self-help best seller lists becomes clear.

(2) *One's ordering system supplies operative assumptions, but is itself rarely available for conscious reflection because one looks out at the world from within its perspective.* The ordering system acts like an unperceived horizon defining what one sees and how one fits these pieces together into a coherent whole. But at earlier stages this horizon is entirely self-evident and tacit—until, that is, another perspective replaces it. Only at later stages does one

have the self-reflective ability to grasp how one's stage of development circumscribes what one sees and how one understands.

(3) *Stages describe qualitatively different styles of viewing reality.* These stages cannot be created by simply summing up prior stages, but require a different ordering axiom to account for each new configuration. By itself, more and more arithmetic did not produce algebra in my 14-year-old mind. Instead, I needed a qualitatively new ability for abstract thinking which could account for both the arithmetic and the algebraic operations. On our imaginary planet, the citizens of one country view reality differently from those of the neighboring countries, and they must learn the language and take out citizenship in each subsequent country they choose to inhabit.

Several structural principles address stage change. (4) *The movement to a subsequent stage requires a "higher order of ordering," to account for the increased complexity.* Therefore, the stages appear in invariant order from simple to complex. Stages cannot be skipped but persons can understand and use any of the simpler ordering systems they have already transcended—in some situations, the simpler systems provide the most elegant and common-sense solution. For example, a child who thinks in concrete operational categories cannot understand the theory of relativity, even though she or he could perhaps recite it. But a theoretical physicist presumably has the ability both to understand the theory of relativity and to explain how it is that two plus three equals five. (5) Research shows, however, that *persons can understand the complexity of from a half to a whole stage ahead of where they are, but they will reframe any greater degree of complexity in terms of their present stage.* Teachers and preachers can expect some of their hearers to take away something different than they said!

(6) *Stage progression, then, is a dialectical movement, with each stage transforming the prior stage and preparing for the next one.* At the same time, (7) *Stages are remarkably stable systems, since they represent entire "logics" or systems of meaning-construction.* Change takes place in such a stable structure only when the stage no longer accommodates the contrary data it must absorb. High school students can be notoriously dualistic in their thinking, seeing complex realities in either/or categories (which they often express as "If I am right, you can't be right"). Eventually, dualistic thinking tends to give way to more relative thinking ("You are entitled to your opinion and I am entitled to mine") and,

we hope, to a considered position within relativism ("You have a truth that I don't, and we might learn from each other"). This transition usually occurs only after logically self-consistent but diametrically opposite points of view collide too frequently to be dismissed as simply an anomaly.[16]

Significantly, structural theories with their stable stages can account for the remarkable consistency within the human personality. In a structural system, there is no theoretical necessity for change. (8) *Without sufficient dissonance to require a new structure, the person will not change.* Therefore, stage change does not inevitably result from advancing age. In fact, substantial empirical data suggests that many adults do not change structural stages after their early twenties. When stage change does occur, it is likely to be a protracted process; many forays into the more complex worldview occur before it becomes more or less habitual. On our imaginary planet, the citizens from one country could make exploratory excursions into the next country before finalizing a decision to take up permanent residence there.

The implications of this latter characteristic point toward another cluster of characteristics. (9) *Stage change takes time, even a long time, and it is not at all inevitable without an appropriate developmental context.* Since stage change in adults is relatively rare, permanent developmental equilibrium is quite possible, and a single transition over the entire period of adulthood not out of the question. Therefore, though simplistic attempts to move people to "higher" stages will most likely prove futile, developmentally sensitive environments can create a context which encourages stage change. (10) *Since the stage where a person levels off will quite likely remain a life outlook for a period of time, a stage also functions as a distinct personality style.* Recall again the inhabitants of the imaginary planet: citizenry of each country represent distinct "developmental personality styles." Some persons adopt the CON perspective, others the SAG and HOT perspectives, and as long as they remain "citizens" of their respective countries, they respond from within that set of conventions. In "real life," these perspectives represent entire "languages" and meaning systems for interpreting one's inner and outer world.

But real people do not turn out to behave quite so consistently as the picture I have so far painted. Persons are far more complicated than any theory can capture. (11) *Individuals may use a variety of meaning-systems in response to a variety of situations.* Extremely stressful situations generally provoke a return to earlier meaning-systems. Sometimes, whole areas of personality may be sealed off from the rest of development and therefore elicit less complex responses. At the same time, in another less threatening arena, one might be tentatively trying out a more complex perspective. A stage is somewhat analogous to stopping the action in a motion picture—we artificially freeze a complex, dynamic personality system for the conceptual convenience it offers. Therefore, (12) *a stage is simply an abstract convention which denotes the most complex meaning-system which a person uses consistently in the ordinary circumstances of life.*

(13) *The entire context in which a person lives carries developmental significance.* Certain predictable or unpredictable life tasks, such as leaving home or receiving a diagnosis of cancer, may provide a context for constructing a new meaning-system. But sometimes a new system appears in the absence of obvious external causes, especially farther along the structural continuum. Some kind of conflict does precipitate, or at least accompany, developmental stage change, but the conflict may be interior, completely obscured to an outside observer—a hidden grief process for example. Conversely, a person may live in a highly conflictual system without any structural change. In some situations, in fact, it becomes far too costly to continue to develop. In the case of a person who lives in a constantly chaotic, unpredictable, oppressive, or dangerous environment, a wary and self-protective stance is both developmentally predictable and environmentally adaptable. Individuals are not isolated automatons, but live in complex systems of communities, all of which constantly exert developmental pulls or developmental constraints, both powerful and subtle.

Structural theories account for the stability of personality through many crises, but they have more difficulty accounting for why change does occur, especially in adults. Since the opposite is true for the life-span theories (which easily account for change but have trouble accounting for intrapersonal consistency), it is clear that we are working with two different conceptions of development. Each paradigm helpfully illumines some aspects of human development but obscures other aspects. Although I will concentrate on the structural theories and their implications for spiritual direction, astute spiritual directors would do well to employ simultaneously a variety of psychological perspectives, including life-span theories.

Using and Misusing Structural Theories

In beginning to apply developmental perspectives, some unwarranted conclusions appear with surprising frequency.[17] Almost invariably, students and researchers assume that they rank higher on the developmental continuum than they actually test out to be. In reality, graduate students in psychology and counseling match the developmental profile of the general American public. The same profile probably describes ministers and spiritual directors as well.

Not only do we often overestimate our own developmental stage, we typically overestimate the developmental level of whole groups. Research on large populations confirms Jane Loevinger's claim that the modal developmental stage of adults in this culture lies midway along the developmental continuum.[18] In Loevinger's terms, the greatest density in the adult population lies halfway between her Conformist and Conscientious stages. Roughly speaking, if a census were taken on our imaginary planet, half the adult population would lie on each side of the border between CON and SAG.

Finally, we usually expect groups to be more developmentally homogeneous than they turn out to be. Most sizable groups, even if they are composed only of adults, will include persons representing three or even four developmental stages. Those who teach adults, preach to them, or see them in medical, legal, or counseling practices or for spiritual direction rarely take into account such developmental complexity.

Several pitfalls seem designed especially for spiritual directors who naively employ the structural theories. We may expect quick developmental progression or assume that our interventions will help a person move to a later stage which we assume must be better than the person's present stage. Stage transition does not occur just because the director or the seeker simply wills it to happen; in fact, attempting to cause stage change directly can be intrusive and manipulative. Sometimes even unconsciously hoping for stage change in our directees results in frustration on our part or guilt on their part. Although our relationship and responses may, in fact, assist a seeker through a transition, that end ought not to be our *primary* consideration as spiritual directors. Rather, our basic covenant concerns assisting seekers as they attempt to respond to God's initiative, in whatever way that initiative occurs.

A more constructive approach to developmental stages understands that each stage has its strengths and limitations, its opportunities for virtue and its unique temptations. Fortunately, as we
shall see when we investigate the dynamics of structural change
more thoroughly, encouraging a person to be exactly where she or
he is on the developmental continuum does paradoxically promote
stage change. Spiritual directors can best participate in the development of their directees by creating an environment which facilitates transition without forcing it.

Another subtle temptation arises when we confuse the map of
the terrain for the terrain itself. With the structural perspective,
this happens when we box people into stages. To the extent that we
see people as stages, we abdicate our role of standing with them as
unique human persons seeking to understand how God calls. Variations on this temptation include assuming that people will move in
a lock-step and/or unidirectional manner and artificially reducing
human complexity and messiness. Or, we may excuse growth in the
name of personality stages or types: "He can't help it because he's
an introvert; she's an adult child of an alcoholic; I'm a conventional
type of person and it's just the way I am."

A final, subtle temptation arises when we expect the developmental theories to supply the content of our education or spiritual
direction, when, in fact, they actually illumine *styles of meaning-
making.* Apart from the context of a living faith tradition, structural theories are unable to specify what we ought to believe, in
whom we believe, or even why believing might be better than not
believing. Structural theories simply illumine the movement from
less to more inclusiveness in that believing. Put more bluntly, we
can reduce the goal of spiritual formation to the highest developmental stage, thinking that the person at the highest developmental stage is more successfully responding to God.[19] At the other
extreme, we can totally ignore the developmental possibilities and
constraints which are simply a part of human nature, constructing
a view of holiness and spiritual development which is either unreal-
istic or which we apply indiscriminately to everyone. Neither extreme takes seriously the fact that humans are unique before God
yet manifest general similarities in style with some other persons.

If these problems await spiritual directors who wish to use
structural developmental theories, how might the structural developmental theories help us? What can we gain when we use this
powerful developmental paradigm in service of spiritual companionship? The most basic benefit, perhaps, lies in increasing our

potential for accurate empathy.[20] To the extent that we grow in our ability to experience the seeker's world from within that very worldview, we enhance our ability to reflect on what is happening between the seeker and God. In addition, as we come to understand the process of change more deeply, we can strengthen our ability to facilitate those changes which lie within the scope of the spiritual direction covenant.

Structural developmental theories articulate the human competencies which our directees bring to spiritual direction. As we examine the personality styles formed when persons pause at different stages, we can pick up numerous clues about which issues will prove salient to directees. We have another tool for assessing the potential a given directee has for "working inside," for noticing and naming feelings, desires, hopes, values and long-term goals. Furthermore, since the direction of development concurs with that of spiritual maturity, indications of increased development add positive confirmations to the seeker's discernment about decisions and actions.

These benefits directly affect what we might do with directees as we listen, understand and respond with more accuracy and clarity. In addition, the structural theories prove their worth at another level. As we come to recognize that we, too, are subject to the same developmental constraints as our directees, we can then look at how our listening, our style, our goals, may be deeply informed and limited by our own developmental stage. This unique opportunity helps us to approach the task of spiritual direction more humbly, recognizing that only God is big enough to encompass all persons, all developmental perspectives. God is bigger than our directees' perceptions of God, or our own: "Let those who are wise give heed to these things, and consider the steadfast love of the Lord" (Ps 107:43).

III. Four Seekers:
A Developmental View

Let me introduce four people, very much like directees I have seen. Imagine, if you will, that these persons recently came to you requesting spiritual direction. Although the following descriptions are typical of persons who actually could contact you for spiritual direction, they are actually hypothetical persons and situations. The first two persons are males in theological studies leading to ordination, and neither is married. The second two are women of approximately the same age, married, and neither is in the seminary. To clarify at the outset, I do not imply any necessary correlation between the developmental stage of these persons and their sex, religious tradition, marital or educational status, or occupation. By holding some variables constant, I simply wish the developmental issues to emerge more straightforwardly.

Tom Z. and Roger Q.

It is October, and Tom Z. has just approached you for spiritual direction, in accord with the policy of his seminary that all candidates for priesthood receive spiritual direction. Tom is a forty-one-year-old veteran, a lifelong Roman Catholic educated in the parochial school system. While serving his second tour of duty in the service, he earned an M.B.A. After being discharged, he started a successful consulting business. He had dated off and on, and was once quite seriously considering marriage. In the end, after thoughtful discussions with several persons who knew him well, including his fiancée, he decided to test a deep-felt and long-standing desire to be a priest. He had come to this seminary after a year of philosophy studies at the diocesan collegiate seminary.

But this year is already proving to have some rough spots. Tom indicates that his peers think he is stuck-up and doesn't like to associate with them. He does, in fact, spend a good bit of time studying or recreating at things which refresh him, rather than sitting in front of the TV or "shooting the breeze." He reports mixed feelings about this peer reaction, knowing that he is causing it by his choices, yet feeling increasingly lonely. Because the formation program feels stifling, Tom struggles to share his life with his fellow-students and the formation personnel. He wonders why, when his life-style as a priest will require autonomy and self-direction, the formation program seems to assume he is an adolescent.

43

Tom finds his courses, especially systematic theology, quite challenging, and has to work consistently to keep up his B average. Although his self-identity doesn't seem to hinge on how well he does in his studies, he wants to be well-trained for the sake of his future parishioners. In the classroom, Tom is somewhat impatient with students who want right answers and a clear system; he feels that real people won't always fit into clear-cut systems. He prefers teachers who offer several methods for approaching situations and problems, and then he finds a method he can call his own.

Tom identifies celibacy as one of the issues he must discern carefully in the next months and years. He is sexually experienced: one brief relationship while he was in the service seemed to mean little, but a more extended sexual relationship over a number of months with Sally, his former fiancée, makes him wonder if he can live as a celibate, or if he is really called to the depth of relationship appropriate to marriage. He appears to relate smoothly with the women in his classes. But he recounts once realizing that, if he is ordained, he will be perceived as representing the church to some very hurting women. He has not considered what this will mean to him; instead, he has put it out of his mind.

Tom prays pretty regularly; if he skips his spiritual exercises, most often it will be on weekends. He usually attends eucharist and the communal recitation of the Office, and spends about twenty minutes reflecting on the Lectionary texts. He speaks about no unusual difficulties or desires concerning prayer. Upon questioning, he seems to have a relatively unformed relationship to the person of Jesus.

About this same time, Roger Q. also approaches you for spiritual direction. He is a fourth-year Methodist seminarian, twenty-seven years old. He has recently been appointed student pastor of a rural three-church assignment after its former pastor retired. He enjoys being received as a pastor in the communities he serves and doesn't bother to clarify his status when community members not affiliated with his church address him as "The Reverend" or "Pastor."

Roger has a reputation for being personable, cooperative, generous with his time, often volunteering for seminary projects. Everybody likes Roger. As a student, he always gets his work done, and quite credibly. Yet each year at evaluation time, his professors usually remark that Roger does not work up to his capacity, and seems to be personally disengaged from the subject matter. Roger expresses some frustration with "process" courses, where he struggles with finding out what it is that the professor is looking for. He also thinks that the M.A. students should have separate classes so that the divinity students can concentrate on their own questions and not have to waste time on the more academically-oriented issues the M.A. students raise. He has several times complained about either the existence or the agenda of the seminary's feminist organization.

Celibacy is also a "live" issue for Roger. One of Roger's best friends at the seminary, who also came from Roger's home church, has recently become involved in a homosexual relationship with another of their mutual seminary friends. Roger is hurt and angry: "They know what the denomination's rules are. Despite all the controversy lately it's still 'celibacy in singleness and fidelity in marriage.' If they want to get into that stuff, they ought to get out. I don't think they should be ordained if they are actively homosexual, but obviously I'm not saying anything to the Commission on Ordained Ministry either."

Roger is regular at seminary chapel. He prefers the traditional service and reacts somewhat critically to worship prepared by the racial-ethnic and feminist organizations. Roger's personal devotions have long included studying the Word. Now that he is preaching weekly, he finds that he pays even more attention to the texts that form the basis of his sermons. He really gets into studying them in preparation for preaching. The language of "personal relationship with Jesus" strikes him as fundamentalist and he's "not into that stuff."

Two people, both seminarians, but their developmental issues reflect more dissimilarities than similarities. In terms of our imaginary planet, Tom Z. responds like most inhabitants of SAG, while Roger responds like most citizens of CON. Formal names for the developmental perspectives reflected in CON and SAG, used throughout this study, are *Conformist* and *Conscientious;* for the approximate correlations between the countries on our imaginary planet and the principal stage theories used in this work, see Table 1.

From the data at hand, we can begin creating a portrait of the developmental stages illustrated by Tom and Roger. Tom appears able to sustain long-term, self-evaluated goals (his long-standing desire to be a priest, his successful business, his underlying motivation for studying, the overarching issue of celibacy as a viable lifestyle for him). He shows differentiated self-criticism, recognizes traits and motives in himself and others, and perceives consequences, alternatives and contingencies (he is aware that his choices are complicating his peer relationships; he struggles with an apparent discrepancy between behaviors useful in an institutional setting and those required in his future work; he resists rigid or artificially clear answers to complex realities). For him, rules must be internalized, self-evaluated and self-chosen; hence, he struggles to share himself in a situation that doesn't make much sense to him. Tom may very well experience some tension around hurting others even when he has kept the rules (he has recognized, but at the moment put aside, the issue of alienated, angry women who will perceive him as part of the "enemy"). Tom seems less interested in what's right in any general sense (for example, celibacy or priesthood) than in what is best *for him;* notice that for him the goal of priesthood does not automatically foreclose questioning celibacy, and that he frames the celibacy issue in terms of relationship—however, this reasoning is so common these days that it might escape notice as a *developmental* clue.

Interestingly, though Tom appears to possess both an inner life and the ability to assess it, his prayer, or at least his reporting of inner movements, seems not quite to have caught up to his developmental abilities. He probably is capable of developing a richly affective prayer life in the context of a personal relationship with God, yet needs to be invited to it in the light of faith. A spiritual director could say to Tom: "Have you expressed your feelings about all this to God?" and have some expectation that he could do so if he chose.

Turning to Roger, we meet a nice guy, fun to be with and consistently helpful. But notice that, for Roger, people ought to be socially acceptable (he is angry at his friends for stepping beyond the pale by their homosexual activity). Roger shows genuine interpersonal reciprocity, but he doesn't extend that reciprocity outside his own group (he doesn't like the cross-cultural worship services; the M.A. students ought to be separated from the divinity students so that the seminarians can get on with their presumably more important questions; personal relationship with Jesus is a "fundamentalist thing"). Roles and their external signs are important (he likes being called Reverend in "his" rural communities).

Roger's preaching helps him to fulfill his role in the church's hierarchy in a visible, credible way and his prayer is oriented to this preaching task. As a student, Roger tends to do things the way the professor wants, and may be studying primarily because it is expected, knowing it will eventually end with his ordination. Roger seems to obey the rules because they exist ("They know what the denomination's rules are"); his hurt and anger seem related to the fact that his long-term friends have challenged the rule system they have all tacitly agreed to live by. Disapproval forms a strong sanction—Roger does not want to "do it wrong" in his classes, but neither does he want to be the one to blow the whistle on his friends' homosexual relationship.

Moving beyond the actual detail provided, to the extent that Roger matches the Conformist developmental stage—in reality, no one ever represents a pure stage, since stages are simply useful abstract generalizations—he would manifest the following characteristics. His sense of self will come from the groups to which he belongs; he will appeal to externals for behavioral norms; his conscious preoccupations will include appearance, reputation, social acceptance, belonging. Moral "should's" could be very strong for Roger, either directed to himself or to others. Sexual and aggressive feelings will feel very dangerous since they threaten one's position in the group; consequently, they will be largely banned from his consciousness.

In terms of spiritual direction, Roger will be able to formulate what's happening inside him in only the most general way. His ability to "work inside," to "notice key interior facts," to use Barry and Connolly's phrase,[1] will not yet exist to any great extent. When asked about how he feels, Roger may answer with what he thinks or does. For example, to the question, "How do you feel about your friends' behavior?" Roger might well reply, "I feel they ought to get out." While Roger's own presumably celibate life-style is implicitly challenged by his friends' actions, he sees the issue as *their* behavior and therefore outside him. His problem is what to do with the knowledge that he has—how to negotiate the competing demands of his peers and the denominational structure.

Spiritual directors generally prefer to work with the Tom's of life much more than the Roger's. Tom can do the work expected in spiritual direction, but Roger never quite seems to get going. We might even find ourselves quite frustrated with Roger, likable as he is, because he never appears to reach much depth. We always end up doing the discerning, basing it on externals. Tom, however, can grasp discernment. With a little help, he can begin to pose the right questions to himself, notice his inner responses, pick up patterns in how God has worked with him in the past, and begin to apply this self-knowledge to his present struggles and questions.

Roger's identity, we have seen, comes to him from the various groups to which he belongs; and cooperation, playing by the rules, and external signs of his status shore up an identity which scarcely exists as an internalized self. If Roger's groups or valued authorities clash at a significant enough level, Roger may have to "go in search of a self" which transcends the groups to which he belongs. Tom has made this shift, and he uses his "self" to judge everything else. But Tom's position also has its weakness: he cannot yet place this "imperial self" in a wider perspective or hand it over freely to some greater good. Extremes of Tom's position show up in self-serving, ideological versions of me-ism. Tom exemplifies a much less malignant version of this position, yet it still shares the same blindnesses.

There is, however, a much more significant issue for spiritual direction to which I have already alluded. At Roger's developmental position, access to inner life is limited, and feelings are global and relatively undifferentiated. To the extent that spiritual direction relies on access to one's feelings, it will be *developmentally* beyond Roger.

Lest you think you will never direct a Roger, empirical studies indicate that the modal level for the adult American population is halfway between the positions illustrated by Roger and Tom. That means, roughly speaking, that there are as many adults at Roger's construction, or lower, as at Tom's construction, or higher. (Recall that the modal level of the population on our imaginary planet was clustered at the division between CON and SAG.) In fact, large numbers of people put the world together in a way developmentally similar to Roger. They are in pews, in seminary formation programs, in the Charismatic Renewal, in women's circles and men's prayer breakfasts, on the Parish Council or Session, and they are some of your neighbors. Are spiritual directors very attentive to the needs of these people for *appropriate* spiritual direction? Do we even think of them in terms of spiritual direction at all? Do we think of them as somehow "less spiritual," as lukewarm or indifferent or shallow, and assume that, if they *really* wanted to, they could develop in their spiritual life? Or can we wholeheartedly affirm that God has their spiritual life as much at heart as those more developmentally proficient? Can we affirm the very real virtues that such persons offer the rest of us?

Mary Beth T. and Katherine M.[2]

Two more persons have recently consulted you for spiritual direction. Mary Beth T. is in her mid-forties, married to her original spouse, with children in high school and college. Her family are long-time Presbyterians—in fact, Mary Beth's maternal grandfather was a minister, and her mother a "preacher's kid." Over the course of the first two meetings, the following picture emerges.

Until recently, Mary Beth saw herself as having lived her whole life "being a good girl." As a child, she was "OK" as long as she was responsible. However, the praise she received from her parents and teachers for her responsibility never quite seemed to make up for the lack of warmth and physical affection traditional in her family of origin. After her marriage, she feels she was acceptable as long as she was responsible. But, over the past few years, she has become increasingly "irresponsible" according to the significant others in her life.

About three years ago, Mary Beth decided that she wanted to resume the college education she deferred at her marriage. Her husband thought it was "crazy, at your age. What will you do with it when you're finished?" Even though she didn't have any logical answers to his questions, she began taking courses anyhow. She spaced out the classes because of the additional strain on a budget already subsidizing one college-age son, and because the resistance at home was considerably lessened if she were home at meal times and not closeted studying on weekends. The classes captivated her imagination, and quite literally she found herself thinking all sorts of formerly unimaginable thoughts.

At about the same time, her consistent church-going began to take on new meaning. She experienced God as personally interested in her whether or not she did everything right. With a little experimentation, she discovered she could imagine God as her loving Father and herself his beloved child, resting on his lap. This prayer became a source of comfort and strength whenever she began thinking she was crazy for attempting this school thing at her age.

But lately the imagery had changed. The resulting confusion brought her to see you, on the advice of one of her friends. Now, it seems, God "talks" like a lover and calls her to union with him. She is anxious, fearful, and "doesn't like this at all." She's tried bargaining God back into the old relationship but he won't cooperate. Right now she is avoiding prayer. She wants to continue to grow in prayer but doesn't want "that kind of intimacy." She wants you to teach her how to pray "now that this has happened."

Yet a fourth person has recently consulted you about spiritual direction. Katherine M.'s spiritual director of seven years is moving out of town, and she is asking that you take on this role. She feels afraid, abandoned and confused, and is seeking help in discerning what God is saying to her. During the first session, she conveys the following information.

Katherine is Roman Catholic, forty-two years old, and has been married for twenty years. Her husband, Ken, is a vice president of a sizable investment firm. They have no children because Katherine is infertile. For many years she had wanted to adopt children, but her husband was opposed because remaining childless allowed them freedom to be together, to travel and to develop careers. This situation caused Katherine great pain for some years, but since Ken was unwilling to budge on the issue, she came to a point of acceptance, using the time freed from parenting for serving others less fortunate.

Katherine employed her degree in education to teach various elementary grades before and after their marriage. She enjoyed her work with the children, but eventually discovered that it was no longer challenging enough. Aided by spiritual direction, which she began seriously ten years ago, Katherine experienced a gradual deepening in her prayer life, growth in relationship with God and desire to live the gospel more radically. Eventually, she quit teaching to volunteer her services in social justice and the peace movement. She has been active in justice issues and education in the intervening decade.

These involvements have proven baffling for Katherine's husband. He views her friends as a bunch of well-intentioned but unsophisticated do-gooders. Katherine has felt continually frustrated in her attempts to explain what for her is a central aspect of the gospel, a clear call of the church and a lived expression of her own spirituality.

Lately, she has begun to experience the tension of living two lives. There are "her" friends and the spiritual growth for her which arises from the challenge of a committed Christian community dedicated to justice issues. Then there are "his" friends and the responsibilities to entertain socially and be involved in business circles. Katherine continues to live this life out of a deep love for Ken and sense of responsibility to him. She feels, however, that she must stifle herself on these social or professional occasions because Ken has made it clear that her friends and her positions on social justice are both naive and offensive to these people.

Increasingly, she has begun to feel like a hypocrite. She wants to modify her life-style, but Ken is opposed. She doesn't want to change her husband, but wishes to continue loving him and freeing him to be who he is. She views her marital vows as sacramental and covenantal. She also feels that a commitment to peace and resolution of conflict must be lived at home. She has several times asked Ken to go to marital counseling with her but he refuses. At the same time, she sees her relationship to God as primary, and is committed, "no matter what the cost," to following of God's will for her.

Mary Beth T. may look quite familiar to you; with variations in detail, she is a quite frequent visitor to my office. As different as they may appear at first glance, however, Mary Beth and Tom actually represent approximately the same developmental construction, Conscientiousness. The abstract nature of the structural developmental theories means that each individual will embody the theory in a unique way, making his or her own concrete decisions in the context of his or her daily life. The theories focus on the meaning-system behind the perceiving and choosing, not the specific content itself. From a faith perspective, furthermore, each person has a unique call from God—structural developmental theories, properly interpreted, allow for this uniqueness.

Mary Beth, however, gives us more clues than Tom about how she got to her developmental position and about what could be an invitation to transcend it. Leaving home has proven to be one of the most significant factors promoting the transition from Conformist to Conscientious perspectives. Mary Beth "left home," analogously speaking, when she went back to school. Other ways to leave the "home" of one's familiar worldview include joining the military (Tom's avenue), coping with divorce, and facing death— any sudden loss or major stress can precipitate the reorganization which results in structural stage change. We see the marital reverberations of one partner's stage change in both Katherine's and Mary Beth's situations. One implication sounds like a truism: crisis may result in significant growth. For spiritual directors, the issue is not so much precipitating transitions as understanding in the light of faith the ambiguity and confusion which transitions almost always entail.

Had Mary Beth come to you three or four years ago, while her developmental perspective was not quite Conscientious, she might have expressed the nagging worry that her desire to go back to school was really just selfishness on her part. Although this scenario is particularly prominent for women, any persons moving from the niceness, helpfulness, and cooperation of the Conformist perspective will meet subtle forces designed to keep them nice and cooperative. It doesn't matter whether the group in question is one's spouse, one's religious community or the society at large; moving past a group's expected level of development results in overt or subtle pressures to stay where one is developmentally. We uncover, then, framed in developmental issues, the individual's need to discern: what really *is* good? What is *better?* Or, as Mary Beth would put it: What is better *for me?*

But, at this moment three years later, Mary Beth's more pressing issue concerns the shift of imagery in her prayer. She's caught off guard, frightened, and would prefer to return to the earlier, comforting imagery. One of the clues that in fact Mary Beth *could* be moving toward a new developmental level is the spontaneous emergence of sexual material previously banned from consciousness (and prayer), especially since the imagery is in the context of the same relationship which supported her through her last transition. But, under the stress of images she judges unacceptable in her relationship with God, her strategy looks like a Conformist one: she appeals to authority for a method of prayer to which she can conform. From her report, God isn't cooperating in the bargaining. Nor ought her director simply provide her with prayer forms for relieving her anxiety about this new development. Rather, the director could help her stay in touch with this inviting God, accompany her in the scariness, and try to help her make some sense of what she experiences. The director and the directee both know that there are some large pitfalls and blind alleys that could sidetrack her at this critical juncture.

There are obvious similarities between Mary Beth and Katherine. They both experience a good deal of pressure from spouses who resist the direction that their lives are taking. They both report confusion, darkness and fear which accompany major transitions and have brought them to spiritual direction. Yet there are also significant differences between them.

Katherine, in fact, embodies yet a third developmental construction, which, following Robert Kegan, I shall call Interindividual. (The inhabitants of HOT on the imaginary planet demonstrate this developmental perspective.) A central characteristic of this position is autonomy, not only for oneself, but for all others as well. Despite pain, Katherine desires to let others—in this case, particularly her husband—be autonomous individuals, to find their own way and make their own mistakes, and to be at different developmental levels. She experiences inner conflict arising around needs and duties; her thinking is multifaceted and transcends simple polarities. She has an ability to tolerate levels of ambiguity that Roger can't, and that even Tom would find difficult. She realistically and rather objectively recognizes her situation, and intuits that not all problems are solvable. A key aspect of the Interindividual developmental stage centers around a broad view of life as a whole, including various abstract ideals such as social justice.

Katherine believes that mutuality and intimacy can coexist with autonomy and she desires this harmony in both life and prayer. It is quite possible that for Katherine the language of death to self and the experience of the cross may be the only thing that ultimately helps her make sense of and live in the midst of these tensions. Katherine's situation reminds us forcefully that all is not smooth and rosy in the farther reaches of the developmental continuum—the difficulties and struggles have a different nuance, but they may perhaps be even more painful since the person sees complexities that escape many of the rest of us. But Katherine may also have more developmental ability for the subtleties of discernment. She may need your presence and support, but she will be able to do a significant amount of discernment on her own.

Now that Tom, Roger, Mary Beth and Katherine have made their appearance, we are ready to elaborate the developmental processes which they exemplify.

IV. Changing and Staying the Same: The Structural Perspective

In the interviews recounted in the previous chapter, we gleaned some impressions about four persons and their present contexts. While parts of their lives are going along smoothly, each revealed discomforts. Tom and Roger must deal with peer relationships, but Roger must also contend with his loyalty to competing groups. Mary Beth's dilemma clearly centers around prayer, the classic domain of spiritual direction. Katherine faces the widening discrepancy between her values and life-style and that of her husband. In their own ways, each is saying, "I've lost my way. This doesn't make sense." How might spiritual directors understand and respond to these discomforts?

Only Tom is required to have a spiritual director as part of his seminary formation. We don't know if he would seek out formal spiritual direction independently. Roger, Mary Beth and Katherine, on the contrary, have chosen spiritual direction on their own. Mary Beth has the least acquaintance with spiritual direction, Katherine has amassed ten years with several spiritual directors, while Roger's spiritual guidance has occurred largely through oversight committees as he progressed through the candidacy process. Does spiritual direction contribute to personality development? If so, how?

Before we can attempt to answer these questions, we must grapple with four significant issues integral to developmental transition. First, how can *both* stability and change happen within the constraints of one personality? An adequate theory of development must address both equilibrium and transition.

Second, precisely how does structural change occur? How could we describe the transition from one stage to the next? Is movement actually continuous, rather than stage-like? Is it purely interior, unaffected by what is happening around us? What role, if any, do "outside" events and persons, including spiritual directors, play?

Third, why do people usually level off at stages noticeably lower than the hypothetical highest stage? Research indicates that development occurs most rapidly in infancy and childhood, slowing in the late teens and early twenties. After that, many adults settle in for long periods of time, perhaps never again manifesting the qualitative new reorganization of perspective called a stage change. Others make one or two more stage changes, and a small number, even three. Why do some persons continue to develop and some do not? How are spiritual directors to interpret this fact?

Finally, what is the proper role of spiritual direction in this developmental process? Is it a director's responsibility to encourage stage change, directly or indirectly? If so, how might this be done? If not, why not? These four areas undergird an understanding of structural change as it will affect our four spiritual directees.

In this chapter, then, we will focus on movement in personality development. After examining the notion of development and distinguishing it from simple change, we will turn to Jean Piaget, Robert Kegan and William Dember for their understandings of developmental transition. With these images of development in mind, we can focus explicitly on the spiritual director's role regarding stage change. Finally, we will return to Mary Beth to illustrate more concretely how the dynamics of structural change might inform her spiritual director's responses.

Change Versus Development

Not all changes qualify as development. A random happening is certainly a change, but such chance events are not considered developmental. Nor are reversible processes necessarily developmental—but the ability to recognize and employ reversible processes *is* developmental.

I remember, for example, how many times as a first-grader I was asked to take three chips and then two more for a total of five. Then, starting with a group of five, I was to take two away, leaving three. This physical grouping and ungrouping is change without being development. But to recognize that subtracting and adding are reversible operations (though not necessarily describing it in such abstract language) does qualify as a developmental change, because it requires a level of cognitive complexity beyond that necessary simply to group and ungroup. Still later, to learn that adding and subtracting are but one pair of inverse operations requires a developmental ability to think about the thinking process.

Thus, for a change to qualify as development, it must demonstrate three conditions. It must increase in complexity, it must encompass and surpass the prior level (it must be a new order of ordering), and once attained, it must not be lost, though it could be unused.

In a remarkably readable philosophical discussion of the principles of change, Paul Watzlawick and his colleagues elucidate the difference between first-order change (within the system) and second-order change (moving outside one system to another or altering the change principle itself). Since second-order change is precisely what happens in structural developmental stage transition, their discussion applies directly to our topic. Second-order change, they observe, has four characteristics: (1) Second-order change is applied to what in the first-order change perspective appears to be a solution, because from the wider perspective, the "solution" reveals itself as precisely the problem. (2) While first-order change always appears to be based on common sense, second-order change usually appears weird, unexpected, and uncommonsensical. There is a puzzling, paradoxical element in the process of change, which accounts for the disorientation which often attends stage change. (3) Applying second-order change techniques to the "solution" means that the situation is dealt with in the here and now. Practically, therefore, attention shifts from "Why (did things get this way)?" to "What (can change)?" (4) The use of second-order change techniques breaks the no-exit circular logic of the attempted solution and places it in a different frame.[1]

One of the inherent tensions in structural theories of development arises at this point. Are they theories of movement or are they theories about stability or non-movement? If we stress stages at the expense of transitions, we will spend our energy describing these plateaus, drawing rich pictures of the behaviors, attitudes and potentials of each stage. Just how one goes about moving from one plateau to the next may be completely overlooked. When that imbalance occurs, it subtly encourages the assumption that everyone *could* climb to the highest stage and bask in the magnificent and panoramic view of the world from those splendid heights. From there, it is but a small step to assuming that everyone *ought* to climb to the top, and suspecting that those who don't are dumb, lazy, stubborn, or even morally inferior. This unhelpful judgment is not confined to psychological development, for in spiritual life people too frequently assume that higher must be holier. How often have persons read John of the Cross only to conclude that they could never be contemplatives because they haven't experienced the Dark Night?

On the other hand, the constructive function of stage descriptions lies in providing the panorama, the range of possibilities shown to exist over large groups of people. This long view helps to keep our bearings with massive amounts of concrete detail, to see how perspectives are related to each other, to ascertain a person's current position on the developmental continuum, and to intuit what his or her developmental "cutting edges" might be.

In order to do structural theories justice, therefore, both the notion of stages and the notion of transitions must be addressed with equal care. In the images of developmental transition that follow, each of the theorists offers some way to balance both stasis and change, and gives some account about how both happen in the same individual.

Piaget on Developmental Change

Four concepts from Jean Piaget begin our discussion of developmental transition: equilibration, assimilation, accommodation and décalage. Piaget assumed that the personality's natural condition is a state of dynamic poise, which he called equilibration. This condition is by no means static psychic inaction; Piaget spoke of "*mobile* equilibrium" while Loevinger evoked the image of a gyroscope, which maintains its upright position only through continuous, balanced movement.[2]

A living organism is affected by everything that takes place in its environment. It takes each experience "inside," as it were, so that it becomes part of its information about its environment. Piaget called this process assimilation. But each experience also changes the organism, if ever so slightly. It must "expand" to accommodate this newly acquired information. Assimilation and accommodation are always partners.

Most of the time we unconsciously absorb new data into our reigning (and largely unconscious) assumptions about reality. In fact, research shows that we overlook or misperceive that which is too unexpected or for which we have no categories or language. But each assimilation inevitably brings some accommodation along with it. After repeated accommodations, the original equilibration or "evolutionary truce"[3] cannot hold all the anomalies it has absorbed, and it begins to unravel. When that happens, a stage gives way to a transition, that sometimes disorienting period between one equilibration and the next. Eventually, a more complex principle of equilibrium emerges and the sense of chaos subsides in favor of a new and more complex view of "the way things are"—the next stage. This new evolutionary truce contains all the earlier data and its organizing principles, now subsumed into a more inclusive system.

Let us employ another image to illustrate décalage, Piaget's term for the process of reorganizing one's knowledge in terms of new logic systems. Imagine, if you will, an expanse of tiered rice paddies constructed stepwise up a riverbank. At the spring flood, rising water fills the lowest field. Initially, water spreads across the flat surface, simultaneously soaking in until it reaches the water table. When it has saturated all the ground at this level, the water again begins to rise, gradually reaching the top of the second embankment. As it tops the wall into the next higher field, the process of spreading out and soaking in occurs again, flooding the second tier. When it reaches the third embankment, the process repeats itself yet again. The lowest paddy, of course, is still submerged, deeper than ever.

Piaget used the term décalage to point out that persons can be at different stages at different moments or with respect to different issues.[4] When a new logic is acquired, one's earlier experience must be reworked in light of this more complex perspective, much like the newly flooded tier first absorbs water until the ground is saturated. Piaget called this recapitulation process *vertical* décalage. In addition, each new logic is at first confined to a relatively small domain, only gradually expanding to encompass more possible applications. Piaget called this gradual expansion of the logic system to encompass new experience *horizontal* décalage. In our metaphor, it compares to the gradual spread of the water all across one field before it rises to flood the next.

Robert Selman's research on the development of interpersonal perspective verified that children do understand certain social concepts earlier than other social concepts. The child's perception appears to radiate out from a center formed by the child itself, with knowledge about the self occurring first, followed by knowledge of relations between two people, and finally by knowledge of group life. In five-year-olds, concepts about self will be the fullest, relatively speaking. Their understanding of dyads consists of two independent selves reacting somewhat like balls bouncing off each other. Groups are, at best, collections of dyads each with an overlapping member. This gradual extension of perspective-taking from self outward illustrates horizontal décalage.

At around age fifteen conceptual development across all three domains—self, dyad, and larger group—seems to come together.[5] The notion of self has not disappeared, by any means, but remains, deepened and enriched—an example of vertical décalage. High school sophomores understand that particular persons do not cease to be individuals when they are part of a group, but also recognize

that the group is more than just a collection of individuals in proximity to one another—concepts beyond the grasp of preschoolers.

To understand just how décalage might be significant for spiritual direction, let us return to the image of the water flooding the
rice paddies. It is not possible to flood the top paddy while skipping
the second tier in the process. And if the ground isn't saturated, the
water will seep away into the soil rather than collect in pools and
rise to the next tier. As Robert Selman's children reveal, it is impossible to develop increasingly complex views of the self while by-
passing the continuing development of relationships. Likewise, the
understanding of groups "brings along" with it the concept of the
self as individual.

The applications within spiritual direction are multiple. Let
me suggest two. Spiritual directors can't simply assume that directees will easily develop rich and inclusive views of Christian community until significant relationships both to self and to "close-in"
groups are also present. Roger's spiritual director ought not expect
that he will speedily adopt a warm and welcoming perspective toward groups that challenge his denominationally based identity—
such as an underground organization of gay and lesbian seminary
students agitating to change the ordination requirements—because to do so would require him to skip an entire stage with its
intervening transition. Second, focusing on only one aspect of spiritual growth to the exclusion of others may unnecessarily limit the
potential for continued development. Mary Beth's spiritual director could concentrate exclusively on the shifting images in her
prayer, but it might also prove very profitable to explore the connections between her deepening relationship with God and those
with her family and with her professors and peers at school.

An even more basic implication exists for spiritual directors—
or counselors, social workers, educators and parents for that matter. Trying to cause stage change directly simply does not work. At
best, we can only contribute to the conditions which encourage
such change. Transitions seem to emerge from within the individual, but they can be fueled or hindered by experience, culture and
pressures to change or stay the same. Even under apparently ideal
conditions, it remains unclear why some persons embark on a transition and others do not.

But it does not follow that spiritual directors, pastors, counselors, educators and parents have no role in promoting structural
development. They can and should assist in the recapitulation process in which newly received graces and insights become integrated

into more and more aspects of life. Mary Beth's spiritual director may help connect her graceful insight that she is a child of God, loved for who she is rather than what she does, to relationships where she still feels the need to earn acceptance. We are much closer to midwives than engineers when it comes to personality development.

Our inability to engineer stage change may appear to be quite unfortunate. Actually, it serves to bring spiritual directors face-to-face with the mystery of our role. It is God's position to initiate spiritual growth, not ours. But the temptation to push directees to advance developmentally is so alluring that perhaps only the fact that it doesn't work saves most of us from regular mistakes in this respect. Paradoxically, however, we can provide a context which encourages stage change precisely by encouraging persons to be most fully where they are developmentally. In terms of our metaphor, spiritual directors and other ministers help with saturating the ground and clearing out the debris so the water can spread as far as possible.

Naturally Therapeutic Holding Environments

Most development occurs, Robert Kegan reminds us, without much conscious intervention or even awareness on our part. It should be worthwhile, therefore, to examine what goes on when development "just happens" of its own accord, and then try to imitate the dynamics we have uncovered. Such "natural therapy" would take place, not primarily through counselors, spiritual directors or other professionals, but through all those relationships and human contexts which spontaneously support people through the sometimes difficult process of growth and change.[6] A grasp of naturally therapeutic environments could then help us understand how such one-to-one relationships as spiritual direction can effectively join the developmental agenda already under way. They could also offer a way to understand how complex social groups function to foster development, and indeed how parenting, curriculum-building, ministry, and even social policy-making might collaborate with the naturally occurring developmental dynamic.

What happens in naturally occurring developmental processes? Enter another new image, "holding environment," originally proposed by D. W. Winnicott, but which Robert Kegan employs within the structural developmental perspective. Kegan suggests that we understand each stage as a "holding environment" or "culture of embeddedness." These colorful terms refer to the entire psychosocial environment in which personality develops. When holding environments serve three simultaneous and interrelated functions, they become effective, naturally therapeutic environments. First, naturally therapeutic holding environments must recognize and confirm the person as an individual, surrounding her or him with a supportive and caring context. Second, they must foster continued development by encouraging a new level of interpersonal differentiation. Third, they must provide continuity through this often stressful process of reintegrating one holding environment into its successor. When the totality of one's world functions to perform all three of these functions in the proper degree and timing, it becomes an effective developmental context within which transitions may occur.

For example, a seeker whose meaning-system functions at the Conformist stage will be embedded in mutuality and in the web of interpersonal systems. This holding environment encourages mutually reciprocal one-to-one relationships. It confirms and acknowledges the capacity for collaborative self-sacrifice in mutuality. It encourages shared feelings. But it eventually should contradict a prolonged continuance of self that is submerged within relationships. It should promote a self that will not be fused with, but still seek and participate in, transformed relationships. It must gradually begin to demand that the person assume responsibility for his or her own initiatives and preferences. At the same time, the crucial interpersonal partners must remain in place, allowing the relationship to be placed in a larger context. If significant persons, such as a spouse or a spiritual director, leave or suddenly repudiate the relationship, the reassimilation of these relationships on the new footing will be severely handicapped.

This situation describes Roger's current meaning-system. Until now, the process of candidacy and seminary has encouraged Roger to define himself by his increasing incorporation into the Methodist clergy culture. He has already formed an identity based on long-term friendships. He has learned how to be a successful student and popular community member. On the other hand, Roger seems to have insulated himself from other perceptions of "truth" articulated by the seminary's racial-ethnic and feminist groups, and his identity has not been formed to any significant degree within the horizon typically held by such groups.

These selves who comprise Roger now appear to be in danger

of severe conflict. The discrepancy between loyalty to denominational polity and loyalty to his friends constitutes the most overt of the challenges to Roger's meaning-system. Although Roger has only indirectly reported it, his professors have already set up dissonances between versions of "truth," and asked him to take a stand for himself. Roger, however, still struggles to find out what each professor wants so that he can respond "correctly." Process-oriented classes implicitly invite Roger to allow the truth (and his identity) to unfold in the course of the work—but Roger finds this search for himself very difficult. The entire Conformist holding environment, while confirming Roger's identity as a member of various groups, now appears to be "turning him out" to find a new source of identity. If it is successful, Roger will eventually have to choose how *he* will respond to his professors, to his friends and to the denominational polity. If Roger's friends should drop out of the seminary, Roger may be able to avoid integrating a deeper grasp of loyalty—friendship with those who disagree with him at some fundamental level—into his new-found identity.

Whether or not Roger and his spiritual director actually discuss any of these issues, the naturally therapeutic dynamics of confirming, contradicting and continuing may themselves prove powerful enough to see Roger through a transition to the next stage, Conscientiousness. But if Roger's spiritual director understands and collaborates in these naturally therapeutic dynamics, the spiritual direction relationship may also become an important part of the natural therapy. Hopefully Roger will eventually come to experience God's personal presence and call within these concrete struggles.

Let us briefly examine one more example of a naturally therapeutic environment, the one in which we find Tom at the point of his first spiritual direction conversation. As the Conformist meaning-system gradually erodes, group-definition may "move over" in favor of self-definition. At the subsequent Conscientious stage, a person is embedded in personal autonomy and self-authorship, with its concomitant investment in the public arena and career. This "culture of embeddedness" confirms independence, self-definition, exercise of personal authority, enhancement and achievement. But eventually it also should begin to contradict the conviction that self can remain the ultimate, and therefore sufficient, norm for judging everything—precisely the point of irritation which Tom reveals with the formation program. During the subsequent shift, the systems themselves must remain in place for eventual reintegration into the new understanding of self in systems—Tom's peers and the requirements of his formation program must remain as part of Tom's concrete context as he begins to forge an interdependent self or they may be excluded from this reintegration.[7] For a summary of the confirmations, contradictions and continuities at other stages, see Kegan's "Forms and Functions of Embeddedness Cultures" in Table 4.

The concept of holding environment can illumine the transition process; consequently it provides valuable clues about the relationship between spiritual guidance and personality development. Spiritual directors are part of the culture of embeddedness in which our directees exist, and we can attend to the dynamics of confirmation, continuity and creative contradiction as an integral aspect of our role. Perhaps part of Katherine's distress at the moment we first met her has to do with losing the continuity provided by her last spiritual director just as she must reinterpret in the light of faith the quality and even the continuation of her marriage.

Mary Baird Carlsen has seized upon this threefold dynamic, confirmation, contradiction and continuity, integrating it into a method for therapeutic intervention in meaning-making. Briefly, therapeutic meaning-making cycles back and forth between the following steps: (1) Establish a climate of trust, a confirming holding environment, by joining the client in his or her presenting problems and pain. (2) Together with the client, examine a wide range of facts, assumptions and speculations which are part and parcel of the client's meaning, gently contradicting the inadequate or destructive perceptions and actions. (3) Open oneself to a wide range of contexts of meaning, differing personal systems and histories, while evaluating all aspects of the presenting problem; model and encourage this same openness in the client. (4) Creatively reconstruct new scenarios through freethinking and imagining. (5) Help clients to think about their own thinking so that they grasp their ways of ordering the world. (6) Continue to confirm and creatively contradict within a supportive environment while the client constitutes a more effective way of being and acting.[8] These six steps emerged from a problem-oriented counseling context, but, with suitable adaptation, spiritual directors can also employ this same process as seekers examine, appropriate and reintegrate their ultimate values and beliefs.

Pacers and Nonrevolutionary Growth

Our day-to-day experience of change is considerably more mundane than that of life-transforming shifts in worldview. Instead, we experience ourselves in a more or less continuous state of flux, the significance and direction of which is often far from clear. Frequently, it is this ambiguous kind of change which brings people to spiritual direction, seeking to ascertain some meaning and direction in the midst of the movement. William Dember's concept of pacer gives us a vivid image with which to shift our attention from stage change to the myriad of smaller changes which go on continually in and around each of us. It will also help to refine our understanding of the spiritual director's potential role within the change process.

Dember's work on motivation indicates that humans are not primarily driven to reduce physiological need states. Rather, they are motivated, at least in part, by complexity and novelty. Each person prefers a particular degree of novelty and complexity, neither too much, nor too little. When persons are free to choose, they will select experiences within their preferred range of complexity, spending the greatest amount of time on stimuli just a little more complex than comfortable. Indeed, they will seek out such persons, things, concepts, values and relationships, which become their own reward. Dember called objects in this range of complexity "pacers."[9] As individuals strive after and master pacers, their own level of complexity grows and they are ready for new, more complex pacers. In summarizing Dember's work, Loevinger concluded that the pacer "appears to be the formula or model for nonrevolutionary growth."[10]

All sorts of things function as pacers; they, too, permeate any naturally therapeutic environment. Three important pacers are culture and socioeconomic status, interpersonal relationships and conscience.

James Fowler speculates that certain conditions widespread within a society may encourage development of the majority of its members up to a certain level. Society can act as a pacer, but only up to a point. If we adapt Fowler's faith development concepts and categories to our ego development system, the following relationships between culture and stage emerge. Preliterate societies with a single worldview encourage adult versions of the Impulsive stage.

Conformity could emerge as a widespread style in cultures which recognize the uniqueness and value of each person, and which have speculative literary traditions. Conscientiousness could only surface in an ethos of ideological pluralism marked by critical methods and empirical inquiry.[11] These relationships do not rule out the possibility that some individuals will transcend these limits, but instead suggest that, until the average expectable level of development is reached, one's very place in history may even pace one's development. To move beyond that point requires a new pacer cogent enough to counteract the historical-cultural forces working to keep persons in line with the reigning system. It is relatively rare for someone to envision a new human consciousness beyond the historical moment in which he or she exists.

One's immediate culture and socioeconomic status are somewhat more obvious in their ability to pace. For example, the growing awareness that women are persons in their own right, not merely appendages of significant male persons, raises a new set of developmental expectations for an increasing number of women and men. Among our directees, Katherine's work for justice, and her association with justice activists over time, has opened her eyes to the possibility of a spirituality which is inclusive on a global scale.

The interpersonal relationships which exist within any "holding environment" provide the most crucial matrix for pacing ego development. The power exercised by a teacher, mentor, therapist, friend, spouse, spiritual director—indeed, the entire network of primary relationships—to challenge one's assumptions about reality and one's place in it can be extremely important developmental pacers. It is equally possible, of course, that these same primary relationships invite one to "settle in"; they can just as easily contradict development.[12]

Although many relationships serve as pacers, spiritual directors may be particularly apt at pacing for several reasons. Spiritual directors provide a regular forum for clarifying and celebrating one's relationship with God, transmitting the principles of spiritual life in a personalized fashion. In many ways, they act as mentors in spiritual life. The director's task typically includes pointing out patterns of maturation (at least with respect to "spiritual" issues), helping individuals question their experience in terms of ultimate meanings and select the path leading toward these self-chosen directions.[13] If the spiritual director—whether consciously or unconsciously—stimulates novelty and complexity to match the directee's preferred range of complexity, the director acts as a pacer.

The psychoanalytic tradition has long recognized the power for good or ill of interpersonal relationships in personality development. Within developmental psychology, however, the power of interpersonal relationships to affect development has been overshadowed by the concept of differentiation, in which the highly developed person often appeared to be increasingly distanced from others. The images generated within developmental perspectives often suggest separation: "launching out," "becoming one's own person," "learning to become more assertive." Pitting differentiation against relationship, however, is far too simple—differentiation and relationship are paradoxically intertwined as two aspects of the same reality. Jean Baker Miller and her colleagues are attempting in their developmental research to equalize this imbalance between differentiation and relationship. Recognizing that all development occurs within the context of relationship—persons move toward a more complex sense of self by participating in more complex relationships—Miller and colleagues highlight the continuity of relationships along the developmental continuum. Relationships do not fall away as the self becomes more differentiated; they change quality to accommodate a more developed sense of agency-in-community. In this light, appropriate professional interaction involves recognizing and supporting the enlarged ability for relationship, which, rather than greater distance, implies a new quality of caring.[14]

If we transfer this insight to the spiritual direction relationship, we uncover at least three developmentally-linked perceptions of the spiritual director. To Conformist-oriented persons, the spiritual director tends to be perceived as an expert or authority who provides correct answers, or at least better ways of proceeding. Conscientious directees may use a spiritual director as a sounding board as they increasingly find and refine their own identities and make their own choices. Interindividual persons may understand their spiritual directors more as co-pilgrims who walk beside them, sharing both the challenges and delights of the spiritual quest. When spiritual directors are able to accompany individual directees all the way through a stage transition, part of that process will include forging qualitatively new director-directee relationships.

Just as external factors affect the possibilities and limits of structural development, so do internal factors. Conscience figures prominently among these internal factors. Somewhat surprisingly for a psychometrically trained researcher, Jane Loevinger recognizes that the growth of conscience will of necessity be so intertwined with ego development that they constitute a single, complex sequence of events, and that the dynamic principles accounting for ego development overlap those accounting for conscience development. Yet, she insists, the two concepts are not synonymous, and neither is superfluous, arising as they do from different realms of discourse.[15]

For Loevinger, conscience encompasses elements of accountability for past actions and feelings, and obligation for future ones. Conscience both judges what has been done and impels toward what could be. Mature conscience requires the capacity for self-reflection, self-criticism, self-evaluated standards and ideals, and some degree of disinterestedness and ability to account others equal to oneself. Loevinger posits that the conscience—or at least that aspect of conscience which pulls one toward the future—becomes itself a moving principle in ego development. As that aspect of the future which is embodied in the present, the (adult) ego-ideal provides a vision of a more organized and mature self, and creates the necessary complexity and tension for psychological growth. Conscience can therefore pace ego development.

Since God initiates all relationships with humankind, we could, in fact, think of God as the pacer *par excellence*. If, as Karl Rahner suggests, humans are beings that lose themselves in God,[16] then the drive toward reality and the drive toward final coherence *are* precisely the drive toward God. Conversely, the more one knows God, the more one knows oneself.

Left to our own devices, however, we are seldom aware of this deeper consciousness. To the extent that we do begin to focus, however vaguely, on this level, we experience a dim but constant anticipation of the positive fullness of infinite reality as the horizon of all our knowledge and freedom. God pulls us toward God's Self, and in so doing, creates the possibility of more complete actualization of human potential.

The concept of pacer helps clarify why virtually every person ceases to develop before reaching the hypothetical "highest" stage. If our life circumstances, including our relationship with God, do not elicit complex developmental responses, they will not be forthcoming. That an individual functions at stages lower than the highest, therefore, does not necessarily indicate immaturity, pathology or immorality. We must view this situation in relation to all the demands placed upon the person—which, from the Christian perspective, includes the action of grace. Furthermore, developmental maturity also entails the ability to choose among a more differentiated range of responses those which best meet the needs of each unique situation.[17]

The variety and potency of forces which encourage us to settle in require equally attractive and potent pacers if we are to continue developing. Education, travel, and even military service have long been recognized as stimulants to development; the concept of pacer suggests why this is so. But external pacers, such as culture, family, education, friendships, vocation and profession can function as pacers only up to a certain point, which we could call "the average expectable level of development." For further structural development to occur, internal pacers must increasingly take over from external ones. This qualitatively new situation defines the transition between the Conformist and Conscientious stages. The fact that large numbers of adults never complete this transition suggests how difficult it can be.

I believe the church could play a significant role in assisting with this transition from external authority to internal authority. Of all the institutions in our society, perhaps it alone is equipped by size and gospel vision to encourage the development of both inner life and broad social consciousness—as well as the integration of the two—all of which pace relatively complex developmental stages. However, as part of the church's historic institutional role in civilizing and ordering society, it has more typically fostered conformity to a cohesive social system and hierarchically ordered authority. In order to pace for complex developmental stages, the church must encourage individual conscience formation, promote open and collegial decision-making, and provide the necessary education for assuming responsibility in church and society. It will have to allow its leadership to be challenged even as they challenge the society, and recognize that the personal and the political are cut from a single piece of cloth. While the church as a whole may not be able to provide such pacing with any consistency, spiritual directors may have more success, especially when they are aware of their potential for influencing the change process from within their own ministry.

Spiritual Direction and Developmental Transition

Let us attempt to bring all these developmental images of change together and reflect further on the spiritual director's role regarding developmental transition. First, let me reiterate that the content, focus and goals always remain those of *spiritual direction,* namely, fostering the individual's response to God and to the call that flows from their relationship. As spiritual directors, our primary goal should not be reduced to developmental change. But we can and should attend to our developmental effectiveness—we will more adequately fulfill our mission as spiritual directors if we can join with the developmental movement already underway by enhancing each seeker's naturally therapeutic developmental environment.

All communication depends on accurately comprehending another person's frame of reference; exchanges in spiritual direction are no exception. Structural developmental theories provide empirically based models for understanding the implicit frame of reference which the seeker brings into spiritual direction. As we increase our ability to attend to seekers from within their own worldview, we likewise increase our ability to respond empathically and accurately.

Since few spiritual directors would be inclined to give their directees a test to determine their developmental stage, how might we assess the developmental stage of a parishioner or directee? Listening with a developmentally sensitive ear allows us to gauge what individuals mean when they use the word "I" to refer to themselves, thereby unself-consciously revealing their preferred meaning-construction. With a thorough grasp of the developmental continuum, stage assessment becomes straightforward, almost common sense perception. As such, it can take place relatively early in the spiritual direction relationship.

Steven Ivy has developed questions around two rubrics, symbolic communication and self-other perspective, for assessing stages in pastoral contexts. In each case, it will be important to listen more to the implied "why?" behind the answers than to the explicit content.

In order to grasp an individual's level of symbolic communication, Ivy proposes that we might ask ourselves the following: What symbols, metaphors and images does this person use to refer to that which is ultimate? Are references to meaning, symbols and metaphors literal or metaphorical, one-dimensional or multidimensional? What level of reflection constitutes the person's sense of meaning and the ultimate? Does it include consistency and comprehensiveness as important elements? How are pain and ecstasy dealt with in the person's sense of meaning?

To understand the self-other perspective, Ivy proposes these questions: What persons, groups and classes are included and excluded as decisions are made and meaning is formed? What criteria are used in the choice of community and authority? Who are significant others in relation to whom the person maintains a sense of identity? How does the individual experience the community's tasks of confirming, contradicting and continuity?[18] Ivy's stage-by-stage summaries of symbolic communication and self-other perspective appear in Tables 5 and 6. His summary of stage-specific pastoral care appears in Table 7.

With sufficient grasp of the developmental continuum, these questions (and similar ones) can help locate the developmental complexity and meaning-making system of a given directee. Yet even though we might misjudge ego level, we will not go too far astray either developmentally or as spiritual directors if we stay close to each individual's experiences, pacing our responses accordingly.

The simultaneous holding and letting go within the continuity of the spiritual direction relationship can be a powerful environment for spiritual development. When we pace, we attend carefully to the trust level present in the relationship before challenging long-held beliefs or actions; we judge the amount of dissonance introduced as we creatively contradict—enough, but not too much. In addition, our own struggles with similar issues can pace by offering a trustworthy and continuous role model at some particularly disorienting or discouraging point in the seeker's journey. Such careful pacing of our responses to our directees' issues and struggles allows seekers more effectively to use spiritual direction in service of their own deepening relationship with God.

Carlsen's model for therapeutic meaning-making also easily adapts itself to spiritual direction. No less than counselors, spiritual directors must also attend to the trust between ourselves and our directees. This trust provides a context for seekers to examine any thought, feeling or action, hope or disappointment, grace or failure; its depth provides one gauge of the dissonance and creative contradiction the seeker can tolerate from us. Spiritual directors can also listen attentively for the whole context of our directees' lives, including their assumptions about God, their goals, secret disappointments and fears. As inadequate perceptions and assumptions appear, we can gently challenge inadequate or destructive perceptions and actions. We can join our directees in examining a variety of styles of Christian life, inviting and imagining new responses to God's call. We can help them think about their own process of deciding and responding, and learn about discernment as they experience it. We can continue to accompany our directees as they move more deeply into their relationship with God, themselves and the world.

In the course of this chapter, we have seen that both pauses and transitions naturally occur as part of human development. Examining some of the external and internal catalysts to structural development and employing a variety of images gleaned from several theories to illumine our understanding of stage change, we have recognized that many small changes, if appropriately contextualized, may lead to qualitatively new meaning-constructions. However, for a variety of reasons, development is a long-range and not always a successful project. A comment remains on whether or not spiritual directors should actively foster stage change in their directees.

I propose that the spiritual director's role in stage change begins, as always, by attending to the seeker from within her or his frame of reference. The content of the spiritual direction session remains that which is appropriate to the spiritual direction covenant: prayer, relationships and decisions in light of God's call. But the spiritual director can attend to this content through a lens which includes an awareness of the individual's developmental stage. Responses can be framed in such a way as to pace with respect to development. When the directee begins to struggle with issues in such a way that a transition to a new frame of reference appears possible—that is, when the *directee* signals from within that the transition has begun—then the director allies himself or herself gently with the newly emergent system of meaning-making. As the transition continues, the new meaning-system frames an increasingly greater portion of the seeker's life. The director may appropriately accompany and guide the process of recapitulation of ever deeper aspects of self-identity in terms of the new vision of God's call (vertical décalage). At some point, the person more often than not "sees" out of the new frame of reference; then the director can participate in the widening of the new logic to include more aspects of the self (horizontal décalage). In this way, a director can foster the person's increasing integrity within the developmental perspective—while also being alert to and creatively contradicting the imbalances, blindnesses and temptations inherent in the new stage.

Furthermore, as directors, we can employ the "natural therapeutic triad" of confirmation, creative contradiction and continuity without becoming overly concerned about affecting stage change. Each accurately framed response assists the directee's assimilation and accommodation, and thereby contributes to the conditions which foster stage change. Every time a person can emerge from embeddedness *in* an issue or problem, however insignificant it appears, into an enlarged perspective *on* it, we have a sign of further accommodation. But the timing for and even the fact of stage change lie within the seeker's developing integrity.

Responding Developmentally to Mary Beth

Let us return to Mary Beth in order to illustrate more concretely how the dynamics of structural change might inform her spiritual director's responses. Developmentally, Mary Beth is breaking out of a self constructed by the groups in which she has been embedded; this process shows up especially as she returns to school from within a family constellation which still resists her new independence. At the same time, her inner life begins to come alive: she thinks new thoughts triggered by her interaction with a wide variety of persons and ideas she meets at the university. Although increasingly excited by these new horizons, she continues to monitor the resistance from spouse and children, trying to balance her new needs and interests and the family dynamics. Her largely Conscientious perspective still shows traces of the Conformist strategy of behaving according to the standards of the groups in which she is embedded. At school, she thinks her own thoughts, but at home she keeps them to herself, relying on her prayer images to encourage and justify her new self.

The tentative balance that she has worked out is now in jeopardy, and from a quarter that she didn't expect. The very relationship with God which had sustained and comforted her as she navigated the shoals between Conformity and Conscientiousness is now contradicting her tendency to settle in at this new truce; to Mary Beth it feels more like betrayal. She still resists sexual and aggressive feelings in her other relationships, so these feelings in the context of her prayer prove especially disorienting. Any overt sexual overtones emerging in her relationship to God, with all the connotations of "breaking the rules" that they would probably carry for her, evoke a sense of shame. She assumes that God couldn't be breaking these unnamed rules, so the problem must lie with her and the way she is praying. Appealing to an expert to fix her prayer is clearly a Conformist strategy. If her director accommodates this desire, he or she might very well undermine the developmental transition which has absorbed the past three years, and make retreat to Conformity in the face of this challenge much more likely.

The model of change proposed by Watzlawick and colleagues suggests keeping the focus on what is happening rather than on what led up to it. In this light, the spiritual director would probably do well to avoid searching through the background material which Mary Beth has spontaneously offered for the cause of her present dilemma. This information is initially most useful for the developmental clues it provides, especially the evidence of a recent transition which is not completely solidified. The material also suggests a strong motif of being a "good girl." Psychodynamically, developmentally and spiritually, this theme may very well prove salient.

Remember that Mary Beth has not received one-to-one formal spiritual direction until now. Forging the basis for a long-term spiritual direction relationship will require initial confirmation and trust building. As she begins spiritual direction, it will be important to clarify what spiritual direction can and cannot do. This conversation about the purpose and goals of spiritual direction can confirm Mary Beth's growth in personal relationship with God, but also plant seeds for the possibility that this relationship will invite her to more complex and personally responsible decisions. It may also provide the first opportunity to contradict her assumption that the role of the director is simply to teach her how to pray in a way which forecloses new complexity.

Spiritual directors must make several determinations at the outset of any spiritual direction relationship. The first one may often be overlooked: can this person profit from one-to-one spiritual direction, or would he or she make as much or more progress utilizing the resources available in congregational spiritual guidance? Is Mary Beth a good candidate for the personalized spiritual guidance available through spiritual direction, or does she simply need reassurance in this crisis?

A second and developmentally related issue concerns the directee's potential to participate in her own discernment. If Mary Beth can notice and stay with her inner turmoil, at least to a degree, then she probably has the developmental prerequisite for discernment, one sign that she is potentially a good candidate for long-term personalized spiritual direction. In the absence of that ability, or if she experiences too much anxiety, her director may first have to set conditions for Mary Beth to notice and name inner movements, perhaps starting with the more comforting ones from her recent prayer experiences. Such an approach confirms the growing inner life which is characteristic of the Conscientious stage and provides practice in a skill essential for discernment.

The necessary awareness for this kind of interpretation will only emerge over a number of meetings with Mary Beth. These determinations resolve overarching theoretical questions for the spiritual director, and could intrude on Mary Beth's momentum if raised with her directly at this point. Meanwhile, her director would do well to take seriously the discomfort she articulated in her first session, but without making it the sole focus of attention. Among other things, her director might confirm the reality and scariness of the new feelings and images she experiences in prayer, her ability to feel and name these and other feelings, her desire to be close to God, and her graced experiences of God the Father's secure embrace.

Simultaneously, her spiritual director might use Mary Beth's own language and images gently to contradict her assumption that sexual imagery or feelings in prayer necessarily mean that she is somehow bad or wrong, or that she has to earn God's love by being "responsible," or that "good prayer" results only in "positive" feelings—all the while paying careful attention to the degree of anxiety that these disconfirmations might raise. At some point, when trust is sufficiently deep and the timing set by Mary Beth's own agenda, the director will need to probe more carefully the focus of her discomfort, the most accurate name she can give it, and its meaning for her. Such concreteness will be essential in framing immediate responses and in uncovering long-range direction. It could make a great deal of difference, for example, whether Mary Beth is simply ignorant of what prayer might encompass, or whether she is afraid of being overwhelmed by sexual feelings which she has been able to keep repressed until now, or whether she is being invited to begin to deal with intimacy issues across all the relationships in her life.

Keeping the focus on the present can include some historical work around the discomfort which brought Mary Beth to spiritual direction, but attention remains on its description, not its causality. How has she prayed in the past? What happened? What effects did these experiences of God seem to have on her and her relationships? What feelings does she now have as she thinks about beginning to pray again? Could she voice her desires and/or her fears to

God directly? As she does so, what happens? Since imaginal prayer has already figured importantly in Mary Beth's religious experience, further work with guided imagination may elicit alternative images which lower her confusion yet still pace the development of affectively experienced intimacy with God.

If the director does pace appropriately, Mary Beth will indicate in various ways her involvement in the process of spiritual direction. She will confirm accurate interpretations, spontaneously offer further examples of the new insights and behaviors which she is testing out within spiritual direction, and struggle with the implications of her maturing relationships.

More examples of developmentally attentive spiritual direction will appear in the next chapters as we examine three developmental stages in some depth.

V. The Stages Elaborated:
The Earliest Self through Conformity

The three most common developmental stages at which adult parishioners and directees cluster are the Conformist, Conscientious and Interindividual stages. Roger, Tom, Mary Beth and Katherine have introduced us to some of the dynamics of these meaning-systems. These three stages and their implications for spiritual direction need to be examined in more depth.

The typical parish or congregation, however, contains a fuller range of developmental stages. Its younger members manifest what Jane Loevinger calls the Presocial, Impulsive and Self-Protective stages as a matter of their *normal developmental progression* through infancy, childhood, and adolescence. Including a full description of each of these stages in a work focused on adult developmental implications for spiritual guidance would make the volume unwieldy.

Still, in order to understand the three typical adult stages which are the primary locus of this work, it is necessary to grasp the full range of the developmental progression. Briefly describing the stages which precede the three upon which we are concentrating will help trace the increasing complexity of the developmental progression. And should an individual regress under the stress of his or her current life circumstances, we will have some sense of the issues and behavior which may appear.

At the other end of the developmental continuum, the opposite situation occurs. The estimated number of persons in our culture at the Integrated stage averages a mere one percent. Thus, each congregation will contain relatively few persons at this stage and neither pastors nor spiritual directors will see many of them. Consequently, a brief synopsis of the characteristics of the Integrated stage, again without the detail accorded to the more typical adult developmental stages, will give a glimpse of the issues and behaviors which beckon Interindividual persons as they continue to develop.

Examining discrete developmental stages is analogous to stopping a motion picture at three different positions, each separated by some length of film. Because of the intervening frames, the action observed in the stills will not appear to be continuous. Concentrating primarily upon three developmental stages, even three consecutive stages, produces essentially the same effect: the "action" appears discontinuous between the stages. Positively, such a procedure allows the contrasts between the perceptions of reality characteristic of each stage to emerge more clearly.

Negatively, however, this move all but obscures the complex series of starts and stops and advances and retreats which cumulatively constitute a transition. It also promotes the false assumption that development proceeds in a stair-step fashion. In reality, developmental stage change occurs through many small assimilations and accommodations. We literally inch along, sometimes going backward, frequently returning to our present developmental configuration, and only very gradually advancing. (Recall that the inhabitants of our imaginary planet could travel both backward and forward as they wished when preparing for a move to the next country.) Transition is a protracted affair, and in adults typically takes months or years—although at a given moment one may become conscious of what has been happening over time.[1] In order at least partially to retrieve the sense of this incremental flow which comprises a transition, we will also highlight aspects of the transitional levels between the stages.

Several cautions are in order before we begin this phase of our investigation. First, stage descriptions are abstractions, generalizations about a coherent worldview culled from a relatively wide range of behaviors. They cannot be "found" through any single behavior or statement. It is inappropriate, for example, to assume that Mary Beth's meaning-construction is Conformist solely because she looks to her spiritual director as an authority who will help her solve her problem with prayer—a Conformist strategy.

Second, no person will exemplify all the characteristics of a stage. The stages are ideal types, which real people only approximate. Furthermore, persons may respond out of reasoning a half-stage above their usual comfort level as they seek to grasp more inclusive meaning-systems, or they may employ a less complex response than they are capable of, further complicating any simple assessment.

Third, it is impossible to say at what point a person actually reaches a stage. When does a baby learn to walk? After a single step, when it can navigate three consecutive steps from the arms of one parent into the arms of the other, or when it can walk freely around the room, starting and stopping and changing direction at will? Developmental abilities appear in nascent form in one stage, emerging full-blown at the next. As the new stage begins to solidify, its developmental perspective is still relatively restricted in its application. As one "reworks" earlier patterns in terms of the new complexity and applies the new logic to increasingly wider realms, the stage becomes a more comprehensive organizing principle.

Therefore, as we make intuitive assessments about the developmental level of a given person, we would do well to treat any particular clue as just that, a clue about the possible developmental stage. It must be confirmed by a wide range of other clues before we could assume that the person generally operates out of the Conformist construction, for example.[2] Once that determination has been made, we must then resist the temptation to treat the stage as a predictor of behavior. External behavior admits of numerous possible causes. We can never assign a developmental stage with any certainty from a single behavior or statement, nor can we assume that within a particular stage construction a person will *do* any given thing. In fact, one sign of developmental maturity is precisely the ability to select (perhaps unconsciously) from among a range of behaviors that which best fits the circumstances.

With these caveats in mind, we begin with an overview of the stages which lead up to the Conformist. Within the context of the Presocial stage, we will pause to introduce Kegan's understanding of the successive shifts between subject and object, an alternate and dynamic understanding of the process of change. As we discuss the Conformist stage, the first stage typical of adults, we will subdivide our discussion into the four domains which together comprise ego development, probing each subdomain for some implications for spiritual direction. At the end of the chapter, Roger and his spiritual director will reappear.

The Presocial Stage and the Subject-Object Balance

This time of initial ego formation precedes the acquisition of language; it cannot be investigated by the means which structural developmentalists typically use. Therefore, Loevinger and her co-workers consider this early period to be theoretical from an empirical standpoint. Based on Margaret Mahler, Loevinger divides the stage into two substages. In the presocial substage, the infant constructs a stable world of objects. In the symbiotic substage, he or she differentiates self from the outer world. A child who remains at the presocial stage long past the appropriate time is referred to as autistic.[3]

This stage, coextensive with the infant's earliest and prelinguistic months, provides the foundation for Robert Kegan's approach to personality development. He asserts that the pattern of our earliest developmental transition, with its tension between attachment and differentiation, remains prototypical for all subsequent developmental transitions—though obviously the process becomes increasingly complex farther along the developmental continuum. Kegan's understanding of the shift from subject to object undergirds our perspective on stage change.

Kegan alternately calls the subject of his investigation the person, the Self or the ego. He prefers to speak of person or Self, but he understands these terms as analogous to Loevinger's ego. Kegan, however, continually stresses the movement that constitutes the central reality of personality. He speaks of stages as "evolutionary truces": not only do stages manifest distinct and separate realities, "psychologics" with consistency and integrity of their own, they comprise an active process of increasing organization in the relationship of the self to the environment. As organizations, stages are both stable yet somewhat precarious; they are truces, they are balances, they can "tip over" given the right conditions. They are therefore markers in an ongoing process.[4]

This process consists in the progression from being *subject to* or *embedded in* a perspective (so that one sees the world from within it), to standing *outside* that perspective and being able to look at it. This change, equivalent to Piaget's dynamic of assimilation, accommodation, and equilibration, Kegan calls the "successive shift from subject to object." The earliest experience of this evolutionary movement occurs in the first months of life. At birth, infants regard their entire world as part of themselves; eventually, as their primary caretakers interact with them, they begin to differentiate themselves from others. In place of being fused with their primary caretakers, they learn to relate to them as separate persons (or "objects," to use the psychoanalytic term for discrete persons or things).

Paradoxically, though stages mark successive differentiations of the self from the environment, they also signal increasing integration of the environment. This dynamic occurs as follows. That perspective which constitutes the context within which one understands reality is itself rarely available for conscious reflection. We are aware of the results of our perspective, while remaining unconscious of the perspective which has led to these results. Precisely this embeddedness leads one to project that reality onto the world as one's very constitution of reality. One assumes the world is "like that."

To illustrate this dynamic, let us jump ahead in our scheme and look at the Conformist stage. In this perspective, our very self is constituted by the variety of relationships in our world. We *are* our relationships. We cannot critique our relationships as separate from ourself because, as yet, no self exists apart from the network of relationships in which we live. But, at some point, relationships can "move over" to become objects themselves; once this happens, we no longer *are* our relationships, we *have* relationships. That is, relationships no longer form the unreflected horizon within which we construct reality, but become themselves available for critique from the new (itself still unconscious) horizon, in this case, of personal identity. We can then internalize relationships precisely because we are separate from them. The new structure, Conscientiousness, becomes the next mediator and, since it constitutes a new subjectivity, will be projected onto reality in its turn. In terms of the earliest of these transitions, Kegan says: "When the child is able to have his reflexes rather than be them, he stops thinking he causes the world to go dark when he closes his eyes."[5]

At each successive differentiation from the environment, then, one can more accurately integrate it into one's own conception of "the way things are." Recognizing that differentiation and integration are two moments of a single psychological "event" corrects a long-standing and deeply entrenched assumption that differentiation alone serves as the sign and norm of development. This assumption has proven particularly problematic when assessing women's development.[6]

Although this process of successive reorganizations is cognitive at root, it nonetheless also incorporates affectivity. For Kegan, affect is precisely the felt-experience of motion (hence the term "e-motion"): "I am suggesting that the source of our emotions is the phenomenological experience of evolving—of defending, surrendering, and reconstructing a center."[7]

Decentering entails "affects of loss," anxiety and depression. From this perspective, a transition is the experience of separating from one's very self, a self which, although no longer useful, one cannot yet quite differentiate as "other." Fortunately, as an old self dies, a new self is born. Transitions consist in successive deaths and births of self, with all the pain entailed in death and the joy entailed in resurrection. The appearance of hope, the antithesis of depression, marks this subtle change. Developmentally, hope represents the possibility of transformation.[8]

These successive shifts from subject to object constitute the evolution of personality, the very motion of development itself.

Movement occurs as each "subject" becomes the "object" of reflection at the next stage. With Kegan, therefore, our approach changes from focusing on stages with transitions between them, to focusing on transitions with balances (stages) between *them*. In fact, Kegan prefers "balances" to "stages," and names each balance by its typical unreflected horizon. For a summary of this progression and its relationship to several other developmental conceptions, see Table 3.

As we progress through our descriptions of the stages, we will note these shifts from subject to object: each one names the central movement from stage to succeeding stage, and gives us a way to grasp the qualitatively new ability of the next stage.

The Impulsive Stage

From the beginning of the Impulsive stage, the child (or adult) may properly be said to "have an ego," since now individuals begin to establish a separate identity. Children affirm this separate existence primarily through the exercise of their own will. They are no longer subject, willy-nilly, to their reflexes; impulses now rule reflexes. But impulse control is still very tentative and undependable —hence the name of the stage. To Impulsive persons, needs seem insatiable and they may fear their own needs and feelings, especially the bodily experience of sex and aggression.

Thinking is preoperational, fluid and magical, lacking as it does stable logical operations. Since thinking is not yet reversible, cause and effect relations are poorly grasped—a cause is whatever happened immediately before. A strength of this stage, however, lies in the birth of imagination. Symbols and images from stories, fairy tales and biblical narratives can be extremely powerful for awakening long-lasting values.

The typical problem-solving strategies at this stage are wish fulfillment and passive dependency. Significant persons are viewed as sources of supply and the child fears their abandonment or aggression. "Good" and "bad" may be confounded with "good to me" versus "mean to me." Authority is arbitrary; roles are stereotypical and confused (adults are not differentiated from parents, for example). Learning proceeds through reward and punishment, as does this stage's moral thinking.

Not infrequently, adolescents and young adults with adult responsibilities still construct the world from within the Impulsive framework. Their typical ethical stance leads them to "look out for number one first" in order to survive in a hostile world. A higher than average percentage of adults who have not progressed past the Impulsive stage inhabit prisons, mental institutions and half-way houses, reflecting this stage's primitive socialization.[9]

The Self-Protective Stage[10]

In the ordinary course of development, the child begins to establish inner controls through anticipating immediate, short-term rewards and punishments. Impulses become the object of the emerging, as-yet-tentative self, the new subject. Since inner controls are at first quite fragile, the child (or adult) may feel somewhat vulnerable. The person's external and internal worlds are still only partially manageable, with the result that he or she must be on guard at all times to control both the situation and self—hence the name of the stage. But, with the capacity to *have* impulses rather than to *be* them comes new freedom, power and agency.

At this level, persons begin to internalize rules, but understand them literally and use them primarily for their own satisfaction and immediate advantage. With increasing ability to take the perspective of others, reciprocity, fairness and immanent justice make their appearance as major concerns. But interpersonal relations are still manipulative, exploitative, ambivalent and dependent, though less frankly so than at the prior stage.[11] Friendship is context-specific and somewhat "fair-weather," based on pragmatic equality and fairness—think here of the typical ten-year-old's sense of teamwork. Life is a zero-sum game: what one person gains, another must lose. The individual still lacks the power of self-criticism; thus, while the notion of blame exists, it is externalized to other persons, things or circumstances, even to a part of the person's own body. What is wrong is getting caught.

Cognitive processes consist in concrete, literal and stereotypical thinking. But, new to this stage, thinking is reversible and the person can conceive of processes and make inferences regarding cause and effect which were impossible earlier. Roles are "given," with behavior often changing to fit the role. Conscious preoccupations concentrate around self-protection, wishes, advantage and control of others, and fears of retaliation, getting caught or being punished. Ritual, understood as a means to gain control of outer events, characterizes this level. Learning progresses through seeking rewards and avoiding punishment.

The newly emerging self at this stage has become a storyteller *par excellence,* appropriating and retelling adventure stories, lives of important heroes, and roles tried on for their potential "fit." Imagination remains active and vivid, but more subject to the logical constraints of the story which contains it. Still in the future, however, is the ability to draw general conclusions about life from the meanings revealed in the narrative.

This stage is typical through late childhood and early adolescent years. One of the more interesting and observable transitions, which frequently occurs during late high school or early college years, is that from dualistic thinking to relativistic thinking. The dualistic thinker sees all issues of truth and morality in terms of in-groups versus out-groups, right versus wrong, good versus bad, or we versus they. Morality and personal responsibility equals obedience to rules, self-control, and the unquestioned assumption that Authority (whatever that is seen to be) is identical to Truth. This same style of thinking characterizes fundamentalism, and those who work with adolescents know that they are the original fundamentalists. Such dualistic thinking is certainly not confined to adolescence, and its presence in an adult *may* suggest the presence of a self-protective developmental stage. If that be true, dualistic thinking will not yield readily. Only when valued authorities themselves present conflicting views of right, order, or truth will this position begin to weaken. Some struggle usually ensues before Authority will be dethroned to authority, Truth to truth.[12]

Spiritual Direction at the Conformist Stage

At this point, we will expand our discussion to include the four subdomains which comprise each stage: cognitive style, conscious preoccupation, impulse control or character development, and interpersonal style. These four subdomains develop independently of each other, Loevinger holds, but a stage's characteristics will only emerge through the configuration of all four dimensions together.

The significant advance which marks this stage concerns identifying one's own welfare with that of the group, however defined. The needs, interests and wishes which formerly constituted the basis of meaning now yield to interpersonal relationships. Now one *has* impulses, instead of *being* them. Or, in subject-object language, impulses become the object and interpersonal relationships the new subject.

A kind of meta-conformity, which includes non-conformity

and anti-conformity, provides the central category and hence the name of this stage. The group will be "close in": for the child, it will ordinarily consist in the family; for the adolescent, the peer group; and for the adult, the members of one's ethnic group, church, and the like. Identifying with a group requires a new level of trust. Consequently, a person who exists in a hostile environment may harden into a malignant self-protectiveness, never developing the true interpersonalism characteristic of this stage.

A group is experienced as a social whole, held together as a shared community of common interests and beliefs in which a consensus of conventions and general expectations exists. A person at the Conformist stage will perceive differences between groups, but will not yet be sensitive to differences between individuals within a given group. Groups themselves are distinguished by external characteristics such as age, sex or nationality. A Conformist person both manifests and expects social desirability; that is, people are and ought to be what is socially approved. The unanimity characteristic of this stage suppresses the possibility of pluralism; groups appear to break up when something happens to upset the sense of commonality shared by each member. Anger is particularly problematic for a Conformist person because expressing anger risks rending the interpersonal fabric which constitutes one's very self.

The Conformist stage typically arises in adolescence, but becomes the permanent style for many adults. Consequently, we can expect to find such persons as a matter of course in congregations and even among our directees *if* there is some expectation in the group that one "have a spiritual director."[13] Roger still constructs the world essentially out of this perspective.[14]

Cognitive Style

The first of the four subdomains comprising a stage deals with complexity of thinking. Conformist individuals exhibit stereotypic thinking, cliches, and all-or-nothing statements, suggesting that they are still more at home with concrete thinking than with formal operations in the Piagetian sense,[15] although they can reverse their concrete thinking and recognize several perspectives simultaneously. Yet, in order to judge among alternatives, they may appeal to the external order for norms. Right and wrong admit of few exceptions; things are the same for everybody. Their relatively unnuanced approach to life encourages a sentimental and idealistic outlook. Their concrete thought focuses on external objects and behavior, including appearance, reputation, social accep-

tance, belonging and material things. They have little ability as yet
to introspect, and what references to inner feelings they do have,
will be global and banal: they will be happy or sad (but not simultaneously), problems will be solved by "understanding," they want
to "love" more, they may complain that someone doesn't "like"
them, and so on. Therapy which depends primarily on inner awareness of differentiated feeling states remains beyond persons at the
Conformist stage. This notion alone will significantly influence
spiritual direction and discernment, both of which rely on an individual's increasing access to his or her inner life.

A major difficulty that this cognitive style raises for spiritual
direction centers around an undifferentiated and banal inner life.[16]
When asked how they feel about something, Conformist persons
may miss the import of the verb "feel," responding instead with a
thought or an action. Alternatively, the feeling reported may be
very general, as "I felt really good about that conversation," or
"My prayer feels o.k., nothing special." One of the spiritual director's tasks will necessarily be to help these persons begin first of all
to *notice* what happens interiorly, then to be able to *describe* inner
movements, and eventually to incorporate feelings into prayer.
The director can continually underscore any feelings demonstrated
within the conversation, and then, increasingly, any feelings present in the memory of past events. The director can also help refine
the global descriptions: "When you say you don't feel very good
about what happened, would it be more accurate to say you felt
guilty, or ashamed, or disappointed, or embarrassed, or what?"

It may be the case that some persons simply need a more vividly developed language to communicate inner richness or assur-
ance that their inner life has meaning before God. These persons
may learn relatively quickly both to notice and to communicate
interior movements. For example, a woman confined basically to
her home and whose feelings are always discounted by her husband
may never learn to pay attention to or value her feelings. But if she
begins to believe that *God* might be interested in how she feels,
affective prayer may bloom.

If someone is solidly Conformist in meaning-construction,
however, the director will most likely find that the ability to notice
and to describe inner life grows very slowly. Change will happen
over months or years, not days or weeks. An experienced spiritual
director described directing one person who never was able, in the
two years that he worked with her, to "move inside," despite his
underlining, questioning and almost step-by-step instructions for

prayer and post-prayer reflection. Such persons are not being indifferent or stubborn when they don't shift from the externals of their life or employ a variety of feelings in their prayer. In fact, since a rich, differentiated inner life characterizes the Conscientious stage, increasing awareness and expression of feelings may indicate a developmental transition.

Conscious Preoccupation

Appearance, both physical and social, absorbs a great deal of Conformist persons' attention, as will social acceptance and adjustment to group norms. They will be keenly aware of or curious about how others in the group see them, including their spiritual directors—we hold more authority than we often realize, or are comfortable with.

At this stage, what persons want for themselves is identical to group values; they want (or want to be) what their groups judge worthwhile. They will desire and work for group status symbols, especially in such concrete forms as an office, a secretary, a car, professional diplomas—the list is endless. They can be humiliated if their reputation in the group is somehow called into question. A slight from someone important, shame at being unable to live up to personal standards or critical judgments from others who transgress the group's norms are among the issues that may make their way into spiritual direction with a power appearing out of proportion to the cause.

The content of spiritual direction with Conformist persons, then, will tend to concentrate on external norms and concrete aspects of observable behavior. Prayer will likewise focus on concrete styles: a routine of personal devotions or formal prayers like the Liturgy of the Hours, the rosary, or daily devotional reading or other traditional prayer forms perceived by Conformist persons to be valued and expected by their church communities.

That individuals readily socialize into certain kinds of behavior and groups, including religious ones, comprises a major strength of the Conformist orientation. The danger, of course, arises with misplaced concreteness, mistaking nonessentials for essentials. What color the sanctuary gets painted may elicit more struggle than a local initiative to restore the death penalty—which may never come up for discussion at all. Since Conformist persons support and contribute positively to the groups to which they belong, a question for spiritual directors, especially those in institutional settings, becomes whether to ally themselves with "correct" behavior or with the seeker's nascent tendency to challenge rules or differentiate their personal desires from that of the group. Encouraging the latter can become especially complicated when directees begin to critique or act against the system in which they had previously been model members: "I used to listen to what the church says about things like abortion, but now I am beginning to think that sometimes you might have to go against the rules." In order to maximize the inner freedom of both the seeker and the spiritual director to search out what God calls them to do and be, spiritual direction should be totally separate from formal institutional evaluations.

Impulse Control

Conformists present themselves as the proverbial "nice persons" who do everything right and feel shame even for inadvertent infractions of rules. They will no longer simply overlook rules, as at the Impulsive stage, nor obey for their own immediate advantage, as at the Self-Protective level. Typically, they will know and readily obey the discipline of the church, the rule of a religious congregation, and the written and unwritten behavioral norms for community life, but they will tend to see all rules and norms as having approximately the same significance and binding power. Furthermore, they tend to obey without question rules that have been only partially internalized: rules are rules, and following them brings conformity to group norms and a sense of belonging of a kind not possible in earlier developmental constructions.

Because rule-governed behavior guards Conformist persons' hard-won control over the impulses, they need rules and cannot readily bend rules or allow others the freedom to do so.[17] On the contrary, clear and exceptionless rules predict orderly interpersonal interactions with others who also obey rules. Conformist persons will forge a strong group identity and may feel terribly threatened by colleagues whose attitude to rules allows a more flexible interpretation. Disapproval, especially from significant persons or those in authority, becomes a very powerful sanction; conversely, approval promotes learning and socialization.

Two major issues for spiritual direction arise here. One has to do with the "shoulds" characteristic of this stage. The strong moral imperative, which Conformist persons both feel for themselves and project onto others, coupled with the tendency to collapse all rules and conventions into categories of similar significance, make these persons tend to be very hard on themselves, and to appear very judgmental of others' behavior. Spiritual directors can support Conformist persons through the contradictions which this world-view will inevitably sustain by gently challenging judgments concerning self and others, differentiating between moral, behavioral and doctrinal issues, and stressing the free and unearned grace of God.

The second issue which the Conformist's characteristic impulse control raises has to do with denial of negative feelings, especially sexual or aggressive ones. Since these areas can be particularly crucial in spiritual development, the astute director may notice a lack of references to sexuality or an apparent inability to direct any anger at God. Should the director gently inquire about either of these possibilities, he or she may be met with genuine puzzlement, blankness or denial: "I really don't have to worry about being attracted to the opposite sex; that's really not an issue for me" or "God never lets me down."

To the psychological eye, this kind of response looks like resistance. As a normal *developmental* achievement, however, such denial represents an advance over the earlier impulse-ridden stage: energy which was formerly invested in keeping impulses at bay can now be invested in other-directed social behavior. The process of distinguishing psychologically unhealthy resistance from the typical Conformist stage construction includes noticing such clues as the following: First, are other signs of the Conformist stage present; for example, are *all* emotions expressed in vague or general terms or just emotions in this area? If all feelings are equally vague, the person may simply be manifesting the Conformist's global and undifferentiated inner life. Second, does the directee show other signs of resistance such as avoidance, embarrassment, or projection when the conversation moves to some aspect of sexuality or aggression? If yes, either sexuality or aggression may be the primary issue, perhaps compounded by the developmental stage. Third, does the directee avoid only these areas as somehow unworthy or inappropriate to discuss with the spiritual director or to bring before God? In this case, the problem may be an idealized view of God, an exaggerated sense of sinfulness, badness or dirtiness with respect to sexuality or anger, or an inflated need to look good in the eyes of the spiritual director.

To the extent that the director actually encounters Conformist-specific behavior in this regard, he or she can periodically assure directees that any "negative" emotions are included in God's loving concern for them, that at some future time they may find these areas more vivid and compelling than at present, and if so, these feelings can also be brought to spiritual direction. Should Conformist persons commit infractions in these areas, they can be quite literally overcome with shame. Assurances of pardon, rituals of reconciliation with God (and perhaps also with the group if the matter is public) may restore some equilibrium and permit further exploration of this dimension before God.

Interpersonal Style

The Conformist's desire to belong obviously influences interpersonal style in significant ways. First, the scope of social interaction remains relatively concrete and "close-in" at this stage. Conformist persons feel trust and warmth from and extend cooperation and helpfulness to groups "like me," such as immediate or extended family, one's religious congregation, parish or denomination, one's colleagues at a particular workplace or in a certain profession, even one's fellow-citizens. Yet two significant limitations characterize the Conformist interpersonal style. First, awareness of mutuality, the ability to participate equally in relationships, is still limited to conscious participation; a grasp of unconscious motivation has yet to occur spontaneously. Second, a broad and inclusive social worldview is developmentally beyond the Conformist person; it becomes ascendant only at the Interindividual stage. Consequently, amid the niceness and loving concern for one's own, malignant or thoughtless prejudices to out-groups can coexist. This developmental constraint helps explain why some religious groups, typically those who attract large numbers of Conformist persons, can be among the most prejudiced in our society —for such persons, being outside the pale should merit *God's* judgment.[18]

Another stage-specific Conformist characteristic, alluded to previously, involves understanding relationships in terms of action rather than of still relatively inaccessible feelings and motives. Thus, for Conformist persons, friends are people you do things with. In a sense, interpersonal style is *the* significant dimension of the Conformist stage. Interpersonal relationships, though tacitly held (Kegan would say subjectively held), comprise the chief focus of identity formation.

What issues arise for the spiritual director? First, interpersonal mutuality can extend to God, as well as to the valued members of one's self-chosen groups. To a more significant degree than possible at earlier developmental levels, God can be a separate person with whom one can have an increasingly deep relationship. The somewhat prepersonal anthropomorphic conceptions of God typical of earlier stages may now become intensely personal, though still concrete and anthropomorphic. The hierarchical, authoritarian and dualistic conception of parent-child relationships which also characterize this stage may carry over into the conception of God, encouraging a power-oriented, exploitatively dependent attitude.[19] Thus, in a malevolent turn of the same dynamics, some individuals may experience God as a personal judge or strict parent who haunts their every infraction of the rules.

Being a valued member of a congregation, religion, or religious community can assume central importance in identity formation. Seeking "God's will," whether through denominational leaders, clergy, formation personnel or spiritual directors, through "God's Word" in scripture, or through religiously sanctioned behavior, can serve as crucial behavioral motivators. However, "God's will" will most likely be understood in behavioral terms rather than in attitudinal or motivational terms.

A delicate issue arises around the spiritual director's participation in Conformist dynamics. It is clearly important to encourage growth of a personal relationship with God. But, because directors will necessarily have to respond concretely to Conformist persons, they may also tend to become more "directive." To the extent that seekers perceive spiritual directors as valued authorities, directors may unwittingly collude in confirming and even strengthening a Conformist orientation past its usefulness. Sanctions by valued religious authorities, especially within the context of a one-to-one continuous relationship, can have tremendous power. On the other hand, spiritual directors may also lose sight of the fact that the Conformist orientation can be valuable in its own right if it is an authentic expression of one's life and call at that moment. As James Fowler says:

> For persons in a given stage at the right time *for their lives,* the task is the full realization and integration of the strengths and graces of that stage rather than rushing on to the next stage. Each stage has the potential for wholeness, grace and integrity and for strengths sufficient for either life's blows or blessings.[20]

Recapitulation
The *strength* of the Conformist stage comes from investing in persons and institutions outside oneself. Socialization into groups

and communal norms readily occurs. But the strength of one stage simultaneously comprises its weakness with respect to subsequent constructions. At the Conformist stage, individuals remain submerged within the various groups to which they belong. The lack of an inner, self-chosen identity allows Conformist persons to take on various identities—to be different persons—as dictated by the diverse groups to which they have committed themselves.

In somewhat more theological language, the *virtues* of the Conformist stage include generosity, consistency, niceness, helpfulness. Conformist persons will actively promote the goals of the groups with which they identify; certainly they will not "rock the boat." They are capable of a new level of trust and interpersonal relations, including a personal relationship with God. Prayer will be action-oriented and concrete (but with so-called affective prayer still beyond their comfort range). Corresponding *temptations* include an outright return to impulsive behavior, resisted by limiting one's negative feelings; literal and concrete interpretations of rules, texts and relationships (including the relationship with God); prejudice against others perceived as different; authoritarianism; rigidity; harsh judgments on self and others for infractions of rules; and succumbing to shame for personal failures.

Some spiritual directors will find Conformist directees frustrating and challenging. To the degree that directors assume that seekers will come with and will grow in self-awareness, self-identity and self-responsibility before others and before God, they may be puzzled and irritated by the apparent inability of Conformist persons to take life into their own hands, to work "inside," or to pray affectively. They may feel that they have to be more directive with such individuals and to assume more responsibility for their spiritual life than they would like. Therefore, they may fall into a parental style without confirming and enhancing the strengths of this developmental type.

Signs of Transition

Although it is impossible to point out any one time or behavior as the actual stage change, some situations and experiences tend to precipitate transition. At this point in the developmental continuum, those issues and experiences include realizing that respected authorities disagree, and that the various groups to which one belongs demand contradictory commitments or behaviors. Possibly, too, an individual may have experienced "failures" to live up to the idealized portrait set by social norms. For example, a person may work assiduously to earn recognition or advancement but be passed over without notice. Another person may be ashamed that less desirable drives and their attendant feelings surface, despite attempts to keep such unruly aspects of personality out of conscious awareness. We have already seen how crucial the experience of leaving home was for Mary Beth, though in her case it occurred emotionally rather than physically.

The beginning of the transition out of Conformity presents the seeker and the spiritual director alike with a crisis—though not one that can be settled once and for all. The seeker must decide whether to explore the implications of unruly emotions or conflicting stories, despite the painful disorientation which may result from the undoing of one's worldview. Some persons will foreclose the possibility of change or even regress to an earlier dualistic level. Such persons, who have in some sense "chosen" to keep life artificially simple and clear, will present a particular challenge to spiritual directors.

For their part, directors must decide what to confirm: the "old" view of the world, the confusion of the present experience, or the possibility of a new self which as yet may be only a hope. Furthermore, what constitutes hope at this juncture? Who is God for the directee now? How can or must the relationship between the director and the directee change?

Transition may happen so gradually that one only recognizes it in retrospect. And, in fact, a transition itself may make sufficient sense of inner and outer challenges that it becomes a quasi-permanent reality construction in its own right. But before we examine the next transition more closely, let us return to Roger, and follow the progress of his spiritual direction through his final year at the seminary.

Roger's Spiritual Guidance

At their first meeting, Roger's director had inquired about why he sought out spiritual direction, since it was neither required nor expected at his denominational seminary. Roger related that both the senior pastor in his home church and his current District Superintendent met with "spiritual advisors," as Roger called them, and each had encouraged him to do the same. He thought a spiritual advisor would probably be a good idea for him, too. This spiritual director's name had come up as a pastor who "did that kind of thing," so he thought he'd give it a try.

What did Roger expect from spiritual direction? "Well, I guess, to meet with someone who helps me keep my spiritual disciplines going. You know, when you have three different churches, you can do an awful lot of running around. My devotional reading went overboard right away. Sometimes I try to pray in the car, putting on Christian music tapes and stuff like that. But I've really got to get back to my daily devotions. Seminary's a pretty unspiritual place, really. Between the head-trips in my classes and the extra time I spend working at the churches and preparing my sermons, my spiritual life has really dried up. I do repeat my sermons in all three churches each Sunday, but preaching every week takes a lot more time than I expected. I also hope you'll give me some ideas for an adult Sunday school class that I want to do in one of my churches."

Roger readily agreed to meeting once a month, and to come to each meeting prepared to talk about how his spiritual life was going and to reflect on other major aspects of his life. The first few meetings, however, also addressed Roger's frustration at his friends' behavior. Roger introduced this topic early in his second conversation: "I just can't figure it. I've known one of these guys a long time, ten years or so, ever since we were in the high school youth group together. The other one I met here at the seminary. They've always seemed like regular guys. This comes out of the blue. I could kill them for being so stupid."

"Why do you think they're stupid?"

"Because they are jeopardizing their future—they could waste their whole seminary education. If this gets to the wrong people, they'll never be ordained. They could make the seminary look pretty bad, too—the gay seminarians are just looking for a cause to get behind so that they can embarrass the seminary and make the rest of us feel guilty. I bet they'd use publicity in the denomination to raise the ordination issue again. If the denomination's position for clergy, "no sex outside of marriage," is good enough for us heterosexuals, and we are judged on that standard, then they better be too."

"Sounds like you are irritated because there is a double standard."

"Well yeah, I am. Don't get me wrong, I know people can't help it if they're homosexual. But they can choose not to sleep together, same as I have to choose not to. And if they're going to do it anyhow, then they could at least be more careful about it. If they got caught later in their churches, everything would blow up around them. My congregations would certainly be scandalized.

We are losing our moral credibility and that's one reason we are losing membership so fast, because we don't stand for things any more. The people in the pews know it. Every time something like this happens, we lose a bunch of people. We can't afford that much longer. So I guess I think it's morally wrong and stupid, both."

Asked what he felt God might be asking in this situation, Roger replied: "I think God is asking them to live by basic moral principles regarding sexual relations."

"That might be God's call for them; what do you suppose it might be for you?"

"Well, I guess to pray for them. I tried talking to my good friend, but there wasn't any way I could get through to him. He says he's tired of living a lie. He doesn't think there should be a double standard, either, but for him the double standard is that I can get married, but he can't. He says they're not going to broadcast their relationship, but they're not going to quit, either. He assumes I won't say anything about it, even though he knows I totally disagree with what they are doing."

The above exchanges reveal several aspects of the Conformist developmental stage. First, Roger requested spiritual direction because respected mentors suggested he seek it out. He selected a male pastor for his spiritual director. Though the rationale for this choice did not surface in their conversations, a Conformist would seek out someone either like him, or like his stereotype of the pastor he wants to become. Roger hopes spiritual direction will help him get back into "spiritual shape," and also provide him data for a class. That is, the spiritual director will do things for Roger, including provide input and answers.

Second, Roger laces his frustrations with his friends with generalizations: about the consequences facing them if they are discovered, about the gay seminarians, about his own parishioners and about the denomination. Roger judges his friends' behavior as wrong neither because they will get caught (a Self-Protective reasoning), nor because of what it might do to them spiritually (a Conscientious reasoning), but because of its potential for disrupting the communities Roger identifies with. Roger's first reply about God's will assumes it deals with others. His second reply remains externally directed. Roger's anger has a righteous tone to it; he is within the pale, they have stepped outside it.

At one point, Roger's spiritual director tried to bring the conversation closer to Roger by naming a feeling he suspects Roger experiences. Roger acknowledges the feeling, but immediately returns to focusing on his friends' behavior; he is either unwilling, unable, or does not see the need in staying with his own feeling response for what it might reveal. The director tries again to bring Roger closer to the situation by asking about God's call *to him*, with slightly better success.

The following session, Roger reports that he has quit trying to talk to either of his friends. "I'm really kind of sorry, we were such good friends. Now I feel like I hardly know them, nor do I want to. It probably isn't the most Christian response to write them off, but I don't want to waste the energy on being angry with them either. I do keep them both on my intercessory prayer list. God will have to change their hearts."

"You're sorry, you say. Any other feelings?"

"Yeah, I hope they don't burn all their bridges before they're ordained."

"That's not exactly a feeling. Anything like sadness, frustration, resignation, or anger?"

"Well, I could be pretty angry, but, like I said, I'm trying not to. It doesn't seem to be very productive, nor particularly Christian. Mostly, I just feel sorry that it all happened, that our relationship changed, and that they might blow everything."

"I'm not as sure as you seem to be that anger couldn't be productive. Do you think Jesus ever got angry?"

"Well, sure. He was certainly angry when he drove the moneychangers out of the temple. But that's different, these were my friends. I've got my own future to think about, so I don't want to get involved publicly. I can always pray for them, and I do."

Meanwhile, Roger reports with some satisfaction that he has been successful at keeping up with his personal Bible study almost every day. "When I get distracted, I use a book of daily Bible meditations. I've been able to get that done and go through my prayer list no matter how pressed I feel. That's what I did during exams and Christmas, with all the extra stuff going on. This week, things are more regular, and I've gone back to my own Bible study. I feel much better about keeping my spiritual disciplines this month than when I came. I am sure it's helping me preach better, too, because I am more focused on the Word again. . . ."

After Easter, Roger noted that he was finding it hard to find sermon texts week after week. His director suggested turning to the Common Lectionary as a foundation both for his preaching and his personal Bible study and prayer. Roger seemed enthusiastic at the idea, and at the last meeting with his spiritual director before graduation, reported on his experience.

"I did get some helpful sermon texts for the weeks right before Pentecost. I think some of those sermons were really good. Last week, I talked about the congregation's mission in the summer time and that we aren't out of church the same way kids are out of school."

"How would you describe your own prayer and devotional reading during this time?"

"Sort of mixed. Some days, it's rich. Other days, I don't really get anything out of the selections. Those days are frustrating, because I don't feel like I get much out of the prayer time either, except the satisfaction that I kept to my disciplines."

"You think your prayer isn't much good on those days?"

"I know in my head that my feelings aren't the bottom line, but when it seems like God isn't present, it's harder to get through the day. I kind of wonder if I am just doing my own thing, like God isn't very enthusiastic about my ministry, and on those days, I'm usually not either. . . ."

After graduation, Roger returned to his three churches for full-time ministry. He thought he'd join the local Ministerial Association's Lectionary study group as a way to keep up his spiritual disciplines in his new setting. He looks forward to being ordained, on schedule, at the end of his second year as a deacon.

At this point, Roger shows few signs that he is ready to renegotiate his developmental perspective. He looked at what his director brought up, but went no further with his leads. He seemed satisfied to have reestablished his former prayer discipline, though he expanded the range of biblical texts considered in his prayer and preaching by basing them on the Lectionary. Roger resolved the collision between the "authorities" embodied in his friends' life-style and the officially sanctioned life-style of Methodist clergy; he effectively eliminated the voice challenging the system in which his identity is lodged. On the other hand, Roger's prayer experiences raise for him the relationship between his feelings, his prayer, and the fruits of his ministry. Had he continued spiritual direction, the discomforts he experiences as "God not being present in his prayer" and "God not being enthusiastic about his ministry" might have provided a vehicle for further differentiation in his inner life, and for understanding the effects of "desolation"[21] on his prayer and ministry. In the absence of spiritual direction, these discontinuities may still contribute to a developmental transition if other naturally therapeutic developmental dynamics occur in Roger's new life situation.

We might be tempted to ask whether or not Roger's spiritual direction was effective. That there were no obvious developmental changes does not, by itself, rule out the efficacy of the spiritual direction. Developmental change may take months or years. It may never happen. The question, therefore, bears reframing. Does Roger's life reveal more fruit of the Spirit as a result of spiritual direction? Has his life more integrity? Has he been faithful to his lights, as he perceives them? Has his director also responded with integrity? Has he confirmed the action of grace in Roger's life, as he sees it? Has he challenged Roger to expand his interpersonal perspective in ways appropriate to the covenant that he and Roger share?

From our vantage point outside Roger's spiritual direction, we might also be tempted to conclude that Roger has allowed his God to be too small, but so, at times, do we all.

VI. The Stages Elaborated: Spiritual Direction at the Conscientious Stage

On the way to the next developmental meaning-construction, we find a transition which becomes a way station for many people, sometimes for years. Loevinger calls it the Self-Aware level.[1] It is both the easiest and the hardest to study—the easiest because it is so typical and examples proliferate, the hardest because what we see appears self-evident and unrelated to development. This level comprises a normal developmental transition for young adults, and many older women begin spiritual direction with this meaning-construction; therefore, we will explore its particular characteristics before continuing our discussion of the Conscientious stage.

The primary focus of this chapter, however, concerns the Conscientious stage and the spiritual direction issues arising from its four interrelated subdomains. At the conclusion of this chapter, Tom and his spiritual director will resume their work, illustrating the process of spiritual direction with a Conscientious person.

The Self-Aware Transition

Recognizing that one does not always live up to the idealized portrait set by social norms may precipitate the movement from Conformity to this transitional level. Its developmental advance centers around two abilities: increasing self-awareness and appreciating multiple possibilities in the same situation. This new consciousness of oneself functions as a prerequisite for replacing group values with personal values, which characterizes the next stage, Conscientiousness.

The Self-Aware person still experiences inner life in a somewhat global, undifferentiated and banal manner, often expressed by rather vague references to "feelings" in relationship to other persons or groups. Typical descriptive terms include: lonely, embarrassed, self-confident and self-conscious. This latter term suggests the name of the level itself.

Rules now have exceptions or hold only in certain contingencies, though still in stereotypical categories rather than as a reflection of individual traits or needs. Individual persons begin to stand out from the stereotypes and roles by which Conformist persons characterize them, but are not yet seen in the uniqueness by which Conscientious persons perceive them.

Interpersonal style includes awareness of self in relationship to the group. Cognition has become more complex, with formal operational thinking clearly manifest. Learning occurs through identification with ideals and models. Though still vaguely conceived, conscious preoccupations expand to include adjustment, one's problems, reasons and opportunities. Talk of personal goals and plans, while present, continues to be concrete and specific.[2]

Sharon Parks's sensitive study sheds light on this stage as a normal developmental transition which young adults must typically navigate, frequently in the context of higher education. It is characterized by probing commitment, fragile self-dependence which responds affirmatively to appropriate mentors, and formation of ideologically compatible but deeply influential communities. In the most positive situation, these affiliations can be communities of care for others and even of prophetic witness; on the other hand, they may provide a base for destructive ideologies as well.[3]

The Self-Aware developmental construction characterizes many women for long periods of their lives, and therefore will be well represented in the typical parish. A group of researchers, Mary Belenky, Blythe Clinchy, Nancy Goldberger and Jill Tarule, describe the particular nuance in these women's experience. If and when the crucial shift out of Conformity occurs, it centers around three movements: from passivity to action, from a concept of self as static to a concept of self as becoming, and from silence to the reliance on an infallible inner sense.[4]

For these women, Belenky and colleagues note, it is usually not the experience of higher education which precipitates this change. They, like Mary Beth, may return to their education as a *result* of their developmental shift out of Conformity. It is as if they have only just discovered that they are worth educating for their own sakes. In or out of school, women in this transition frequently distrust logic, analysis and abstraction, and instead turn to their experience to validate what authorities present as true. In situations where their inner voice is silent or they lack personal experience, they often apply a "cafeteria approach," trying on a variety of options, trusting that eventually one option will work. Thus, direct sensory experience is particularly important for these subjective women. The arts may be an exceptionally enriching source of data with which they can vastly increase their inner experience.

Because they have cast off their former style of relating, but have yet to develop a consistent, secure, enduring self-concept with which to anchor transformed relationships, these women often feel they have lost *all* relational moorings. Panic and self-doubt may alternate with the exhilarating sense of birth or rebirth.

Almost half of the women Belenky's team interviewed exhibited characteristics of this developmental construction, suggesting that a transition out of this position may be particularly problematic for women in this culture. As a result of a variety of circumstances, they may develop an inner voice, but keep it to themselves because they fear that, if they say what they really feel, they may rupture the thread of connection binding their social world together.[5] Mary Beth adopted this strategy, thinking thoughts formerly unimaginable, but keeping them quiet at home, where they were likely to meet with resistance or subtle ridicule. Only later will these Self-Aware women be able to integrate their self-consciously chosen identity with care for others in a way that sacrifices neither.

Because so many adults settle at the Self-Aware level for long periods of time, at least some persons receiving spiritual direction will manifest the characteristics of this stage. Prior to this developmental position, we could hardly expect persons to seek spiritual direction at all—they would scarcely perceive any need for it unless they were in a social group which expected it. At the Self-Aware level, however, the newly acquired ability to introspect makes an additional spiritual direction focus possible: that of helping the person to notice and share aspects of their growing interior lives.

Recapitulation

The *strengths* of this position include the beginning of personal vision, deepened interest in interpersonal relationships, and increased flexibility in respecting rules and relationships with others and oneself. A young adult at this construction may be governed by an ideal, searching for a community embodying this vision. Loevinger's Sentence Completion Test reveals a clustering of global and undifferentiated references to God, death and religion from persons at this level; such responses indicate awareness of ultimacy in values and relationships but with little of the potential depth and vigor attached to the same notions later. The *limitation* of the Self-Aware level, then, lies in the still incomplete interrelationship between the newly perceived multiplicity and a self-chosen value system.

The *virtues* of this level include helpfulness, patience, honesty —Self-Aware persons are good citizens *par excellence.* Perhaps its *temptation* is to settle in—and unless life deals a challenge, many do. *Transitions* from this level may be precipitated by leaving home, as in the Conformist transition, and by disruption of a primary relationship; for example, through death or divorce. Such external pressures, coming together with the beginnings of self-criticism and self-reflection, invite and challenge one to adopt a Conscientious frame of reference. Such a transition is not at all inevitable; in fact, it demands a kind of moral courage. William Perry notes the cost and the risk involved in the shift to relativistic thinking alone:

> Our records suggest that this development becomes a positive experience only where two processes run in parallel: (1) The confrontation with diversity occurs in ways which allow a person to moderate its impact by steplike assimilations and accommodations . . . ; and (2) The analytical and synthetic skills of contextual thought are developed . . . to provide an alternative to helpless despair in a world devoid of certainty.[6]

In discussing alternatives to growth, Perry also remarks that individuals find their greatest sustenance in a sense of community *in the risks of caring:* "The educator's effort would be, then, to increase the student's experience of recognition and confirmation as a member of the community by virtue of the courage with which he undertakes the risks of care."[7] So, too, the spiritual director's work involves welcoming persons into the community of those who risk caring about ultimate values and concerns.

Spiritual Direction at the Conscientious Stage

With the Conscientious stage we come to what may be the most significant developmental construction with respect to spiritual direction. From this point on the developmental continuum, seekers possess all the key structural prerequisites for effectively using spiritual direction in their search for increasing spiritual integrity. After briefly describing the central developmental advance which characterizes this stage, we will examine each of the four subdomains which together comprise this meaning-construction, commenting upon some of the ramifications for spiritual direction.

The essential characteristic of the Conscientious stage involves the critical appropriation of one's formerly tacit value system. This appropriation is forged by interrupting the reliance on external authority and relocating authority within oneself. Eventually, the interpersonalism which organized the personality at the Conformist stage yields to new awareness of self as an internally organized, consistent identity. This self-as-organization can judge relationships; it *has* relationships rather than being determined by them. The self-constituted self becomes the new subjectivity within which reality is constructed, and interpersonal relationships the new "object." The developmental strength of this stage is the ability to reflect critically on self and outlook, like Mary Beth's often exhilarating experience since her return to college. But this stage's limitation arises at precisely this point as well: the Conscientious person tends to be excessively confident about conscious mental processes and to judge everything from within the self's perspective, something Tom seems inclined to do with respect to his peers at the point when we met him.

This stage receives its name from the word "conscience," since the major elements of adult conscience become developmentally ascendant at this construction. These elements include long-term, self-evaluated goals and ideals, differentiated self-criticism, and sense of responsibility for living up to goals. In a word, the person is now genuinely reflexive,[8] manifesting a rich and differentiated inner life.[9]

Let us see how the Conscientious meaning-system manifests itself over the four dimensions of ego development.

Cognitive Style

For Conscientious persons, conceptual complexity has become the rule rather than the exception, making it possible to see consequences, alternatives and contingencies. Individuals can now think in systems as well as establish priorities among the elements of a system. Thus Conscientious persons can see themselves in the context of, though distinct from, community and society. No longer are they simply defined by the contextualizing relationships in which they were formerly embedded.

The concept of psychological causation arises spontaneously at this stage. Conscientious individuals experience many shades of emotion and observe a similarly expanded range of emotions in others as well. Their deepened ability to perceive patterns allows them to recognize traits and motives in themselves and others, and to understand personality itself as a system. As the understanding of others deepens, it leads to recognizing a broader social context and to increasing mutuality in interpersonal relations.

Consequently, spiritual directors may now deal with persons who feel as if their moorings have vanished.[10] The "new" contingencies may surface as a series of qualifications to almost every possibility. Formerly clear moral norms based on behavior sanctioned by external authorities may now appear to give way to a quicksand of relative and apparently subjective standards. The foggy areas can extend to an evaluation of motivation as well; directees may now recognize that motivations which appeared pure and idealistic are simultaneously self-serving and flawed. Simple views of the world have become impossible, a loss that some persons may even need to pause and mourn—in a very real way, they have had to leave behind childhood to take on this frame of reference. This experience of losing external certainties could drive a person to pursue spiritual direction as an attempt to establish an inner direction amidst apparent chaos. Some form of the question "What does it all mean (to me)?" is both a possibility and a motivation from this point onward.

If confusion and grief over lost certainties become too great, paralysis may also set in, especially early in the transition when there may appear to be too many possibilities and contingencies to move at all. William Perry sensitively illustrates the pain and disorientation present in the relativism of this position.[11] He also points out the *kairos* inherent in this struggle: it is possible to foreclose the effort, having sensed its cost, and return to an artificially simple world. But returning to an artificial simplicity after a glimpse of the possibility of relativity and contingency takes an immense amount of psychic energy. One must, quite literally, defend oneself from complexity, even in one's inner life. It is quite possible, Perry's research shows, to retreat.[12]

But it is also possible to come to grips with a relativistic universe. Perry contributes two observations which indicate clearly the moral nature of this position's dilemma:

> 1) Theologically speaking, [Relativism] represents the point of critical division between "belief" and the possibility of "faith." Belief requires no investment by the person. To become faith it first must be doubted. Only in the face of doubt is the person called upon for that act of Commitment that is his contribution, his faith. In [Relativ-

ism] one can no longer "believe" in the simple, unquestioned sense.

2) If one later commits oneself to a faith in an Absolute, *there is a criterion which reveals that this Commitment has been made in the context of a relativistic world.* This criterion is one's attitude toward other people with a belief or faith in a different Absolute. . . . The moral obligation to convert them or to annihilate them has vanished.[13]

But having seen and accepted relativism, there is still a further trap: in a relativistic world, one may become detached, avoiding personal commitments to anything or anyone. That is, one may choose alienation. Perry highlights two forms: passively delegating all responsibility to fate—or to God, or using excessive activity or perfectionism to seal oneself from the implications of deeper values.[14] Either possibility may tempt religious persons, albeit each in its own way.

What implications for spiritual direction appear in this shifting of meaning-systems? It is possible to speak of each developmental transition as a "crisis of faith," since each is characterized by the breakdown of one frame of reference and the emergence of another. But only at this stage does it become possible self-consciously to appropriate religious values, behaviors and beliefs.[15] Spiritual directors, then, could expect some form of acute or chronic crisis of meaning intertwined in this transition.

The variations can be as numerous as the persons. For some, the crisis may center on images of God, God's authority, or God's power in a world where evil seems to prevail. For many women at this stage, inclusive language clothes a revolution in their entire repertoire of God-images as they become increasingly conscious of the ways they have internalized androcentric conceptions of the divine. For others, it may focus around rebellion against or collapse of structures which have previously been given divine sanction, such as the authority of the church with respect to moral norms, the form of religious life, the place of women in society, or the understanding of the family. Crisis may brew as a result of losing an idealized view of the clergy or other valued religious authorities through some scandal or slight. Whatever the cause, the spiritual director's challenge lies in deciding whether to legitimate or to abort the crisis.

Because such crises of faith leave persons quite literally "off balance," directees are thus particularly vulnerable to our influence at these times. Spiritual directors can as easily encourage identity foreclosure as identity formation, collude in a retreat from the issues, as pace dealing with the painful vacuum between one set of images and another. We may ever-so-subtly encourage seekers to adopt our own values, norms and behaviors or to launch into the sometimes protracted and frequently frustrating process of forging their own self-chosen spiritual identity.

How free can spiritual directors allow seekers to be as they search for their own spiritual identity before God? In what ways will or won't we support the fragile and unique spiritual direction that directees may be painfully constructing—especially if it appears to us that the emerging identity is more rigid and less inclusive than the former? After all, retreat is one potential choice, as is pausing in mid-stream before taking the plunge. Perhaps the timing isn't quite right yet; in the short haul, such temporizing may look like outright retreat.[16] Understanding the complexity of developmental transition and the often lengthy time span it occupies may give us a broader and less judgmental perspective on directees who don't develop as we might prefer.

With the rise of relativity, it becomes impossible to rely exclusively on external norms as the sole basis for decision-making—the various "authorities" disagree. Discernment, the name that the spiritual tradition uses for the ability to discriminate between choices, becomes increasingly possible and significant for assessing increasing numbers of moral and spiritual contingencies.

The vastly increased awareness of *inner* movements characteristic of the Conscientious cognitive and emotional complexity provides rich material for discernment. A new voice, "I feel," now begins to speak louder than the ecclesial, societal and familial voices of earlier meaning-constructions and carries increasing weight in decision-making. With the appearance of mature adult conscience, then, the possibility of discernment in its rich, inner self-directing sense at last becomes possible for directees themselves. This new possibility creates a watershed in terms of spiritual direction.

But the particular blindness of the Conscientious perspective also makes discernment more crucial than ever before. Because one's own self becomes the norm at this stage, a person of this meaning-construction might readily say, "I have prayed about it and I have decided . . ." in a way that forecloses input. Since careful discernment includes considering the impact of one's decisions upon others and contextualizing decisions within the long and frequently ambiguous spiritual and ecclesial tradition, spiritual directors may need to challenge an overreliance on the directee's own self as the sole norm for discernment.

Conscious Preoccupations

A sense of being the author of one's own destiny surfaces at this stage. Conscientious individuals value achievement, but use internal rather than external standards to judge this performance. Conscious preoccupations include obligations, ideals, traits and achievement. New to this stage is the understanding that persons are not always aware of their behavior or motivation; though the term "unconscious" itself may not be used, the concept is operative nonetheless. Conscientious persons learn best through challenges to their ability, self-initiation and personal development—precisely what Tom felt to be lacking in his seminary's formation program.

Self and self-identity move to center stage in individual consciousness. A longer view of time and a sense of self come together to create an enriched capacity for long-term goals, ideals and values. Since spiritual direction involves one person assisting another to discover and live out his or her deepest values and goals before God, this ability—to recognize, cherish and work for long-range goals and more inclusive and personalized values—itself qualitatively extends the scope of spiritual direction.

This stage's cognitive style implies the ability to "demythologize"[17] former meaning-systems, and in fact, it is a prerequisite for clarifying meanings and systems until now only tacitly held.[18] The demythologizing could well extend to the person's own self-image, since awareness of one's motivations comes to the fore at this stage.

Formerly significant issues may now lose their meaning for the seeker. Symbols appear to "flatten out," and life to have lost its direction and compelling power. Directees may become aware that they see things others don't seem to see, that they no longer fit so neatly into the system, that life has become more complicated. The former ways of praying and images of God may drop away leaving them confused on this front as well.

Yet it is equally possible that the structural components of this stage *open up* life. Where one person is lost, another can have a sense of embarking on an enlivening journey, or of growing up and "finding" herself, or of taking responsibility for his own life. The *structure* of a given stage will be made concrete by specific contents and emotional tones, and indeed this variety forms a part of each individual's uniqueness. Human complexity alone suggests that for most persons such a major transition will not be an all-or-nothing affair: through a series of advances and retreats, individuals eventually forge a unique personality style in response to physical, environmental, social and intellectual stimulations. In addition, our theological assumptions assert that God works freely and uniquely with each person. At this point in the developmental continuum, however, uniqueness can be embraced to a new degree, since one is able to reflect consciously on one's self-identity before God.

Impulse Control

At the Conscientious stage, rules become internalized, self-evaluated and self-chosen. No longer are they seen as absolute, but instead encompass exceptions and contingencies. Assuming responsibility for oneself includes adopting inner, moral, self-evaluated standards. The experience of guilt also changes: whereas Conformist persons feel ashamed for breaking rules, Conscientious persons feel guilty for the consequences of their actions. This shift signals the rise of true (adult) moral conscience because motives rather than behaviors become central in moral evaluation.

This transformation of impulse control raises new dynamics within spiritual direction. For example, the self-evaluation which is the strength of this stage can also encourage a hypercritical stance toward oneself and others, religious groups and spiritual director included—at least when compared with prior levels of impulse control. Directees may express confusion over what is really wrong or right or even how to make such a judgment in the face of so much relativity. Eventually, some may settle on the reduced claim: "I don't know whether this is right for everyone or not, but it seems right *for me.*" We have already noted that careful discernment helps transcend any naive pursuit of what "feels good" in the moral realm ("it can't be wrong, it feels so good"). This discernment contextualizes what is "best for me" in the light of a deeper sense of self in community and a correspondingly deeper realization of one's need for salvation.

Or again, as directees begin to see through their own actions and motivations, and recognize how flawed and two-faced they may be below the surface, any previously unexamined assumptions that one can save oneself or earn one's own salvation will be ripe for reexamination. The spiritual director can employ this deeper self-knowledge to stimulate a more radical knowledge of and reliance on a God who saves out of pure graciousness.

Interpersonal Style

The turn to the inner life characteristic of the Conscientious person simultaneously allows broadening and deepening of all other relationships. Developmental readiness for intimacy appears at this stage, resulting in increased potential for mutual, intense relationships. A sense of responsibility for others and a concern for communication, especially of differentiated feelings, sustains these relationships.

Reconstructing the sense of self-in-relationship has tremendous implications for spiritual direction. First, one's conception of self in relation to self changes. Persons become truly reflexive, not as an occasional insight, but as a characteristic way of seeing. Directees can recognize strengths and weaknesses in their relationships, personality traits and responses.

Second, self-objectivity extends to objectivity with others, the prerequisite for deepened reciprocity and intimacy in interpersonal relations. However, spiritual directors also receive the breakdown or frustration of this turn to mutuality. When directees do not experience themselves treated as unique individuals within significant relationships, such as when judicatory boards or religious congregations resort to filling slots, when authority appears depersonalizing, or when one's spouse does not share an interest in inner life, the resulting crisis can even challenge basic vocational choices. This dilemma might be expressed as "I don't see how I can keep growing any more; there's no support for my inner life any longer," or "There's no way we can communicate on the level of feelings and values and what's important to me." When Conscientious persons make this kind of statement, they imply that other persons or institutions should somehow accommodate their newly forged self-identity; when Interindividual persons say something similar, it may function simply as a statement of fact and serve as a launching pad for constructing a new sense of self in the midst of the resulting tension. Katherine's further reflections on the stalemate between herself and her husband will begin to reveal which meaning-construction is more salient for her; in either case, she seems poised to raise this issue with her spiritual director.

In another twist to the possibilities and problematics of the Conscientious frame of reference, individuals may expend themselves out of a deepened sense of ideals, relationships between persons and systems and an enhanced sense of self. There is, in a sense, more of oneself to give than at prior developmental positions. The limitation that Conscientious persons labor under, however, makes it appear to them that caring for others is antithetical to caring for themselves. Hence, directees may resist suggestions that they include themselves in their own caring, or feel guilty when they do quit constantly pouring themselves out for others. Although Conscientious individuals can learn strategies to prevent their own burnout, the ultimate resolution of this dilemma awaits a reframing of the possibilities of care to include oneself within its scope.[19]

Increased potential for interpersonal relationships also extends to relationship with God. The locus for meeting God moves *inside* the person; God can now be "my God," rather than the God of one's parents, church or society. The desire and concern for communication and the differentiated range of feelings can extend to one's relationship with God and others. Prayer, perhaps for the first time, can be truly affective. The question: "Have you expressed how you feel about that to God?" will make sense to Conscientious persons, even though they may not be in the habit of so doing. Some persons may find it relatively easy to express "positive" emotions, but communicating sexual, aggressive, or angry feelings toward God or others may be another matter. Directors can again profitably underscore the person's emotional responses, encouraging directees to express their broadened range of feelings directly to God.

Recapitulation

The *strengths* of the Conscientious stage, then, include the emergence of adult conscience with the concomitant abilities to grasp long-term, self-evaluated, self-chosen goals, and the reflexivity and psychological-mindedness which accompany a developed and differentiated inner life. Its *limitations* include the possibility of losing one's moorings for the short or long term through confronting a more relativistic world; idiosyncratic, self-centered and subjective judgments about self and others; and excessive confidence in one's own assessments and critical reflections. Sometimes behaviors toward strangers may be as exclusive as those of Conformist persons, but organized around a different understanding of "the way things are."

The characteristic *virtues* of Conscientious persons include inner moral standards, integrity, truthfulness, understanding, empathy, altruism, even a kind of humor which persists through successive developmental transformations. Its characteristic *temptations* include: avoiding—through alienation, cynicism, or activism—the responsibility entailed in self-appropriated standards; hypercritical self-examination; excluding oneself in the scope of care; getting sidetracked into a search for inner religious experiences or ideological formulations; and seeking to control others, judging them by one's own norms.

The traits and abilities which make either spiritual direction or any insight-oriented psychotherapy possible exist as a matter of structure in the Conscientious person: reflexive awareness of one's inner life, self-chosen standards and goals, extended vision about goals and commitments, adult moral conscience. Indeed, prior to this stage persons may not spontaneously seek out formal spiritual direction. But to the degree that spiritual directors expect all directees to respond like Conscientious persons, they may find themselves disappointed with directees who are not, and may never be, at the Conscientious stage.

Before we leave our discussion of this stage, let us rejoin Tom and his spiritual director.

Tom's Continuing Spiritual Direction

As we did with Roger, let us return to the early stages of Tom's spiritual direction, noting the qualitative difference in Tom's understanding about the process and his hopes for its outcome.

In addition to the details already noted, Tom's initial conversation clarified his reasons for choosing this director, an adjunct faculty member and Roman Catholic laywoman, from the list of spiritual directors. Tom noted, "I thought you might understand my frustration with seminary right now—you're far enough outside the system not to buy into everything without questioning it, but since you teach here and see some of the guys for spiritual direction, you probably will also understand what I'm talking about. I assume you won't have any vested interest in decisions about ordination. Besides, you have a good reputation."

"But I won't just agree with you about everything," she replied. "I'm not exactly 'nondirective,' as they say. I'll push you on things I think you need to be pushed about."

"That's exactly what I'm hoping for—someone who will help me sort out what I actually think from what I'm 'supposed' to think and who I am from any stereotypes of 'seminarians.' That's the only way I'm going to know if I belong here or not."

Tom described his expectations for spiritual direction: "I guess I already told you some: to become myself, to see if I really do have a vocation and to learn to pray better."

"We don't have to confine our conversations to prayer, by any means, but let's focus some time on this aspect of your life each time we meet. By way of helping us both be aware of what goes on as you pray, may I suggest you do some journaling these next couple of weeks? After you finish your prayer time, give yourself about five extra minutes. Use that time to look back on what happened while you prayed. Note insights, thought processes and conclusions, but also your *feelings* and how they shifted during the prayer time. We can discuss what emerges the next time we meet."

Two weeks later, however, Tom picked up at a different place. "Do I need to talk! Last week, the formation director asked me why I seemed so aloof from the other guys. I said I didn't know, but then I thought, 'what the hell,' and told him all the things I told you last time, how the formation program makes me feel like an adolescent instead of an adult, and that the other guys seem so much younger than I. He said I could learn a lot from them, and besides they would be my support-group all through studies and after ordination, so I might want to put myself out a little and get to know them and let them know me. At least that was the gist of what I remember.

"But, I don't want to—I don't have time for TV, and the stuff the guys talk about is boring. I get enough at meals without looking for more. I've been frustrated and irritable since Wednesday when we had that conversation. In fact, the last few days, when I went to pray, I just thought about what the formation director said, and kept wondering if I should quit right now. Sally's still waiting."

"Let's back up a bit. You're overwhelmed at the conversation with the formation director, or—how would you describe your feelings?"

"I'm feeling embarrassed—no, infantalized. I'm an adult. I made all my own decisions about who I'd see and what I'd do for years. Now I feel like a kid who's had his fingers slapped because he didn't want to play with his cousins. It's humiliating."

"Any truth to it?"

"Sure there is—that's why I'm embarrassed."

"So it would be simple to bail out, especially because Sally's waiting?"

"Yeah. (ruefully) I guess I did kind of jump to an extreme conclusion, didn't I? I've only been here a couple of months, and I am slow to get to know people. . . ."

Later in the conversation, Tom's spiritual director picked up on his prayer: "You said all you did during your prayer since Wednesday was think about the conference with the formation director and stew, right?"

"Um-hum."

"Did you look back after you were finished praying and look for the dynamic movement of that prayer time?"

"No, I completely forgot, but I did before then."

"What did you notice?"

"At first, it felt strange. I got self-conscious, and started looking at what was happening while I was praying instead of after, and it got in the way. But about the end of last week, I kind of quit watching myself. On the day when we had the reading from the first chapter of John's gospel—you know, where the two disciples of John the Baptist start to follow Jesus home—an interesting thing happened. When Jesus said 'Come and see,' I both wanted to and didn't want to at the same time. Like, the guy was fascinating, but I had planned to go home. . . . You know, now that I hear myself saying that, it sounds just like what I am doing right now: I am intrigued but at the same time, I want to go home."

"What does 'I want to go home' mean to you? Can you say more?"

"I miss . . . sad . . . no . . . lonely. I miss my life and my ability to control what I do and how I do it . . . what does that feel like? Maybe like I'm going to lose myself. . . ."

This vignette suggests that Tom can notice his inner responses, and that these responses are nuanced and varied—Tom described himself as intrigued, self-conscious, infantalized, embarrassed and lonely. Presumably, he will be able to notice the patterns in God's work with him and his responses to God and others; he has already begun connecting what happened in his prayer with what is going on in his life. Unlike Roger, Tom expects that spiritual direction will be based largely on his self-discovery, with the director facilitating his process.

Since Tom's prayer around the call of the disciples continued to deepen as he shared it with his spiritual director, she suggested he not move on to tomorrow's Lectionary passage as is his usual pattern, but instead return to that "call" text. Perhaps he would like to ask Jesus what kind of person Jesus is, perhaps he would like to tell Jesus that he is ambivalent about following him, perhaps he would just like to go and spend another day listening to him—whatever Tom felt moved to do in Jesus' presence. Tom thought that he could do that, and he also remarked that he thought he would do something, maybe go to a movie, with one of the men with whom he felt more affinity.

At their next session two weeks later, Tom began: "I still feel lonely. It's a pretty strong feeling, and it's been there since we talked last. I did ask Rick (one of the seminarians) to go to the movies on Friday and we had pizza before. It was fun, and I think we could be friends. One of the things that attracts me to him is that he's not a T.V. watcher, either. He's on the fringe the way I am. We decided we would like to get together pretty regularly.

"The other thing I did was to volunteer to plan the big Thanksgiving dinner for all the faculty, staff and students. The committee was formed this week. It will be a good way to get to know Mrs. Peterson (the President's secretary) and Mary, one of the women who's in my Old Testament class. She's getting her M. Div. too—did you know that, in her diocese, if lay women want to become parochial ministers in charge of parishes, they have to have an M.Div., same as the priests? I didn't know that before."

"How did the loneliness affect your prayer? Did you happen to bring it into your prayer?"

"No, it never occurred to me to do that. . . . I knew I was lonely though, especially one day, because I noted it in my journal. The other days, I guess I just ignored it."

"You could, you know, bring the whole feeling to God, or perhaps to Jesus, since he's been the figure appearing in your meditation lately. What would you think of that?"

"Well, just talk it out, you mean?"

"Yes, or write it out in your journal, perhaps, letting the dialogue flow without planning or censoring it."

"Won't that be just me talking to myself? How do I know the other part of the dialogue is really God?"

"You won't necessarily be certain, but we can learn to tell the difference between God speaking and your unconscious speaking as we go along. There will be a difference. You don't have to make any decisions based on what comes out of such a dialogue alone, but it might reveal some things you haven't quite said to yourself yet."

"That last part sounds a little bit scary. Maybe I don't want to know the things I haven't said to myself yet. . . ."

Sensing that Tom has the developmental ability to appropriate his own discernment process and to pray affectively, Tom's spiritual director supports deepening both capacities. She encourages him to locate the authority for his behavior within himself, choosing to keep rules or to follow social conventions, rather than just "falling in line." She helps him transfer his ability for reflexivity to his own prayer by encouraging him to look back over what has happened throughout the time he set aside for prayer. She knows that if Tom is to examine the whole course of his thoughts, beginning, middle and end, seeing if they are wholly good or pinpointing where they went astray, as Ignatius of Loyola suggested,[20] his ability to do so will depend on this reflexivity. In the early stages of Tom's work with this spiritual director, it appears that he has all the developmental prerequisites necessary for Conscientious decisions, adult conscience and discernment, though these responses are not yet habitual.

Tom's spiritual direction proceeded more or less in this vein throughout the academic year. With his spiritual director's encouragement, he continued to bring both his thoughts and his feelings to prayer, addressing God about his day-to-day struggles and joys. Gradually, Tom's loneliness and isolation decreased; the circle of friends and acquaintances among both his fellow seminarians and the lay students in his classes slowly widened. In fact, he became quite good friends with Mary and her husband and family, a relationship begun as they worked on the Thanksgiving dinner.

At the close of the academic year, Tom returned to his diocese for a summer internship in a rural parish with a large migrant population. He planned to resume his spiritual direction when he returned in the fall.

In late June, however, Tom's spiritual director answered her phone to hear Tom say: "I know we didn't have an appointment until August, but I really do need to see you before then." They confirmed an appointment for the following morning.

"I've been seeing Sal," he opened the next day. "You remember she lives only about fifty miles from my parish. It takes me less time to drive to see her than to see you. We started with getting together over coffee, just to catch up. I realized how much feeling for Sal I still have. I'm really confused. If it weren't for the strength of these feelings, I would have thought all the other indications for continuing in seminary were still 'go.' But now I'm not sure at all."

Tom elaborated on things he and Sally were talking about: his doubts and confusion, their feelings for one another, Sally's life in the meantime, and—just two days ago—her sense that she's going to have to move one way or the other on their relationship pretty soon.

Tom continued: "She can't—or won't—fence-sit much longer. I realized for the first time how I've been unconsciously counting on Sal being there if I leave the seminary. I've been tying her with this thread. I feel pressured to make a decision. . . . I could just leave; we'd be married by the time classes start in the fall."

"Given what you have said today and how I've come to know you over the past year, that seems a little bit abrupt. What's behind it?"

(Sigh) "When I realized how much I've been unconsciously hanging on to Sal, and that she's not going to wait much longer, I think I panicked, because later in the day, I proposed we sleep together, and we did that night. I'm so confused and I feel really guilty."

"Can you describe in more detail what your sense of guilt is related to?"

"Let's see . . . I've led Sally along, but I wasn't doing that consciously. But having sex at this point is really different from before. Then we were headed for marriage, but at this point, I *claim* I'm not. I feel like I've misled her into believing there's something to hope for."

"Maybe there is. What do you think?"

"Well, I still don't know if I should be a priest, but neither is it clear to me that I shouldn't—unless this situation is a sign itself."

"As I listen to you, you seem agitated and driven."

"You're right. It's all I've been able to think about for days. When I sit down to pray, it all comes up immediately, I go over everything again, and when I finish I am exactly where I started. Right now, if I left the seminary for Sal, deep down I think the reason would be because I've led her on, not really because I want to. I do love her though."

"But there is a piece of you that is driven by guilt, is that what you are saying?"

"Yeah."

"Perhaps that guilt is what you should take to God in prayer and see what happens. Meanwhile, while you are in the process of discerning what all this means, how do you think you might respond to Sally?"

"I guess I need to tell her that I think I panicked, that I have been relying on her being there if I left, and that I think I wanted to keep her tied into relationship to me, that I see that better now, and that I am sorry for using her."

"What about further sexual relations?"

"I think we better not, not so much because the church says it's wrong, or because we might get caught, but because I don't really know what my motives are. I don't want to keep using Sal for my own security. We were both chagrined afterward. She knew I was coming to see you, and encouraged me to do so. She said she had to get some space herself. So she will feel ok about at least a moratorium, I think. . . ."

Knowing that Tom must have something unusual on his mind to be calling her out of season, Tom's spiritual director readily agreed to an appointment. The quality of the relationship that she and Tom forged over the year grounded Tom's urge to call her, but her continued helpfulness will flow not only from her ability to "stay with" Tom in this crisis and to confirm his appropriate behavior, but also to nudge him, as he is able, to widen his view of reality and to imagine more alternatives. Hence, she turns the discussion toward Tom's immediate response to Sally. Though the meaning of Tom's recent behavior may not become clear for some time, she asks him to accept responsibility for his part in this confusing situation, yet without reacting precipitously. That is, she helps set the conditions in which Tom might hold a multiplicity of viewpoints simultaneously, acknowledge his (and perhaps Sally's) largely unconscious collusion in this situation, and become aware of its ripples outward into the broader family, seminary and church communities. She doesn't judge Tom's behavior before he does, but does ask him to begin to examine it from several new viewpoints. She asks Tom to keep becoming more transparent before God by assuming he will be transparent with her. How deep and far this process moves will, of course, depend on Tom.

VII. The Stages Elaborated: Spiritual Direction at the Interindividual Stage

Our last stage exploration includes the transitional level leading to the Interindividual stage, which Loevinger calls Individualistic; the Interindividual stage and its implications for spiritual direction; and a brief description of the Integrated stage. Katherine's later fortunes in spiritual direction close this chapter.

The Individualistic Transition

As with the Self-Aware transition, we can briefly summarize this position since it contains the gains of the Conscientious stage and the seeds of the Interindividual stage. Recall that, although the structural developmental theories account for generalizations in worldview, each person embodies them uniquely. Farther along the developmental continuum, this individuality becomes even more important because enhanced originality characterizes increasing developmental complexity. This uniqueness is especially evident from the Individualistic level onward—hence the name of this level.

The heightened recognition of individual differences which marks this position leads to a new toleration of self and others. The moralism typical of a Conscientious person begins to give way to awareness of inner conflict and toleration of paradox and contradiction. Feelings and needs are vividly conveyed, and opposite needs may coexist in the same moment. The conflict between personal freedom and interpersonal responsibility emerges as typical of this level. Conceptual complexity continues to develop; consequently Individualistic persons can grasp the discrepancy between inner reality and outer appearances, between process and outcome, and between psychological and physiological causation. Because of an increasingly refined sense of time, a true notion of development—impossible before the Conscientious stage—becomes a natural mode of thought. Conscious preoccupations center around the distinction of inner life from outer. Learning occurs though active pursuits.[1]

Martin Rock's empirical research confirms that Individualistic persons show a marked shift in self-awareness and self-reflectivity. It also indicates that Individualistic self-reflection is more integrative, more oriented toward finding causes and reasons for one's own experience, more understanding of self in the context of relationships, and more aware of psychological development over time.[2] All these capacities greatly enhance the process of spiritual direction.

The *strengths* of the Individualistic level, then, include new discriminations which prepare for the Interindividual stage, namely: distinguishing between process and outcome, differentiating between inner and outer life, becoming aware that individual selves differ in significant ways, and recognizing that emotional dependence coexists with independence in other facets of life. Seekers may now be more interested in the *process* of the spiritual journey and less concerned about arriving at the destination. They will be able to recognize an increasingly broad spectrum of social problems, yet may lack a sense of urgency to take a personal stand on justice issues; that call becomes a serious issue at the Interindividual stage. They may struggle to tolerate more inner conflict and wrestle with paradoxical ways to understand an increasingly complex world. For example, a person at this level values both intimacy and achievement, but has difficulty finding realistic standards for combining these values.[3] The *limitation* of this level consists in the inability structurally to integrate individual and group needs, intimacy and achievement or the demands of personal freedom and interpersonal responsibility. Individualistic persons tend to see the alternatives as forced choices.

Katherine brings both this transitional level's strengths and its dilemmas to her new spiritual director. But she also reveals a readiness to deal with her conflict through the Interindividual stage's unique structure for meaning-making.

Spiritual Direction at the Interindividual Stage

Because personality structures are stable, and therefore slow to change, it would be somewhat rare to meet truly Interindividual persons before mid-life, although a few reach this level in their college years. Persons may be propelled to this new form of meaning-making by becoming disillusioned with what life has brought and the choices one has made, by recognizing that more than half of life has passed, or having one's ideals and logical reason collide with dilemmas of responsible commitment. Rather than using self as the norm, Interindividual persons can see the self in conjunction with and as an actor in many systems. Consequently, the ability to let both oneself and others be individuals, with the resulting "opening out" to a broader social perspective, comprises an integral dynamic of this stage. In Kegan's subject-object language, the prior subject, the self-composed self, becomes the new object with this rise of interdependence. As Joann Wolski Conn puts it: "There is now a self which *has* control instead of *being* control."[4]

Loevinger calls this stage Autonomy. At this point, I depart from her system of naming stages because, without further clarification, the term "autonomy" so easily obscures the developmental strength of this stage. For Loevinger, autonomous individuals not only act autonomously themselves, but they must also allow all others the same degree of autonomy. From this enhanced sense of autonomy arise relationships of deeper mutuality and equality. Unfortunately, in our society, "autonomy" more typically connotes an enclosed, isolated, nuclear self, completely unaffected by other persons or systems—precisely the opposite of the developmental strength of this stage. To avoid this misconception, I here adopt Kegan's stage terminology. "Interindividual" much more readily conveys the strength of this stage construction in our culture.

Thus, the Interindividual stage's developmental advance centers around the willingness to allow others to be responsible individuals, finding their own way and making their own mistakes, and the enhanced possibility for intimacy and mutuality which results. At this stage, individuals also perceive the limits of autonomy, and consequently recognize the inevitability of interdependence. Finally, Interindividual persons exhibit a broad view of life as a whole, including such abstract ideals as social justice.[5] Sharon Parks aptly summarizes the joys and pains of this stage:

> The person can recognize and know with the whole self the truth of the interdependence that we are. This knowing involves the feelings of delight, wonder, freedom—and often a deep sense of the tragic arising from the capacity to see what others cannot or will not.[6]

Cognitive Style

With new capacities to grasp paradox rather than forced choice, to perceive complex patterns between individuals and systems and between systems themselves, and to tolerate ambiguity, Interindividual persons transcend the limitations of Piaget's formal operational thinking. This complex thinking is evoked by situations where two contradictory statements may both be true or where a statement may be true and not true at the same time, or where formal logic remains insufficient to judge the *adequacy* of certain actions in their contexts. The contextual thinking necessary to respond to these situations requires a meta-logic for communicating simultaneously with other things, other persons and one-self.[7] James Fowler describes such contextual understanding as "dialogical knowing."[8] The ability to think with this nuance results from acting, over time, on long-term commitments, such as when parents live out the lengthy process of child-rearing.

For Interindividual persons, discernment necessarily becomes a more complex undertaking because the range of alternatives and their implications have increased radically over earlier cognitive styles. For example, they can see themselves as participants in sinful structures and readily grasp second-order concepts of institutional oppression and social sin. They can recognize that the call to conversion comes both personally and institutionally, and that they must attempt to effect change on both levels. The sense of sin, repentance, and just action have all broadened. A director's question, "What do you sense that God is calling you to do about what you now see?" takes on considerable power at this stage.

Conscious Preoccupation

Inner life continues to deepen. Interindividual persons consciously express vivid feelings, including both existential humor and poignant sorrows. Sexual feelings emerge naturally from within a context of mutual relationship. The concept of development now includes physiological and psychological development and motives; psychological causation and process comprise natural categories of thought at this stage. Self-fulfillment becomes a conscious goal, yet one contextualized both by the various roles in which individuals find themselves and by their social context.

This expanded view of self-in-relationship, with its newly defined potentials and limitations, suggests that seekers may need to reexamine all their former commitments and life choices. Some apparently firm commitments could drop away, but those that remain must be reappropriated. Katherine's narrative suggests that her relationship with her husband may require such reworking. Reexaminations of this magnitude call for careful discernment. Ignatius of Loyola cautions directors of the Spiritual Exercises not to influence the outcome of this invitation and its subsequent struggle—an appropriate counsel at this crucial juncture, when seekers respond to the call to increased unity between vision and action.[9]

The critical judgment of the Conscientious stage, necessary for identifying oneself apart from one's relationships, yields to a willingness to *be grasped* anew by the symbols of these life choices. Paul Ricoeur described this reappropriation as "willed" or "second naivete."[10] Seekers may now be invited to relativize—but not obliterate—the critical distance so essential to the Conscientious stage as they move toward a renewed vision of life purpose.

Impulse Control

Interindividual persons strive to be realistic and objective about themselves and others, and more gentle and compassionate as well. A measure of freedom from earlier stages' oppressive conscience comes with recognizing that not all problems are solvable. A certain mellowness results from the surrender of some aspects of one's carefully constructed world. Truly principled moral reasoning can emerge from these new perspectives. Behavior becomes an expression of moral principle, flowing from a desire for congruity between inner and outer life.

Interindividual persons add a new toleration for their own inner ambiguities to their Conscientious impulse control. The ability to entertain multiple viewpoints which typifies this stage extends to the self as well—"I" can be comprised of many competing voices and impulses. As part of this increased integration, the unconscious may again be allowed to speak, perhaps through "negative" feelings previously banned from consciousness. For example, sexual references, newly contextualized by mutual interpersonal relationships, may spontaneously reappear—Mary Beth's prayer images manifest this characteristic, though other aspects of her reality-construction have yet to "catch up" with this pacing imagery.

One of the possible ways that this level of impulse control might appear in spiritual direction centers around the sometimes painful adjustment between vision and self-ideal, and the limitations inherent in particular life-circumstances. Seekers recognize, sometimes ruefully, that they have needs which cannot be ignored any longer, although they may have previously been quite successful in doing so. These needs may easily conflict with duties they have assumed. They are invited to reintegrate their vision with awareness of their own and others' limitations in such a way that the vision is both kept alive and yet tempered by a new realism—precisely the challenge facing Katherine. A positive resolution of this developmental transition, as with other reintegrations, is not automatic. It requires deep faith to launch once again into the process of transformation. The Interindividual person sees more and ultimately risks more in the hope of further integration of self-in-systems.

Interpersonal Style

As the sense of autonomy within oneself develops, so does the reality of one's irrevocable commitments. Recognizing that autonomy is mutual leads inevitably to interdependence in one's interpersonal relationships. Further, recognizing the legitimacy of perspectives other than one's own raises the issue of interdependence with groups or structures whose values and goals may be antithetical. Hence the ability to learn from different viewpoints, so significant in ecumenical and intercultural discourse, becomes structurally ascendant at the Interindividual stage. Transcending and integrating these antitheses and reconciling oneself to that which is unattainable remain the tasks of the Integrated stage.

Two spin-offs which may appear in spiritual direction include incorporating the self in care and freeing God to be God. Since one's self was the touchstone for evaluating and assessing reality throughout the Conscientious stage, one could not step outside its limits and include self in the group to whom one responded with care. When Conscientious persons do include themselves in care, it forms a special case, but Interindividual persons reframe the entire issue of care and care-giving in a way that dissolves the apparent contradiction between "selfishness" and "responsibility." Thus, Carol Gilligan speaks of an ethic of care "which reflects a cumulative knowledge of human relationships, [and] evolves around a central insight, that self and other are interdependent."[11] This issue is not confined to women, but represents one of "the paradoxical truths of human experience—that we know ourselves as separate only insofar as we live in connection with others, and that we experience relationship only insofar as we differentiate other from self."[12] Only at the Interindividual stage does sufficient complexity and depth exist for reframing and therefore resolving the issue of self-care as a matter of the way one views reality.

Second, seekers may now experience God as autonomous, as Other, to an entirely new degree. To the extent that images of God rely on images of self, God-images fall away, inadequate to this new relationship with self and God. The phenomenological experience often consists in darkness and obscurity about who God is while simultaneously being drawn into the darkness to meet this Other One in paradoxically deepened intimacy. John of the Cross' wisdom about what he calls the "dark night of the spirit" appears to address a death to self in some respects similar to that occurring when the Interindividual stage challenges the Conscientious stage's secure, solid ego.

As persons live more and more out of an Interindividual framework, spiritual directors may need simply to accompany seekers in their own processes. Two reasons lie behind this judgment. Growing autonomy extends to spiritual life as well as other aspects of human existence. Directees assume greater responsibility as individuals before a God who, to speak metaphorically, is also more autonomous. In addition, the spiritual director's own level of ego development may neither have reached the Interindividual stage, nor have transcended it. Thus, in a very real sense, the spiritual director can only act as a fellow-traveler at this complexity of ego integration.

Recapitulation

The *strengths* of the Interindividual stage entail the following: a vision and commitment beyond the self, but which still includes self as an integrated and valued component of the vision; increased tolerance for the autonomy of others, including one's own unconscious self and God. The *weakness* of the Interindividual stage is that, at root, one remains divided. The locus of the division resides in one's inevitable participation in structures and institutions whose goals and values differ from one's own and which stubbornly refuse to respond to individual action.

The *virtues* of the Interindividual stage include increasing intimacy with self, others and God; a sense of cocreating with God; commitment to social concerns unrestricted by the boundaries of one's own social group, class, religion or nation; and integrity resulting from enhanced congruity between inner life and outer actions, between moral principles and behavior. The *temptation:* avoiding the self-emptying required for granting others autonomy, for building relationships of authentic mutuality and appropriate intimacy, or even more significantly, for confronting the sinful realities of the structures in which one can now see oneself inevitably embedded.

The Integrated Stage

Since this stage is rarely found, it is difficult to study empirically. Furthermore, the more complex the stage, the more likely it is to be skewed by the psychologist's own perceptions of an "ideal person." For these reasons, Loevinger describes this stage only in broad strokes. Its essence involves transcending and coping with the conflicts and differentiations of the Interindividual stage, reconciling the unattainable where necessary. The struggle for personal identity unifies a spectrum of life activities. Intimacy and mutuality combine with agency in a singularly unified personality. Integrated persons also manifest a broad range of social and cultural concerns.[13]

Neither James Fowler nor Daniel Helminiak manifest Loevinger's reticence about describing the end-point of the developmental continuum. Each of them sketches an "ideal person" to culminate his developmental theory. Fowler bases his description of maturity on Christian theological concepts. Persons who live out Fowler's universalizing faith are incarnational and disciplined; they are activists who make tangible the imperatives of love and justice. They are heedless of their own self-preservation as they redefine the usual criteria of normality and subvert limited and limiting social structures. Their communities and their compassion are universal in extent.[14]

Helminiak relies on Bernard Lonergan's philosophical system to "project a theoretical account of the ideal perfection" of the final stage. Helminiak's Cosmic persons continually manifest a process of integration and authentic self-transcendence. They are open to all that is and willing to change as circumstances demand. They are alive to the present moment and in touch with the very depths of themselves, living a deep harmony between themselves and all that is.[15] Loevinger, it seems, describes a few real people, while Fowler and Helminiak draw pictures of the normative persons whom they assume would evolve in an ideal developmental situation.

We now have sufficient context to address a troubling issue implied in the very developmental categories themselves. A theory which postulates a developing ego implies that ego or self becomes stronger, more autonomous and more differentiated as one progresses through the stages. The classic literature of spirituality, however, is filled with images of self-emptying, self-denial and asceticism. Are not these two sets of images antithetical to each other? Does not the ascetical tradition, through a simplistic or even destructive anthropology, betray modern critical views of the human person? On the other hand, could the pursuit of self and development simply mask our capitulation to the basically anti-ascetical lure of hedonism and narcissism?

From the perspective of the entire developmental continuum, we can see that *every* transition requires, quite literally, a self-transcendence, a death to a self that makes a particular kind of meaning.[16] The Conscientious stage's blindness lies in assessing everything by the norm of the individual self—here the temptation to make self-fulfillment the ultimate goal can be particularly attractive. But the Interindividual and Integrated stages reveal the limit of this reality construction; true fulfillment arises from handing oneself over to a larger vision and purpose. The Interindividual and Integrated stages each require dethroning self as the norm of reality. But the language of emptying and discipline speaks its deepest challenge when, in fact, there is a self to hand over, and when there exists a cause, a value, a vision or a Person of sufficient transcendence to be caught up with. Perhaps only from the perspective of a self-composed self can one hand oneself over without self-annihilation. Thus, the developmental continuum itself reveals that images of growth, development, self, abnegation, discipline, and death to self undergo transformation of their meanings.[17]

Therefore, developmentally astute spiritual directors recognize that the guises which clothe the call to death to self vary by stage, and at times they will ally themselves with a seeker's fragile and newly emerging sense of self. We must also be aware that these images vary in their relationship to sex, class, culture—all of these realities individualize ego development and make concrete God's workings in the lives of directees. But the theory of ego development itself reveals that a bigger, stronger, more independent ego is neither the simple and predictable end result of the developmental continuum nor the enemy of self-denial.

Two other important caveats bear repetition as we leave this discussion of spiritual direction with persons at various developmental levels. First, we must place these successive transformations of motive which we have called ego development in a wider framework of God and God's activity. That is, God is not only the God who can most readily be apprehended by the Conformist or the Conscientious or even the Integrated meaning constructions. As we become aware of the deconstruction which inevitably attends each stage, one may be less apt to assume that God is "like that." It is, I submit, the spiritual director's most basic role simultaneously to stand for the transcendent God and to facilitate the seeker's experience of this God in ways which he or she is most capable of apprehending.

Second, the implications for spiritual direction raised in this discussion are only typical and suggestive of the issues which might appear. Individual experiences and the particular tone of these events cannot be specified by a structural theory, which by its nature stresses *form* over *contents*. Furthermore, to the extent that spiritual directors force these stage descriptions onto conversations, or see individuals as "stages," they are guilty of misplaced concreteness in the use of the theory. Persons are not reducible to stages—even though a stage-concept may be useful for grasping why a person sees something a certain way. The two are vastly different. Let us look at the continuing spiritual direction of one person at the Interindividual stage.

Katherine's Dilemma

Several clues from Katherine's first two visits with her new spiritual director suggest that she views the world from the Interindividual perspective, but that this construction awaits more complete integration. The clearest indicators of the Interindividual stage include the following: Katherine sees herself simultaneously as an actor in various groups and systems, she struggles to allow her husband to order his world differently from hers, and she seems poised to reexamine her major commitments, especially her marriage. Increasing discomfort about certain aspects of her relationship with her husband fuels Katherine's need to find a new spiritual director; she wonders how to discern in the new complexity with which she is faced. At the same time, Katherine seems caught between her own needs and desires and those of her husband, still seeing these alternatives as a forced choice.

The several social structures in which Katherine acts include her nuclear family, comprised of herself and her husband (and her as yet unmentioned extended family); at least two circles of friends apparently at odds with one another; the church, supporting Katherine through worship, spiritual direction, social justice vision, and context for her social activism; and an ecumenical "community" of justice activists, grown more extensive through the years. This latter group has encouraged Katherine's widening interest in the world political arena, introducing her to persons and systems far different from her own upper-middle-class American culture. At their suggestion, for example, Katherine agreed to visit three Central American countries as part of an ecumenical fact-finding mission examining the United States military's role in the region.

A developmental interpretation of Katherine's struggle with

her husband acknowledges the tension which arises as she recognizes that her husband's autonomy, although as real as her own, does not reinforce her value system. In her incomplete resolution of this dilemma, her husband's autonomy and her own seem to be "faced-off." Katherine *says* that she wants to let Ken be Ken, not some creation of her manipulations. But, at this moment, his desires and decisions seem to threaten her increasingly strong desires and decisions.

Early in Katherine's third meeting with her new spiritual director, the following exchanges occurred. Almost as an aside, Katherine noted she still felt sad about "losing a good friend and confidant" in her former spiritual director. When asked if there were other feelings mixed in with the sadness, Katherine paused. After a moment, she acknowledged ruefully: "Yes, there are. . . . (pause) . . . Really, I'm angry that I have to stop my process and bring someone else on board at such a frustrating time. . . . I feel cut loose and adrift. . . . In fact, (heavily) I feel downright scared that Ken and I might be headed for a showdown. If so, I am going to need someone to ask me some hard questions. I think Kay (her former director) would have been able to do that for me."

Remembering the first words Katherine had used to describe herself, "afraid, abandoned and confused," Katherine's director asked her to say more about how she felt that first time they had met. Katherine reported being afraid that either she would never get un-stuck, or that if she did, her marriage might be in trouble. "Really, I am afraid that God might ask me to choose God over Ken, and that would be a terrible choice." "Confusion" related to wondering what God really did want of her. "I used to feel I had a pretty good idea, but right now, I'm not at all sure. I wish I didn't fight with Ken about these friends, but I can't just go on acting like I am the same person as I was ten years ago. I'm not." "Abandoned" had to do with losing her other spiritual director, and to the anger which she realized lay just under the feeling of abandonment. But, reflecting further, Katherine confessed that she felt that somehow God had abandoned her into a world which was much more confusing than formerly; old certainties had evaporated. "I see now how all these feelings form a web and that they encompass several people: Kay, you, Ken, and God. No wonder I feel scared."

This brief exchange provides several developmentally suggestive clues. First, despite the fact that Katherine understands the process of spiritual direction, she still needs time to mourn the loss of her former spiritual director and to establish a trusting and confirmatory relationship with her new director. One of the first agendas between Katherine and her new spiritual director consists in the building of a relationship safe enough for challenging questions to emerge, a process taking its own time. Furthermore, since Katherine's former director left in the midst of her transition to the Interindividual stage, the way Katherine relates to a spiritual director will also be ripe for reintegration. Therefore, her new director must be able to encourage Katherine's autonomy and self-direction within spiritual direction as well as in her other relationships. To the director's suggestion that Katherine might now be ready to ask herself her own hard questions, she responded somewhat skeptically: "Maybe so, but right now I don't feel I can do it." Yet, Katherine seemed relieved to realize that all the hard questions did not have to be asked immediately, and that when she was "ready," the questions would emerge from within her own life and prayer.

Second, Katherine reveals an ability to allow a range of emotions, including less-than-comfortable ones, to emerge into her consciousness as part of herself. Underneath sadness, a conventional and socially acceptable feeling upon the loss of a long relationship, Katherine recognizes both anger and fear. Anger is directed first at her former spiritual director for leaving her in the lurch, but it implicitly includes her new director, who may not "come through" for her in a crisis. As Katherine recalls the feeling of abandonment she reported several weeks earlier, she recognizes that God is also implicated in her anger, since it feels as if God has "turned her out" and then abandoned her into a much more complex world. Fear about the potential threat to another significant relationship, that with her husband, comes crowding into her consciousness behind the anger. Would God call her out of that relationship and then abandon her?

To assist in forming a working relationship, to learn about how Katherine views herself and God, as well as to give Katherine an opportunity to recapitulate some of her recent gains, her spiritual director suggested that she review some of the ways that God had worked with her in the past, bringing to their next conversation a few of the most significant. Three weeks later Katherine reported the following:

"I started out doing what you suggested, but the whole thing about being childless came up instead. I found myself reliving everything again. The pain of realizing that I was never going to have children was really hard at first, especially when it became clear that I was the one who was infertile. (That was before all the new technology, so finding out that my tubes were too scarred really did mean that there was no hope that I could conceive.) It took that hurt quite a while to heal. Ken was very supportive during that time, assuring me that he didn't love me any less because I couldn't bear children.

"A few years later, when we were better established, I began to talk about adopting—I think I had held out this hope all along. But by this time, Ken had grown used to being childless, and wanted to continue as we were. Since we couldn't agree on adopting, we never did apply. It took me several years to come to terms with the fact that I would not become a parent in any usual sense. I don't think I resented Ken for his position; I think I just accepted things as unchangeable. What eventually helped me move on was an image that came to me one day as I was praying. In that New Testament story where Jesus gathers the little children and says, "Suffer the little children to come to me," the words went on in my mind, "You know these children weren't mine, either." I realized that my life wasn't worthless or marred by being childless. The release was tremendous. I cried for days, but after that I began to look for opportunities open to me because of my situation. All through that time, I had a sense that Jesus understood my situation and encouraged me to make a difference where I could at school.

"Since this memory was so vivid, I returned to it for the next several days. I can recall clearly how hopeless and stuck I felt then, but what struck me this time is how similar that sadness and frustration are to what I feel now. My vision about my future got totally rearranged, and at first, I was almost overwhelmed with sadness, anger and confusion. Eventually, all that sorted itself out. I can still recall those feelings vividly, but I can also recall the way they resolved into purpose and, eventually, energy. I know that Jesus accompanied me then. I hope he will accompany me this time. After remembering that other time, I am more encouraged."

In this conversation, Katherine revealed a well-developed ability to work inside, to connect present feelings with past ones, and to see interrelationships between her feelings and her prayer, her inner and outer life. The perspective gained through recall allowed her to hope that she will not remain stuck in her current situation forever, and that she does have some allies in her present process. She understood that a resolution to her present dilemma will emerge over time, as it did in the earlier experience, and that she can tolerate not having everything worked out immediately. She began to relax a little and take some pressure off herself and her relationship with Ken.

Katherine was able to do all this without much overt assistance by merely responding to her director's invitation to recall God's work with her in the past. She adapted the resulting reflection to her experience, intuiting that she should stay with the movement released by the recall. As a result, she noticed a significant connection between an old experience and her present process. Her director basically affirmed the direction in which her prayer took her.

Some weeks later, Katherine explored more extensively her sense of being hypocritical and of living two lives. As Katherine's awareness of the United States's unjust level of energy consumption and its control of the world's resources grew, her sense of participating in this imbalance grew accordingly. She became convinced that, in order to cease feeding the problem, she must simplify her life-style. Acting on her conviction created the conflict with Ken, who enjoyed the comforts and convenience of their upper-middle-class life-style. She went on to acknowledge, "I guess I really do too, and it's too easy to see Ken as the enemy here. I think I'm expecting Ken to do something for me that I will have to do for myself. If Ken were supportive, it would be easier to change my life-style, but I'm beginning to realize that I will have to find ways to simplify in the midst of our life together." Katherine's realization opened the possibility that spiritual direction may focus, in part, on helping her develop eyes to see her own inevitable participation in structural evil, and its implications for her spiritual life.

A key insight about being a hypocrite occurred during this same conversation. Katherine's director questioned whether God's leading would create such frustration and confusion inside of Katherine. "Was it possible," he wondered, "that she was being deceived by the appearance of good rather than experiencing a true call from God?" He reminded her of Ignatius of Loyola's image about the difference between water falling onto a stone or onto sponge,[18] wondering if the degree of tension and frustration was more like the water dropping on the stone. Katherine looked first startled and then relieved. "Yes, I think you are right!" After a pause, Katherine almost whispered: "Maybe my fear about having to choose between God and Ken is groundless. That would be a relief."

Katherine's spiritual director suspected that, even if Ken

wouldn't join her in marital therapy, she could profit from some therapy of her own, an intuition confirmed during their first of several conversations. Shortly thereafter, Katherine sought out counseling with a family-systems therapist, who helped her recognize the systemic and intergenerational aspects of her struggle with Ken. As Katherine began to "detriangle"[19] herself from Ken and his business friends, she found herself easier about entertaining them. As she became less anxious about having to choose between Ken and God, Ken became less irritated at her friends as well. Ken and Katherine even made a "friendly pact" to divide up the front yard among their opposite political issues and candidates: Katherine got one sign, Ken the next. Their "equal opportunity yard" became a source of humor among them and their circles of friends.

Katherine's continuing spiritual direction benefited from her therapy as well. A systems approach assumes that Katherine's relationship with Ken is related to her relationship to God; if she can change either her relationship with Ken or her understanding of God's call, the "problem" should also shift. Katherine's Interindividual developmental stage suggests that she can both understand how this process works, and can consciously participate in her own "detriangling." In spiritual direction, Katherine continued to grow in her ability to confront and challenge God in her prayer, more secure that her anger would not displease God, but might even indicate a growing responsiveness to God's call.

These positive outcomes did not preclude some painful struggles. Katherine continued to fight more with Ken, though she worried less about it than previously. She continued to struggle with issues of appropriate life-style, but she was not so quick to assume God was calling her to "heroic" renunciations. Some of Katherine's choices inevitably felt like compromises; what one part of herself wanted to do, another side knew would unnecessarily complicate Ken's business relationships as well as their own relationship. She learned that the sacrifices can't be all on her side, but neither could she simply "do her own thing," come what may.

Within the last two months, a new theme has appeared in Katherine's conversations with her spiritual director, Katherine's participation in church structures. She is increasingly irritated, even frustrated, by the "emptiness" of worship, the sex-exclusive language, and her pastor's refusal to establish a social justice committee within her parish. She finds herself enacting some of her "old patterns," as she calls them. Her prayer has focused on letting go, on getting herself out of the way, so that God might change hearts and open doors.

At present, Katherine's irritation with sex-exclusive God language is spilling over into her prayer, especially her God-images. "If God isn't He—which I know in my head—then who is God? How can I imagine God? When I pray, I unconsciously fall back on my old images, but then I recognize what I am doing, and I get all tangled up. Who is God anyhow?"

Katherine's spiritual direction over the past eight months confirms her deepening Interindividual perspective. She has grown increasingly responsible for her own actions, including the course of her own spiritual direction and discernment. She has differentiated herself more from her husband, allowing deeper intimacy to develop. She is more conscious of the interdependence between Ken and herself, and of how her relationships to Ken, her spiritual director and God are intertwined. She has accepted greater responsibility for participating in unjust structures, and is seeking ways to respond to structural as well as personal sin. Her need for resolution has diminished; she is more able to enter into a process than arrive at a conclusion.

Spiritual direction provides a context for Katherine to discern her actions and motives in increasingly complex systems. She has learned more about how she can be "tempted under the guise of good," to pit her desire "to follow God no matter what happens," against her relationship with Ken. As they began honoring their differences, Katherine and Ken shared occasional moments of playful humor.

Katherine's director also respected the characteristics of the Interindividual stage as they impacted her spiritual direction. He took care to establish a trusting relationship with her, recognizing that she needed both to mourn the loss of her former spiritual director and to maintain a consistent spiritual direction relationship within which she could reinterpret the entire process from her new developmental perspective. He stayed in the background as much as possible, encouraging her to follow her own inner movements and ask hard questions of herself. As their spiritual direction relationship solidified, Katherine's director was increasingly able to challenge her overtly. He recognized that Katherine could profit from therapy, and helped her transfer her therapeutic learning to her relationship with God. He confirmed her growing interpersonal differentiation, noting that she did not estrange herself further either from Ken or from God; on the contrary, both relationships seem stronger and more intimate, though stormier.

As Katherine begins to indicate that her relationship with God may be ripe for reinterpretation, her director prepares to accompany her into the darkness and confusion which may attend the loss of her former way of relating to God. Both Katherine and her director are learning to "see how things develop."

VIII. Developmental Dynamics in Congregational Spiritual Guidance

It is 10:50 on Sunday morning. Inside the sanctuary of East-minster Presbyterian Church, the organist begins the pre-service music, and strains of Bach drift out the church door. In the basement, a variety of people emerge noisily from their Sunday-School classes, greeting acquaintances from nearby rooms. Parents collect their preschoolers, who carry the fruits of their morning's activities; the older ones make their way up to the sanctuary to meet their families.

The Community Center's wheelchair van pulls away from the front entrance, having discharged its two regular passengers into the care of the greeters who take them to their accustomed places. The ambulatory seniors greet their long-time friends, providing each with an order of worship. At the same moment, a guest is introduced to a parishioner from the same hometown—they have just discovered that they have friends in common.

Elsewhere in Eastminster's somewhat cramped plant, the choir, already robed, has finished its warm-up, and is processing toward the sanctuary door, music folders in hand. The remainder of those leading this morning's worship service gather in the pastor's study, where the assembled group learns of the sudden illness of a session member and the death of another congregant's mother. They pause for a brief prayer, asking for open hearts for all at this morning's service and remembering these new sufferers as they do so. The chair of the Stephen Ministry[1] mentally checks the list of ministers available—Bob's recuperation sounds as if it will be lengthy. The pastor is not yet robed; she has been detained by a member of the session and their earnest, quiet conversation has just ended.

Sunday after Sunday, with minor variations, a similar scene occurs in thousands of churches. Similar rituals, similar needs, similar yearnings exist whether the church be Eastminster, St. Teresa Catholic Church or Wesley United Methodist Church. Do the structural theories of development which we have explored at length offer any creative insights about what goes on in parish after parish? What relationship does the spiritual director's work have to that of pastors and other ministers in congregational contexts? Can our awareness of the possibilities and limitations of the meaning-systems employed by Roger, Tom, Mary Beth and Katherine also illumine the lives of members of Eastminster Presbyterian Church? Such questions set the agenda for this chapter.

Spiritual Guidance in a Congregational Context

Up to this point, we have given our attention largely to spiritual direction, dwelling little on spiritual guidance in general. Now we address these more-encompassing spiritual guidance processes. Likewise, we have mainly focused on one-to-one relationships as the interpersonal context of spiritual direction. Now our attention shifts to a new interpersonal context for spiritual guidance—the congregation.[2] This shift in focus and location accompanies a change in emphasis from the more specialized, spiritual direction, to the more typical, spiritual guidance. After discussing the rationale for this shift in focus, we will examine the developmental features characteristic of congregations, reinterpret the images and processes which foster developmental transition as they appear in this new context, and suggest a method for assessing the congregation developmentally. The chapter will conclude with a return visit to Eastminster Presbyterian Church, attending most carefully to one facet of Christian life, the call to live justly. We will examine some of Eastminster's naturally therapeutic developmental dynamics with respect to justice, and note how its pastoral staff enhances these developmental dynamics.

Since there may be many understandings of spiritual guidance, it is important to clarify what I mean when I use this term in relationship to spiritual direction. I have earlier described spiritual direction as a specialized form of the church's mission of pastoral care to its members. In spiritual direction, a competent person makes spiritual guidance concrete and personalized, tailoring it to the circumstances of individuals or small groups. But some persons prefer to use other terms to describe this process, including "spiritual friendship," "spiritual accompaniment," "spiritual counseling" or "spiritual guidance." When I use the term "spiritual guidance," however, I refer to all the pastoral responses which have been called "care of souls" or "cure of souls" in the fifteen hundred years since Gregory the Great wrote his treatise on pastoral care, insofar as these pastoral functions raise our awareness of God's call and our appropriate response. Spiritual guidance occurs through such varied pastoral activities as regular pastoral calls on congregants, letters of counsel or condolence, confessional or penitential guidance, preaching and worship, visits to the sick and imprisoned, sacramental preparation, pastoral counseling, and education in the texts, traditions and disciplines of the Christian community. Spiritual guidance employs all the means, including spiritual direction, that the church offers for the healing, sustaining, guiding, reconciling and nurturing of its members.

By virtue of their office, pastors are responsible to oversee the spiritual guidance of the congregation and its members. They may or may not carry out that mandate through explicit one-to-one or small-group spiritual direction. Generally, only a relatively minor percentage of their time can be spent seeing individuals. By contrast, spiritual directors may or may not be ordained and may or may not serve as pastors, but they participate in spiritual formation by virtue of their baptism and membership in the Christian community.[3] Their particular contribution occurs precisely in their ability to focus on individuals and their spiritual journey.

Two principal reasons underlie our shift in focus from the individual to the congregation. The first flows from the nature of spiritual direction, and the second from the nature of spiritual guidance. Theologically speaking, spiritual direction is essentially ecclesial; it is one of the ways in which the church fulfills its mission to nurture its members. This ecclesial dimension is most concretely embodied through the local worshiping community. Therefore, participating in a Christian community, generally (but not always) a local congregation or parish, makes concrete the ecclesial parameters in which spiritual direction appropriately occurs. This local community complements individual prayer with public worship and intimate conversations with full sacramental life. It offers both support and accountability. In other words, one's local Christian community provides a necessary counterpoint which helps to insure that individual spiritual direction does not nourish idiosyncratic, privatized, elitist or esoteric religious experience divorced from all other Christians.

Of course, the local worshiping community is comprised of fallible human beings and structures, and it may undercut as well as nourish discipleship and intimacy with God. But even when this undermining appears to be happening, severing connections with all concrete church communities risks the loss of a critically important dialogue partner. At times, our discipleship may be tempered and honed precisely through resistance to the limiting or oppressive dynamics of a given church situation. In God's wisdom, even the church's fallible bumbling may invite us—painfully, it is true —to a more adequate meaning-construction by contradicting our embeddedness in one limited ecclesial perspective. For the church's part, when the connection between spiritual direction and the local congregation is severed, the church loses an opportunity to learn a purer witness to Christian community.

The second reason to examine the formational dynamics of the congregation flows from the nature of spiritual guidance. For most people most of the time, spiritual guidance takes place in and through the ordinary life of the believing community, by means of its continual reenacting in word and sacrament of our fundamental beliefs about God, humans and world. It is within a particular believing and worshiping community that we learn, often by osmosis, the stories, actions, affections and commitments which comprise a Christian way of living.[4]

Because the congregation is the ordinary context for nurturing Christians in their call to discipleship, we may be tempted to treat it as therefore less important. But precisely because it is a *primary* formative context, it ought to receive careful attention. Therefore, in order to grasp the full significance of the developmental context of spiritual guidance, it is necessary to focus explicitly on the formative dynamics occurring in and through the congregation. How can they be enhanced? How can developmental theory contribute?

Developmental Features of Congregations

When compared to single persons, congregations raise different developmental possibilities and limitations. As complex as any given human being is, the congregation is vastly more complex, manifesting within its membership every era of the human life cycle and each stage of development. In terms of our imaginary planet, it is as if all six countries exist simultaneously within a typical parish. Furthermore, congregations seem to take on a life of their own which transcends that of any individual member, including the pastor.[5]

Compared to such institutions as hospitals, businesses and schools, parishes have more diffuse relationship boundaries, and huge, often unarticulated expectations of its pastoral staff. Congregations tend to be more constant over time than many other social institutions. Individuals and families come to, remain in and leave their congregations for a variety of reasons which may have little or nothing to do with the stated purpose and mission of the congregation. Members may or may not be moved to seek spiritual guidance in any overt manner, but the pastor enjoys unique access into the lives of the congregants at moments which are particularly laden with developmental potential: birth, coming-of-age, leaving home, marriage, illness and death.

Factors which prove salient in individual persons' transitions may prove equally potent within congregations. Three characteristics of the congregational context prove particularly fruitful developmentally, namely, rich symbolism, multiple possibilities for perspective-taking, and potential for meaningful participation in a community of care.[6] Let us briefly examine each of these developmentally influential dynamics embedded in ordinary congregational life.

Since our understandings of self, world and God rely upon images, symbols and metaphors, the constructing, deconstructing and reconstructing of images, symbols and metaphors necessarily intertwines with spiritual development. Church life is filled with symbols and symbolic actions, drama and narrative, plot and characters, both past and present. Myth-sized realities of life and death, sin and salvation, repentance and forgiveness, dying and rising are the stuff of the Christian story. Its heroes and heroines come in all shapes and sizes, some existing in each particular setting. As we tell and retell the Christian story and our own stories, symbols and characters come alive in our imaginations, inviting us to live into these expanding visions and to embody the Christian story through our own stories.[7] The community's potential for transmitting the central myths, images and affections of the Christian way of life constitutes one of its most significant contributions to spiritual guidance, even though—and perhaps because—it often operates below our conscious awareness. These myths, images and symbols can be appropriated—differently, to be sure—by persons at all points on the developmental continuum.

Perspective-taking refers to all the ways in which one person attempts to perceive, feel and understand the experience of other persons and groups.[8] Robert Selman has demonstrated the significant role that perspective-taking plays in moving from simple, undifferentiated and face-to-face relationships toward complex, multileveled relationships (including both immediate relationships and those with people from other cultures and situations whom we may never meet in person). Every time we succeed, even partially, in putting ourselves inside the experience of another, we participate in our own movement from being embedded within a limited perspective to seeing others more accurately. Eventually, such steps toward self-transcendence may carry along our entire world-view to a new stage.

The congregation offers a wide variety of possibilities for perspective-taking, a mini-experience of the human condition. All ages and personality types appear next to us in the pew, and have the unpleasant habit of staying there when we least want them to. Sooner or later, even in the most homogeneous church communities, we will come face-to-face with otherness: persons who don't like us, who make decisions contrary to our wishes, who gossip or cheat or ignore us, who smother us with love or advice, who manipulate us into doing what we would rather not do, with whom we exchange angry words, who pray or worship in styles very different from our own, who squash our initiative, who challenge us to be more than we are at the moment and perhaps think we can be.

Churches can be full of opportunities, geared to different ages and developmental stages, for expanding our perspective-taking: faith sharing, life-story conversations, support groups for persons of certain ages or experiences, service groups, study groups, work parties, recreational gatherings—all can find their home within the formal or informal structure of the congregation. The stories of our traditions and holy people draw us outside our own experience into that of these characters and struggles. The attempt to care for members of the congregation in their times of need provides us with experience and challenge to extend our care outside the boundaries of our church family. Pastoral care does not reach its fruition when human needs are relieved, but only when those very persons are set free to serve others in behalf of the Good News.[9]

Human persons need to participate actively in decisions which affect them, to author their own presence and actions, a need which exerts a powerful developmental pull. Theologically speaking, though human beings are created and contingent, they still possess the potential to become cocreators with God. When this possibility is systematically stifled, the self, mind and voice remain largely those of others, not one's own,[10] and the potential to cocreate with God lies dormant.

Parishes provide ample opportunity for participating and decision-making at a variety of levels, including the church's physical and financial upkeep and its various committees, classes and ministries. But ultimately more significant is the potential to help shape and execute the worship life of the community, to participate in its struggle to address the structural evils in its milieu, to reflect and choose ethically in an increasingly complex world, and to pursue one's own vocation with its means of holiness.

Clearly the church community contains a variety of both subtle and overt means of grace, and also numerous subtle and overt means of fostering or hindering human development. Attending to the life and purposes of the church from a developmentally informed perspective fosters the ability of its members to respond to God's call with greater complexity and power.

Developmental Processes in Congregations

The same images and models which illuminated individual developmental transition can also assist us in examining the congregational context. The "natural therapeutic triad," as we have earlier called it, helps assess the "how" of fostering developmental transitions within the congregational context. We can teach ourselves to search for the balance between confirmation, creative contradiction, and continuity within a variety of church structures and programs. The developmental potential of the dynamics and decisions of the pastoral staff, the religious education curriculum, the outline of sermon topics, the composition and goals of various parish subgroups and committees can be enhanced by consciously reflecting on the optimum balance between confirmation, challenge and continuity.

The notion of pacer can help determine the degree of challenge which will prove fruitful. We can heighten our awareness of how much diversity and challenge a group or individual can sustain before being overwhelmed and paralyzed rather than motivated. We can identify what or who sponsors each of the parish's constituencies. We can ask in what ways the parish structure itself, as well as the various programs or groups within the parish, paces or fails to pace the growth of its members.

Likewise, with some thought, Carlsen's model for therapeutic meaning-making can be adapted to non-crisis parish life:

(1) Establishing a climate of trust grounds congregational dynamics just as surely as it does one-to-one relationships. The parish's ability to function as a holding environment for all the developmental perspectives represented within its membership can grow by consciously attending to that which fosters trust between the members of the pastoral staff, between the staff and the parishioners and among the parishioners themselves. Actions which the pastoral staff can model include: knowing parishioners' names and

their general life-circumstances; visiting them on their own turf; scrupulously maintaining confidentiality; affirming and supporting delegated leadership and allowing various ministries and committees an appropriate level of decision-making in their particular tasks; affirming and utilizing the personal gifts of members as well as affirming the particular spirit and gifts of the congregation itself; soliciting and responding non-defensively to constructive critique; accepting pastoral authority without using it in a heavy-handed manner; fostering a variety of subgroups within the congregation for expanding personal contact beyond the reach of the pastoral staff; and utilizing appropriate times and places to share personal struggles, learning with members of the congregation. Creative pastoral staffs will undoubtedly expand this list of possibilities.

(2) Carlsen's second point suggests that appropriate groups periodically examine a wide range of facts, assumptions and speculations which are part and parcel of the parish's (or committee's) meaning-system. Some means to structure such reexamination might include requesting that each major committee or ministry prepare a mission statement; providing regular retreats for reexamining the underlying vision which motivates various groups; establishing a policy that all members of the pastoral staff and committee chairs receive regular evaluation and feedback; and encouraging many levels of informal communication and sharing around values and goals.

Any group will undoubtedly encompass a variety of views and visions, some more and some less adequate to the church's mission. Whenever significant persons or institutions begin to contradict inadequate or destructive assumptions or behaviors, conflicts inevitably will arise. A developmental perspective suggests that conflict can serve developmental transition—as long as the anxiety which it generates remains within reasonable bounds. Thus, stifling conflict, or even too quickly resolving it, may undermine the positive developmental possibilities inherent in conflictual situations and personalities.

(3) Opening to a wide range of contexts of meaning, differing personal systems and histories requires that the pastoral leadership has developed sufficient sense of self and pastoral identity that they themselves not be overcome with anxiety in the face of differing perspectives and conflictual situations. Perhaps modeling such openness in their pastoral responsibilities constitutes one of their chief developmental contributions.

(4) As Carlsen attempts to help clients change inappropriate behavior and the structure of the meaning-system within which they act, she employs free-thinking and imagination. Such free-thinking and imagination are as important in the congregational context as they are in one-to-one situations, because imagination allows one to envision how things might be different. Pastorally, the church must invite—indeed, incite—a gospel vision of the reign of God for this time and place. What could God's reign look like? What concrete steps might help this community move, if ever so slightly, in that direction? Preaching and liturgy lend themselves particularly well to nourishing this Christian and prophetic imagination, but Christian education is likewise filled with possibilities for developmentally-geared vision sharing.

(5) Just as Carlsen assists clients to think about their own thinking processes, the pastoral staff can help the members of the congregation reflect self-consciously on their own processes. To the extent that parish groups become more self-reflective and discerning about their own processes, they may assume more responsibility for their own lives and decisions. While the fullest self-awareness and appropriation will occur in persons who have attained the most complex developmental levels, different degrees of self-reflection and appropriation can occur all along the developmental continuum. Posing this possibility in the appropriate developmental terms is another example of pacing.

(6) Finally, therapists must remain in relationship to their clients, continuing their confirming and creative contradicting as their clients learn more effective ways of being and acting. Translated to the parish context, continuity of leadership through times of parish transition and upheaval greatly fosters the internalization of expanded parish vision and mission. Inevitable staff change-overs should involve a wide range of parishioners in an intentional process of rethinking and reenvisioning. In this way, the transition itself can help the parish both to solidify its contributions to the life of the church and to appropriate a shared vision of its future.

Developmentally-informed pastoral interventions, the above suggestions demonstrate, need not be particularly esoteric or complicated. Often they are a matter of common sense and good human relationship skills, but they become developmentally powerful when honed to the particular developmental contingencies of one's parishioners. In so doing, the naturally therapeutic developmental dynamics within the congregation are enhanced.

As we continue to explore developmental contingencies which

play themselves out in the parish context, a few brief cautions bear mention at this point. First, the developmental strength of the congregational context lies in its complexity and diversity. Both theologically and developmentally, it is inappropriate for the pastoral staff to assume they either can or ought to control all these dynamics; clearly it is humanly impossible to do so. The Holy Spirit's promise to be with the church means that the necessary pastoral care of the congregation lies diffused throughout its membership. As the church calls forth that pastoral care, it provides opportunities for its members' growth and development, both psychologically and spiritually.

Nor is it necessary to assess accurately all the developmental possibilities inherent in the congregation. We simply wish to see with developmental eyes, so that, in our congregational care, we can respond with increasingly accurate empathy. Neither the goal nor the content of spiritual guidance comes from developmental theory. It merely suggests a variety of styles—stages—and processes which we employ as we struggle for the prize: the continual embodying of the reign of God in the world.

Assessing the Congregation Developmentally

Researchers have created reasonably accurate and reproducible methods for determining the developmental level of individuals. The same is not true with respect to groups. No empirical tests for determining a congregation's developmental level exist. The current state of the art in developmental assessment suggests that we best approach the question of the developmental level of congregations intuitively rather than empirically. Thus, let us employ stages and transitions as metaphors for congregational styles of being and meaning-making, metaphors useful insofar as they help us understand and interpret otherwise complex or chaotic details about congregational life.

Jane Loevinger makes a few suggestive remarks about the developmental level of groups which may provide some clues about how to proceed. Nation-states, she observes, appear to operate at a Self-Protective level, looking out first for their own interests even when they appear to be offering aid to other nations or people. For their part, societies are built on, value and reward conformity, and pace their members up to the Conformist stage. Loevinger notes the paradox inherent in asking how societies can promote stages above Conformity—since by its very definition, Conscientiousness implies at least partial liberation from Conformity, and societies cannot pace their own dissolution.[11] It is not surprising, therefore, that the modal developmental level for individuals in our society is Self-Aware transition between Conformity and Conscientiousness.

Let me draw some working axioms from these admittedly sketchy comments about group developmental assessment, axioms I believe remain consistent with the structural developmental paradigm. First, a group (of any size) which appears beleaguered, or whose economic, political, cultural and spacial arrangements appear threatened will respond self-protectively, just as individuals who must fight for their place in family or society and who feel they may never let down their guard lest they be overwhelmed likewise operate out of environmentally useful self-protective styles.

Second, non-voluntary groups, such as societies, offer powerful and largely unconscious encouragement for individuals to merge into a monolithic worldview—that is, to become socially acceptable. These kinds of groups literally or figuratively punish those who break out of its ordering system, they censor and edit the versions of "reality" permitted, they celebrate certain virtues by their public heroes and myths, and they rely on tacit acceptance from the vast majority of their members (and conscious choice from a good percentage of the remainder) for their continuation. Voluntary groups function in a similar manner, but these groups must "woo" their adherents through arrangements which meet their adherents' needs, either consciously or unconsciously.

Third, from the developmental distribution curve, we can expect groups of any size at all, congregations included, to contain a solid core of Conformist members. Some more particularized groups may consistently reward internalized decisions—in such cases, their membership may contain a higher than average number of Conscientious members. Rarely will any group be characterized by an Interindividual developmental construction; even though it may have members who clearly function from that perspective, it will still include a strong enough cadre of Conformist and/or Conscientious members to weight the group's meaning-making style toward one or other of these less-nuanced perspectives.

Finally, in groups of more than a few adult members, we could expect a range of developmental perspectives of three or even four stages. This latter axiom seems to offer the most potential for our congregational reflections.

How will such a developmental range of three to four stages show itself in the congregation? Let us return to Eastminster for an example.

About eight years ago, it became painfully clear that Eastminster's neighborhood was in transition. "White flight" took some of the well-established professionals to the suburbs. The median income in the city dropped as some of the area's manufacturing firms closed their doors and moved outside the unions' organizational range. City unemployment rates clung stubbornly toward the top of the state levels. Homelessness rose, with more than an occasional person sleeping in the lot between the church plant and a boarded up factory-outlet store. Eventually, the pastoral staff and the session began to ask themselves what role Eastminster should play regarding these dynamics. One of the ideas which kept emerging from their informal discussions concerned the increasingly difficult housing situation in the neighborhood. Eastminster's session decided to test the congregation's willingness to continue to explore the issue of homelessness and its potential responses. They began with a brief survey of the members' perceptions, feelings and motivations about becoming involved in neighborhood housing, polling the older children and teens as well as the adults.

The replies the session received varied tremendously. Had the session examined them developmentally, the following categories and examples would have typified the results:

Pre-Conventional (Impulsive and Self-Protective Stages)
1. Actions motivated by avoidance of pain or punishment:
    "Let's do something so I (or my kids) won't get into trouble with drugs."
    "No. We don't have enough money and we'd have to cut all our other programs to take on these people."
2. Desire for personal benefit or reward:
    "I'd feel good if we could help."
    "If we could get the homeless off the street, the value of our property would go up."

Conventional (Conformist and Self-Aware Stages)
1. Approval:
    "My Mom and Dad say we should try to help the other families" (from a grade-school child).
    "All the people on our block are against it. We think it's the city's responsibility and they can more easily get the money."

"The Pastor really wants us to get involved in this as a church."

"If others will chip in, I will too."

2. Honor or reputation:

"I don't want these types hanging around our plant. It makes us look bad, and it could be dangerous as well."

"We Presbyterians are known for our social concern."

"We've always taken care of our own in this town."

Post-Conventional (Conscientious and Interindividual Stages)

1. Respect for and maintenance of the community:

"I/we should help these people because I would want them to do the same for me. I've been one paycheck away from disaster before, too."

2. Justice and care:

"I have enough to eat and a roof over my head, so I feel obligated to share with others who have less than I do."

"They should have a chance to get on their feet, simply because they are fellow human beings."[12]

At this point, Eastminster's session was mainly interested in the strength of the congregation's assent or dissent with the proposal. However, reading the results developmentally focuses, not on whether the replies are positive or negative, but rather on the meaning-system behind *either* decision. If the congregation does elect to become involved in neighborhood housing, the task of responding to homelessness could be done from a variety of perspectives. As Morgan and her associates comment:

> . . . there's little doubt that the more altruistic, the more self-less the motive, the wider will be its sphere of influence and application. Justice and care take in more considerations than simple obedience to social conscience, and they endure longer. But it may take all of us a while to get to the point where we consistently elect projects on these bases. This in no way negates the work we do along the way.[13]

In other words, God can and does work through a community which is itself very much in process. In the very act of responding out of our best insights to the needs before us, our own community members may eventually broaden their perspectives. In heeding the plight of the disadvantaged from within our own limitations, we all hear the gospel more clearly.

Developmentally assessing and responding to a congregation can proceed quite informally. The following can be done by anyone willing to observe sensitively.

(1) Listen for the spoken or implied "why" underneath the decisions or actions proposed; these indicate the developmental meaning-system employed in reaching that conclusion. When interpreted developmentally, Eastminster's initial poll could provide the session with a reasonably useful assessment of the range and frequency of various developmental perspectives in the congregation. They might learn, for example, that the largest percentage of comments, both positive and negative, occurred at Self-Aware style of meaning-making, but that a surprisingly strong number of Conscientious responses also appeared.

(2) Attempt to get "inside" the point of view represented. Ask others to make a similar attempt to put themselves inside differing points of view. Not only does such a procedure assist with understanding the other perspective, the act of perspective-taking itself sets the stage for expanding the reigning meaning-system. Eastminster's session had already begun this kind of perspective-taking in its own informal discussions, imagining several possible scenarios and surfacing some of the pros and cons of each.

(3) Ask questions and carry on discussions in an ascending degree of developmental complexity, beginning with meaning/fact and moving to interpretation/comparison/classification, and then to analysis/synthesis/evaluation. Employing mental processes in ascending order allows all persons to participate to the degree of complexity that paces them. Persons who typically employ concrete-operational thinking will spend significantly more time and be far more comfortable with discussions involving meaning/fact activities. Persons used to formal or post-formal thinking find discussions which involve analysis, synthesis and evaluation of proportionately more significance. Beginning with the simpler forms also includes older children and youth, while subsequently adding the more nuanced thought processes will tap the more synthetic thinking processes typical of the later developmental stages.[14] As Eastminster's pastor and session plan their follow-up report and strategy, they will do well to proceed in like fashion.

(4) Recognize that a discrepancy generally exists between what people say and how they eventually act. Articulating a more

complex rationale generally precedes acting on it. For example, we all know from experience that it is relatively undemanding to speak about acting justly, but far more difficult to put that speech into action. When speech and action begin to come together, a stage has been truly internalized. This process of décalage, as Piaget called it, frequently accompanies a transition to a new developmental perspective and continues as the new stage solidifies. Eastminster's session will need to keep in mind that the vision of its congregation's involvement in neighborhood housing may be widely appealing, but the work of carrying out the vision much harder to sustain.

(5) Look for master stories and images, the myths of the congregation. They will most likely be unconscious, but they act as powerful carriers of meaning-making, sometimes setting limits on the developmental system within which the congregation acts.[15] Doreen's "presence" in the congregation—we will meet her shortly—seems to be gradually taking on a symbolic function for Eastminster's members.

(6) Look at images and assumptions about power and authority. Are they assumed to be hierarchical, rigid and authoritative? Do they reside "outside," "inside" or both? Are persons empowered to take control of their own lives? Is Eastminster moving toward a congregational focus primarily on the strength of the pastor's or the session's authority or charism? If so, how might that energy be affirmed, and mobilized, and yet challenged toward a more complex and internalized decision?

(7) Look for a variety of ways of involving parishioners so that the strengths of their developmental perspectives may be magnified. For example, Conformist persons may appreciate a ministry of serving food in the downtown shelter, helping a child at the day-care center, or visiting a homebound elder, or any other, generally face-to-face, situation with observable results. Parishioners whose worldview is primarily Conscientious or Interindividual can be challenged to activities which move beyond the immediate to situations involving structural responses, such as lobbying for more just housing policies and budgets.[16]

Becoming a Just Community:
Eastminster Presbyterian Church

Because the biblical concept of justice places significant developmental demands on any faith community, it could be enlightening to examine one congregation's attempts to live the gospel call to justice. Not only is the concept itself abstract, but living justly requires the ability to identify with increasingly larger groups, including those who may differ widely from one's own religion, class or nationality.

Fully two decades ago, the Synod of Roman Catholic Bishops succinctly summarized the challenge which justice places on the Christian community as a whole:

> Action on behalf of justice and participation in the trans-
> formation of the world fully appear to us as a constitutive
> dimension of preaching of the gospel, or in other words, of
> the Church's mission for the redemption of the human
> race and its liberation from every oppressive situation.[17]

Faithful living of the gospel, the bishops insist, must involve acting to bring about increasing justice for the oppressed, equalizing access both to the world's resources and to the power of self-determination. Just how complex and demanding this call to live justly can be appears by examining the intricate interpenetration between forms of injustice. For example, east-west militarism thrives on increasing consumption of the earth's non-renewable resources, creates a permanent underclass of service people around military bases, encourages one-product, capital-oriented economies in less-developed regions, which in turn tend to generate another underclass of poorly paid workers. Similar systemic interconnections appear when probing other forms of injustice. As the world shrinks, the interdependence of human beings also becomes more evident; the very survival of the human species will soon require respect and dialogue with persons and cultures vastly different from oneself.

Scarcely less difficult is the challenge which just living poses to each individual congregation. Ronald Marstin frames the challenge this way:

> The faith that is satisfied with the welfare of its own is
> faith at a standstill. The mark of a developing faith is its
> embrace of the outsider. And, where universality is the
> measure of its maturity, maturing faith will be recognized
> by its concern for the outsider *as such*, its persistent out-
> reach to those still excluded.[18]

However, the ability to include in the scope of care a wider and wider circle of persons who are very different from oneself and whom one may never know personally is a quality that becomes ascendant only at the more complex end of the developmental continuum. How might a typical congregation comprised of persons at a variety of developmental stages respond to a call to live more justly?

Before we return to Eastminster, one further developmental comment is necessary to set the stage. Biblical justice calls for an increasingly inclusive community, which consciously challenges the unjust structures both globally and within its own boundaries. Growing into this ideal vision of just living, however, involves at least three developmental transformations: (1) moving beyond one's own needs into a sense of community (the transition from Self-Protective to Conformist); (2) then moving beyond personal interaction to structural analysis (the transition from Conformist to Conscientious); and finally (3) moving beyond one's own group, class, religion or nationality to the inclusive community of all people (the transition from Conscientious to Interindividual).[19] The developmental strength of the congregation lies in the possibility that all three developmental stages will exist with integrity among its members. The developmental challenge lies in providing each perspective with developmentally specific confirmation as well as constructive challenge around the demands of justice while remaining a continually sustaining presence in the lives of its parishioners.

To illustrate the developmental dynamics in which congregations and their staffs operate, let us return to Eastminster and follow one thread of its congregational life, its call to live justice concretely in its milieu.

Nobody quite remembers when the idea of low-income housing under Eastminster's auspices began to capture the congregation's imagination. It was certainly not articulated seven years ago when the congregation called its present pastor. Somewhat stung by their former pastor's abrupt departure, the congregation's strongest stated goal concerned resurrecting its former stability. A few members, however, could see that more systemic issues within the church and its milieu would mitigate against a simple return to the status quo. The most obvious among them were the region's deteriorating economic climate and population shift toward the suburbs, leaving a smaller—and aging—population at Eastminster.

Any attempt at a status quo was immediately and concretely

challenged with the arrival of several competent women's dossiers. Some persons on the search committee insisted that in justice the women be given serious consideration. Others countered that, at this point, calling a woman as pastor would be too divisive and that the congregation wasn't ready for such an innovation. In the end, one candidate, Carol, won over both the search committee and the congregation by her straightforward assessment of the church's underlying needs, her ready laugh, and her passion for the neighborhood, which, she said, resembled her own as a child. Carol's fit in the congregation proved deeper than her somewhat disorganized preaching, which, as one member assessed it, tended to run on too long, like pearls strung on a string.

The early years of Carol's tenure as pastor were remarkable in their ordinariness. Sensing that Carol liked them, the parishioners warmed to her open and informal style. Pot-lucks at the church hall, once a regular feature of congregational life, were revived. They soon acquired a reputation: children were welcome, hilarity and bedlam were endemic. Their attendance grew. Then someone suggested a group prayer time after dinner—deliberately short because of the attention span of the smaller children, and thus was born the Bible study and prayer on the following Sunday's biblical texts. Carol more than once mentioned at the Presbytery meeting that she gleaned some of her best sermon ideas and illustrations from that rather uncontemplative setting.

Gradually, the demands on Carol's time multiplied. Never one to stand on clergy prerogative, she tapped several members of the congregation and proposed that they and she investigate Stephen Ministry. Carol and three others completed the training and began a regular program of visiting the shut-ins. Within a year, the original three persons recruited six more, and among themselves handled the organizational aspects of their growing ministry. Carol supervised the newest ministers, provided twice yearly sessions to update and improve their pastoral skills, and tried herself to visit the homebound once every month or six weeks. Some of the most moving funerals of late had involved the ministers who had so faithfully visited these parishioners over the last months of their lives.

Meanwhile, Carol began to forge relationships with her clergy peers in other area churches. The alliance solidified around a common clothing and food bank, housed in an empty storefront less than a block from Eastminster. Because of its proximity to the church, it seemed natural for Eastminster to supply both goods and services. Four of the congregation's couples and a widower became regulars at Fish, as they called their "store," each specializing in some aspect of begging, collecting, sorting or distributing goods. Once their begging uncovered not food, but a lawyer who volunteered his services for those unable to pay. When these referrals became too frequent, the lawyer collared a colleague, and sometimes an intern as well.

Sometime during those years, the church "acquired" its first homeless person, Doreen, a woman who steadfastly resisted being moved to any shelter or group home. She instinctively gravitated toward the small house adjacent to the church in which Carol lived, as had the pastors who preceded her. Every day of the week, at precisely 6:00 a.m., Doreen rang Carol's doorbell for her breakfast. Carol used to joke that Doreen was more consistent than any alarm clock. Although Doreen would never come into the sanctuary on Sunday—it made her nervous to be inside with so many people, she said—she soon became known to all the congregation's regular members. At first, they tried a variety of solutions to the "problem" of Doreen's living situation, all of which she resisted. Finally, they settled on simpler forms of assistance: one person kept track of her Social Security money, doling it out for food throughout the month, and each fall someone would see that she had a warm coat and substantial shoes. Mostly they just greeted her as she sat in the warm curve of the basement windowsill on cool days or in the shade of the parish house on warm ones.

Doreen became a fixture at Eastminster, though not everyone was comfortable with her. Carol began to recognize Doreen's symbolic role in the congregation more than a year later: when the group who gathered weekly to make stained-glass windows began to plan a large piece to commemorate the church's upcoming seventy-fifth anniversary, they worked Doreen into the design.

The congregational stresses and strains were remarkable in their ordinariness, too. The formality or informality of the worship style, a bone of contention for some time, continued to raise division among the members. No worship committee seemed to be able to work together amicably. Eventually the choir director wooed five members of the choir away with him when he accepted a higher-paying position in a church with a worship style more suited to his own. The choir had still not recovered in strength or smoothness fully a year after their departure. And a handful of parishioners, disgruntled with the disappearance of their treasured music, regularly threatened to shift their membership.

Three years ago, the budget seemed to mitigate against calling even a part-time youth minister, and the gradual erosion of the youth program had Carol increasingly concerned. The police picked up one of the seniors with marijuana about the same time, setting off a serious parental ripple. The session could not postpone wrestling with the quality of the youth program any longer, though Carol observed they seemed inclined to ignore it if not prodded.

The budget situation also was not likely to improve significantly in the short run. The church secretary, hired eight years ago for twenty hours per week, but usually working substantially more, told Carol that she must look for a full-time position when her children returned to school the following fall. If the church couldn't find the money to pay a full-time salary, Carol told her—and later reiterated to the session—then in justice the church could not expect her to keep working out of loyalty or duty. Carol would greatly miss Pat's steady presence, astute analyses, and competent and confidential dealings with the people who came through the church offices. Perhaps Pat would still feel able to continue using her gifts with the new-member class, though Carol would also understand that, in justice to her family, she may need to cut back there, too. Carol and Pat promised to continue their conversations over the next few weeks.

Three years ago, then, as Eastminster's session polled the membership on the issue of housing, the church's life did not differ startlingly from others in a similar milieu. Its population decline had slowed and the membership stabilized at about one hundred households. The age distribution had improved somewhat, with more young children than a decade ago, though worrisome patterns appeared among the youth. Although the congregation's racial mix had increased slightly, its percentage of Caucasians still overshadowed their percentage in the neighborhood. Nor was Eastminster a welcoming environment for the Cubans who were moving into the area in noticeable numbers.

Encouraged by the results of the poll, Eastminster's session continued to explore the possible ways the congregation could respond to the homeless. They began simply. At the session's fall retreat, they decided to set aside most of their time for prayer and discussion on the question: How is God calling me personally to respond to the homeless in our area? They reasoned that, before they could expect the congregation to commit themselves to such a focus, they themselves should lead the way. They surfaced their desires and their fears, trying to pay attention to the message that both carried. By the end of the weekend, the new session members felt as committed and comfortable with the emerging consensus as the longest-serving members. Each person selected a concrete way that he or she would begin to address the issue of homelessness, trusting that the precise ways the church might be involved would unfold in the future.

At the retreat's closing session, they sketched some further steps for the congregation. They asked Carol to prepare a series of sermons which could help the congregation reflect theologically on the call to shelter the homeless. They tentatively suggested the "biblical notion of hospitality" for the early fall and "ministry for the long haul" for Lent, but encouraged her to follow her own best sense of the congregation and the material as it unfolded.

They affirmed one of their members, whose background included some community organizing, when he offered to approach city hall and sound out sources of funding, zoning requirements, and the city's willingness to collaborate, should a concrete building project take shape in the future. Before much time had elapsed, he realized that Eastminster needed to repeat the same process at the national level; although considerably shrunk in the past few years, federal funds seemed to be available for subsidized housing. Relatively quickly, he established links with their congressional representative and senators. His initial report brought home the immensity of red tape involved in either federally or locally subsidized housing.

The second task that the session asked Carol to spearhead during their retreat consisted of sounding out other churches in the area. Could Eastminster join with one or more of these churches in a common response to area homelessness? If so, what might their joint response be? Carol's inquiry bore fruit so quickly that it surprised everyone. Within weeks she brought back a request, posed to all the area churches, to commit their congregations to house the overflow from the downtown shelter one night every two weeks between December and March. The theoretical suddenly became practical as, after considerable congregation-wide discussion, Eastminster agreed to participate. What had been the session members' personal commitment now began to include the entire congregation.

The congregation's initial hesitation about having "those people" on their premises quickly dissolved. In fact, since they arrived at 8:00 p.m. and left at 6:00 a.m., many parishioners did not see any sign of them—that made things easier on one front, Carol observed to the session, but kept most members insulated from the real people who slept in Eastminster's pews.

Other than the session members' personal commitments to the homeless issue, the fact-finding, the two sermon series, and this outreach constituted the congregation's corporate response during that year. At next fall's retreat, with Carol's encouragement not to judge themselves or each other, the returning session members spoke about how they did or did not fulfill their personal commitments. One of the most obvious conclusions to their sharing seemed both elementary and very important: those persons who had group or personal support for their commitment were much more likely to have carried it out.

Carol posed a new question for their consideration: Should the session ask the congregation to commit themselves to an active and ongoing response to the homeless? Yes, came the session's unanimous response, but they quickly added several cautions. Not all members of the congregation would respond enthusiastically to this focus, and the session needed to honor their choice not to become involved. Nor would all members be drawn to the same one or two expressions of this focus, so they should encourage a variety of responses from which people could choose. And, from what they observed about their own behavior, communities of support would greatly encourage faithfulness.

The session members decided that they should propose this focus at an upcoming congregational meeting, and speak personally about their own experiences of commitment and conversion. Meanwhile, Carol and the Christian Education chairperson would brainstorm some concrete ways the education program could provide both experiences and input, geared to various age groups, about the larger justice issues underlying homelessness.

The session made two other decisions that afternoon. The first reaffirmed the congregation's continued participation in the shelter overflow program. However, they noted that several faithful women had ended up bearing the brunt of the three hundred sandwiches the church supplied on its shelter nights. The session decided to ask each of the parish's groups to take responsibility for one time of sandwich-making, under the leadership of the regular crew. Even if the congregation's involvement with housing went no further, the session members reasoned, many more members could and should be involved personally in carrying out this level of congregational commitment. And should the congregation decide to extend its commitment in related directions, more people would understand that much behind-the-scenes faithful and thankless work would also be required.

Ida, whose arthritis made it difficult to participate in the more physical aspects of the church's life, came up with the second idea: "Why not begin a regular time in which we pray for the church's guidance on these decisions?" She belonged to the little knot of seniors who met at worship every Sunday. She was sure that they would be more than willing to adopt this as their special contribution. The session happily affirmed her suggestion, and so was born the regular prayer for congregational guidance, which Carol later thought was far more significant in unifying the congregation than anyone recognized at first.

Several notable events occurred that year. The congregation did affirm the focus on ministry to the homeless in their neighborhood after two lengthy congregational meetings. Doreen died after a short bout with pneumonia, and her funeral at Eastminster drew a sizable number of the congregation. Habitat for Humanity built a house in town, to which two of Eastminster's couples devoted their summer vacations. The civic-planning group, as they began to call themselves, drew up a proposal for subsidized housing to be sponsored jointly by Eastminster and the federal government; it was eventually adopted by the congregation but rejected by the government.

About mid-way through the year, the vacant building on the other side of the church parking lot came up for sale. It would lend itself to being converted into a big kitchen and dining room, Carol noted. The church could feed people even if they could not permanently house them. The prayer circle shifted to this question; the study and the informational meetings began again and a steady stream of people looked at the somewhat depressing building they were considering for purchase. The decision involved more than a building, they began to realize. It also entailed a food budget, cooks, and maintenance after the building was refurbished. Even though they could do much of the renovation themselves, the project would be a long-term and expensive venture, committing the congregation well into the future. Eventually they took the leap.

That was two years ago. Eastminster's kitchen now serves whoever arrives every Monday, Wednesday and Friday between 6:00 and 7:00 p.m., sometimes as many as one hundred fifty persons. The church pot-luck, grown to fit the new space, claims Tuesday evenings. Several homeless persons usually wander in and join the parishioners, confused by what day it is, and stay right through the prayer and Bible study following the meal. For the second year, the federal government failed to fund Eastminster's application for subsidized housing funds.

As Carol prepares her annual report for the session retreat, she will comment appreciatively that the Kitchen Ministry really runs on its own. She is seldom called in to help with a crisis; usually she just takes her regular turn at serving and cleaning up. She reminds herself to thank the congregation for their substantial output of both time and money for the more than twelve hundred meals per month served in the course of the past year.

It is, she reflects, about time for her to move. Perhaps at the end of this coming year. She resolves to discuss it with the session next week.

Although much could be said about Eastminster's developmental dynamics, recall some ways that Carol, the session and the entire congregation foster naturally therapeutic dynamics as they grow in their life together.

Carol's first couple of years at Eastminster could be characterized by its confirmative style. The people sensed that she liked them and understood their values and culture. They grew to trust her ministry among them.

Carol's manner of instituting the Stephen Ministry served as a model for her work with other ministries, including housing overflow from the shelter and the Kitchen Ministry. She accompanied the congregants whom she asked to spearhead the Stephen Ministry and could subsequently communicate her understanding and support for their sometimes stressful ministry. In supervising sessions, she personalized this confirmation, but did not hesitate to challenge problems as they arose. Drawing the individual Stephen ministers into funerals initially raised their anxiety level, but the response from every minister after his or her first funeral was uniformly positive. At the organizational level, Carol tried never to undermine the coordinator's decisions in the day-to-day workings of the group. She also maintained continuity with the shut-ins by continuing to visit them regularly.

Carol does not try to submerge the conflict that inevitably surfaces within the congregation and its subgroups. Nor is she loath to raise unpopular subjects when necessary, reminding the session, for example, that they had been taking advantage of Pat's generosity and overlooking their responsibility to the needs of the youth. Carol asks for and receives regular feedback herself, and promotes the same kind of feedback, especially in the session. She is willing to field tough questions and to accept criticism, some of which surfaces at each congregational meeting. She can turn her sense of humor on herself, which often breaks the ice on such occasions.

Finally, she participates in Eastminster's continuity by doing herself what she asks of the session members, and by involving the congregation in her upcoming transition.

During the past eight years the session has grown in its ability to recognize and draw on the naturally therapeutic dynamics as well. Neither the session as a group nor individual members have been exposed to the theoretical discussion of structural development undertaken here. As they move into more complex modes of meaning-making, however, they take into account the meaning-systems that they have transcended. They understand how many of their companions "see things."

The session members have also grown increasingly comfortable with free-thinking and imagination, and encourage both their own members and others in the congregation to dream about alternatives. They are willing to pay attention to feeling as well as thinking in their decision-making. They intuitively recognize that both face-to-face involvement and communities of support will be necessary to involve substantial numbers of Eastminster's congregation in enormous undertakings such as the Kitchen Ministry turned out to be. But they also provided openings which led some of their members to address systemic and structural aspects of their ministry to the homeless. Perhaps Eastminster can evolve new ways to continue its political participation, even though, at least for now, the subsidized housing seems unattainable.

Gradually, Eastminster's programs are challenging persons at a variety of developmental stages. The chairperson of the Christian Education program, herself a teacher, has given much thought in the past three years to raising justice issues in the curriculum in a developmentally sensitive manner. One immediate result: the youth program has stabilized, and is gradually growing in depth.

Eastminster is not utopia. It is filled with ordinary human beings with their peccadillos and their fights. It has not turned into a community of integrated human beings. It is certainly in process. Yet it is a community that has grown in its ability to respond to people who at first seemed very foreign to them, but whom they now recognize as not so different after all. They have learned to share their economic resources, but, more importantly, themselves, and have grown in the process.

IX. Spiritual Guidance as Connected Learning

At the end of our foray into structural developmental theories and their implications for spiritual direction and congregational spiritual guidance, we come full circle to focus again on images, but now of developmentally effective spiritual guidance. I hope our path has been more akin to a helix than a circle: although we will again generate an image to help us grasp our role in spiritual guidance, we have advanced our vision since we began this journey by adding a new interpretive grid, structural development.

In the most formal and particularized mode of spiritual guidance considered in these pages, spiritual directors explicitly covenant with each seeker to assist her or him to listen as attentively as possible to God's call in the midst of everyday life and to respond with integrity. Spiritual directors likewise pledge themselves to seek holiness, even as they assist their directees to attain their own unique holiness. We have also considered the minister's covenant with the congregation to assist it and its members to listen for the call of God and to respond with integrity. Such spiritual guidance lies at the heart of all pastoral functions, although this central pastoral responsibility is carried out in a more diffused and frequently more implicit manner than is the spiritual director's covenant.

But spiritual guidance is not the exclusive prerogative of pastors or spiritual directors, however formative they may be. Family and friends exert a subtle yet powerful impact for good or ill (usually some of each) upon spiritual growth. The faith community's many persons and programs, especially its worship, form and constrict the spiritual life of the congregation. Even such aspects of "secular" life as occupation, civic participation, and recreation can form us spiritually by offering wider contexts to live out the call to discipleship.

Spiritual direction assists the seeker to notice the action of God in the dailiness of life; to listen actively to the nascent language of the soul; to celebrate God's presence and call; and to respond consciously and freely to God, others and the entire created world in all its diversity and ambiguity. Other spiritually formative persons and events should enhance these same responses. All those involved in spiritual guidance, whether as seekers or guides, will hopefully be challenged to stretch, to learn, to grow until their last breath.

Our final task, then, centers around generating an image of

163

developmentally effective spiritual guidance of sufficient breadth to sustain spiritual guidance's broad context and constituency. Ideally, such an image should apply to all the "countries" on our imaginary planet, incorporating the developmental dynamics which assist their citizens to move from one country to the next. Such an image should also unite our understanding of both developmental stages and transitions with the theological and pastoral goals of spiritual direction. Accordingly, it must address men and women equally, and touch all aspects of the human person, not just cognitive development. Likewise, it must equalize our perception of who develops and who facilitates development.

In our search for a useful image for developmentally effective spiritual guidance, the insightful study by Mary Belenky and her colleagues, *Women's Ways of Knowing*, provides an entry point. They first describe five different styles with which women construct the world of knowledge (which correlate with the stages of ego development elaborated in these pages). They name these styles "Silence," "Received Knowledge," "Subjective Knowledge," "Procedural Knowledge," and "Constructed Knowledge." The authors devote the remainder of their study to probing the dynamics of two pervasive contexts common to all women: family and school. Although their analysis focuses on the developmental pitfalls and promises which family and school hold for women, these contexts equally influence men. The dynamics which the authors uncover, while essential to women's development, should also enhance men's development by challenging and contrasting with male-centered developmental pacers.

At the close of their discussion of an educational system which fosters women's epistemological development, Belenky and colleagues develop an image which they call "connected teaching." Adapted to our considerations, connected teaching offers us a potentially powerful and explicitly developmental image to add to our earlier images of spiritual guidance, which I will call "connected learning."

I propose that effective spiritual guidance operates as connected learning. As we probe the genesis and implications of this image of spiritual guidance, we shall dialogue with Belenky and her colleagues with respect to family and education. Finally, based on this conversation, I shall expand the image of spiritual guidance as connected learning.

Belenky and her colleagues recognize that women at particular stages tend to share common family dynamics, suggesting that families limit the developmental potential of their members. The family comprises not only the first formative community, but also the community which makes the strongest and most long-lasting claims upon us. Each child is supported by its family to develop only to a certain point, at which most persons tend to linger throughout much of their adult lives. Families, perhaps more than other social institutions, pace their children's growth to an "average expectable level of development." All other communities, including the church, support, enhance, substitute for, or attempt to undo the developmental contingencies already in place from our earliest years lived in the family context.

Yet the family does not exist in isolation. The social forces that operate on families during children's formative years continue to shape their experience long past their actual years in the family. Thus the jobs, schools, social services and expectations for some families—often the economically, racially and ethnically marginalized—are quite likely to be hierarchical and to demand conformity, passivity and obedience, a poor climate for advancing beyond the Self-Protective or Conformist stages. But the same social institutions serving the economically and socially privileged will far more likely encourage creative thinking and active involvement in forming social relationships, considerably more optimal conditions for lifelong development. Families, like the individuals which comprise them, exist within a web of interacting dynamics.

It might seem impossible to escape the determinism of such all-permeating and often subtle forces which pace development. However, families do develop, and sometimes in surprising ways. What appears at first glance to be a closed system actually turns out to be an open one. With sufficient perspective, it becomes clear that developmental dynamics do not just flow in one direction. Parents' and children's development are inevitably intertwined and interlocking. Children make developmental claims on their parents which are fully as challenging to the parents' development, though different in particulars, as those which parents make on children. Parents and children evolve in tandem, each supporting and challenging the other to develop more complex ways of responding as they play out their lives together.[1] For example, an Impulsive preschooler encourages his Conformist parents to begin to speak for themselves (as Conscientious persons do): "I am talking now, and I do not like it when you interrupt me. You may speak in a moment." Young adults ask to be treated as individuals in their own right, nudging their parents toward the Interindividual perspective. In addition, both children and parents form relationships outside the family context, which in turn introduce further developmental dynamics into the family system. The question, "Mom, why do we do it this way?" invites Mom to reflect consciously on why their family operates the way it does; potentially its members could choose to affirm or change either their practice or their perspective.

Similarly, parishes and spiritual direction relationships operate as open systems set within other equally open systems. Not only do pastors challenge parishioners developmentally, parishioners also challenge pastors. Church communities challenge and support families, but are challenged and supported by families in return. Directees pace their spiritual directors even while directors pace their directees. The Conformist directee "asks" her Conscientious spiritual director to respond empathically to a person with whom the director cannot make a strong inner connection; that is, the spiritual director is invited to develop a more Interindividual perspective. Finally, the relationship with God—the focus of both the pastoral and direction relationships—potentially breaks any human system wide open, as God freely invites both individuals and communities to transcend their current situations.

Since Belenky and her colleagues were investigating the dynamics which influenced the development of women's concepts of self, mind and voice, they examined the patterns of silence and speech as a context of development. They asked what kind of discourse families permitted and what kinds they discouraged. The dynamics of silence and speech which they uncovered highlight the learning environment most conducive to development—for both parties. Their guiding questions adapt to our context as well.

First, they ask, what are the rules (spoken or unspoken) about speaking and listening? Do both parties listen to each other with respect and care? Second, who assumes the role of learner? Do both parties actively and consciously attempt to learn from each other? Third, what kind of questioning occurs? Are questions genuine or merely rhetorical? Do they draw out and enlarge upon both feelings and ideas, plans and possibilities for compromise, occurrences and interpretations, hopes and accomplishments? Or do questions reproach and constrict? Fourth, are feelings and appropriate intimacies permitted?[2] Or must everything be kept on an intellectual and impersonal basis? Or are the two intertwined? Finally, are conversations seen as collaborations in which the parties share and build upon each other's ideas? Do some conversations specifically attempt to nurture both ideas and people? Or are conversations held to outdo the other?[3]

The metaphor of silence vividly describes those who have no voice, those who are not only unseen but unheard as well. Belenky and her colleagues explore this silence resulting from powerlessness. But there is another kind of silence essential to spiritual guidance. This quality of silence allows one to speak when ready to speak, and avoids prying or putting another in undue tension. It respects the choice to keep some thoughts to oneself. It offers space for the growth of creative imagination and ultimately of contemplative prayer. With respect to spiritual guidance, we can ask: Do speech and silence exist together in conversation and relationship? Are times and places of quiet not only allowed but encouraged? Is there sufficient stimulation for the development of inner life through story and symbol, art, music and literature?

Moving to the educational context, Belenky and her colleagues continue to probe the dynamics which best enhance the development of self, voice and mind. Connected teaching, they observe, confirms the other as a knower in his or her own right, and who brings unique experiences as a valuable base for further knowing. Connected teaching relates knowledge to life, does not denigrate practical knowledge as inferior to "pure" knowledge, and encourages all learning to make a practical difference. In connected teaching, the standards of evaluation are constructed collaboratively. In connected teaching both parties, and not just the "student," reveal the thinking process with all its gaps, inconsistences and incompleteness. Connected teaching recognizes the need for both structure and experiment, and provides sufficient parameters without eliminating flexibility.[4]

As a sophisticated example of connected teaching, Belenky and her colleagues point to the social-science research methodology called participant-observation. In this method, investigators actually take part in the enterprise they are studying, undergoing experiences similar to those of other participants, precisely so that they will be better able to understand in the same way that the other participants do. They use their own reactions to formulate hypotheses about other participants' reactions.[5] Likewise, spiritual directors and pastors join all other seekers in the Christian story and in the life which flows from it.

Erik Erikson once described participant-observation as a "technique of *disciplined* subjectivity."[6] Disciplined investigators cannot collapse their perspective into that of the group, thereby negating the "observer" aspect of participant-observation. Participant-observation's strength as a method comes from combining subjectivity and objectivity into an integrated perspective, in which one stands at the same time both inside and outside the event studied. In participant-observation, empathy does not dissolve into identity.

Such disciplined subjectivity provides a particularly apt description for an effective spiritual guidance relationship, whether between director and directee or between minister and congregation. By virtue of their own status as seekers, and through participating in their own spiritual guidance, spiritual guides discern and follow their own Christian call. In that very process they simultaneously prepare to understand the experiences of their parishioners and directees as they experience them. Yet pastoral spiritual guidance demands that guides also remain just slightly outside the seeker's experience in order to supply confirmation, creative contradiction and continuity as called for in the particular guidance relationship. Without ever abdicating their pastoral responsibility, effective spiritual guides seek to share responsibility and power to the degree appropriate, to draw out the effects of grace already present in each person, and to create an environment in which the relationship with creation, self and God matures to the fullest degree. In so doing, spiritual guides participate in the very conditions of their own continuing development. Effective spiritual guidance operates as connected learning.

In pursuit of our image of spiritual guidance as connected learning, we can now ask: Do both parties share the teaching and learning? Is the message courteous to each learner?[7] Do both parties reveal how they arrived at the position they now hold? Do both parties allow the Christian story to challenge and form them? Do both tell their stories of faith and their stories of doubt? Does the relationship maintain the naturally therapeutic dynamics of confirmation, creative contradiction and consistency while allowing for new ideas, actions, and even ways of being? Is the relationship based on cooperation and mutual enhancement, rather than on power and subordination?

What then can we finally say about spiritual guidance as connected learning? It recognizes that all members of the Christian community participate in spiritual guidance for each other. All must struggle with the implications of the Christian story as it comes to us through the often ambiguous heritage of the scriptures and traditions of believers throughout the centuries. Each one of us must embody the Christian story concretely and particularly in all aspects of our life, not just the "religious" ones. Any event and relationship potentially bears God's revelation to us at a given moment.

Spiritual guidance as connected learning builds on strengths present in individuals and in the community of faith. It recognizes that God calls and gifts each person for a particular work in the world. It recognizes that each of us brings unique experiences and graces to the task of discipleship, and seeks to enhance the gifts of that varied experience. It both confirms and challenges the variety of developmental perspectives that individuals bring to their relationships with God, self, others, and the world.

Spiritual guidance as connected learning recognizes the necessity for appropriate structure—but a structure which more closely resembles a semipermeable membrane than a concrete wall. The parameters and structures of connected spiritual guidance serve as a holding environment, providing a safe place for asking difficult, even frightening questions about what is ultimately meaningful, for trying on new images of self in the world, and for coming to terms with the implications of God's ever-new call.

Spiritual guidance as connected learning understands and accepts responsibility for inevitable differences in power, seeing them as functional and shifting, rather than immutable and fixed. It grants as much power as possible and appropriate to the one who has less, seeking ultimately an egalitarian relationship of coseekers.

Spiritual guidance as connected learning supports efforts to become as self-directed as possible at each developmental level, to participate actively and consciously in one's life in God. It supports efforts to collaborate, to engage in two-way conversations, whether between parents and children, pastors and parishioners, or directors and seekers and, above all, between seekers and God.

Spiritual guidance as connected learning supports efforts to feel and to express feelings appropriately. But it also supports efforts to think with increasing clarity and complexity, and to choose with increasing freedom. Connected spiritual guidance seeks to unite thinking, feeling and choosing as three complementary aspects of the human response to God's call.

Ultimately, spiritual guidance as connected learning recognizes that it is a limited human enterprise, which receives as gift both its goal and its life.

X. Development in Human Development

In the years since the first edition of this book appeared, an interesting phenomenon has occurred among those who write about structural development. All those theorists who have continued to produce scholarly works have, without exception, moved away from focusing almost exclusively on the individual person. They have all begun to examine the complex interrelationship between individual development and the communities in which the individuals live.[1] They now seem compelled to work with such questions as "What difference will our contemporary times make in our understanding of human development? What will these times require by way of development if we are successfully to negotiate the challenges facing humans at the turn of the millennium?" In this chapter, I will summarize some of their findings. We will then sit in on several vignettes from Eastminster Presbyterian Church's present life, including its Kitchen Ministry, as its members struggle to come to grips with the future of their homegrown ministry in a period of increasing scarcity for those lowest in the socioeconomic strata of society. Their struggles will take them out to their neighbors as they learn to become "public church." The chapter concludes with some comments about spiritual direction in this increasingly complex milieu.[2]

Both James Fowler and Robert Kegan have pondered the demands that late twentieth century culture poses for human development. Though they focus on somewhat different aspects of our cultural situation, they come to strikingly similar conclusions about the complexity to which our culture has paced human development. In the developmental stage terminology employed in this work, both Fowler and Kegan assert that our recent cultural complexity demands of adults that they function with the nuance and balance of the Interindividual stage. But the earlier chapters made it abundantly clear that many fewer than half of all adults will reach this stage. What then are we to make of this dilemma? As spiritual guides for individuals and congregations, how might we begin to address this situation? These questions will occupy the first part of this discussion.

The Postmodern Challenge

In *In Over Our Heads: The Mental Demands of Modern Life*, Robert Kegan sets out to look at the "curriculum" of contemporary life in relation to the capacities of the adult mind, particularly in terms of structural development. He argues that we unconsciously expect the contemporary teenager to develop the order of conscious complexity required to participate in a traditional, pre-Enlightenment world. We just as unconsciously expect of adults a consciousness threshold consistent with modernity. As if that challenge were not sufficient, we now live in a world becoming still more complex, often described by the term "postmodernity." It requires, yet again, a qualitatively more complex order of consciousness.[3] Translated into the stage language used in this work, "competent" childhood requires the complexity of the Conformist stage, "competent" adolescence and young adulthood require the complexity of the Conscientious stage, but "competent" adulthood increasingly requires the complexity of the Interindividual stage of structural development. For much of our lives, an inevitable mismatch exists between the complexity of the culture's "curriculum" and our capacity to grasp it.

James Fowler also analyzes our culture. He does so from the angle of our recent "culture wars," his term for the contentious bickering between broad political coalitions. He grounds this analysis using a developmental substrate, with telling results. Two broad coalitions surface, which he names the "orthodox temper" and the "progressive temper." The "orthodox temper" displays a cluster of characteristics that includes an understanding of authority as external to self, lawful, fixed, and unchanging; adherence to universally binding moral rules and to religious beliefs established in traditions; an economic understanding of freedom as "free market system"; and an understanding of justice as personal and social adherence to the laws of God. He describes the "progressive temper" as a quite different cluster of characteristics, including an understanding of freedom as protection of the social and political rights of individuals, and of justice as equality for all persons and groups and the ending of oppression in the social world. Fowler notes the source of the problem:

> The two dominant tempers are grounded in convictional emotion, both tend to resist or bypass rational argumentation with the other. These two coalitions appeal to their own cultural canons; each confines its discourse largely to the community of its own adherents. Engagements with representatives of the other temper tend to be conducted in terms of debate rather than of dialogue; their representations of each other occur primarily in caricatures and stereotypes.[4]

The orthodox temper exhibits many of the structural features of the stage we have been calling Conformist, while the progressive temper exhibits characteristics of the Conscientious. It is clear why so many political issues end in stalemate when these two worldviews face off. To compound the problem, neither manifests the complexity that we have seen will be necessary to meet the demands of the increasingly complex global village of the twenty-first century.

Fowler sees the solution to this political impasse in developing a substantial minority of persons who transcend these polarized world views and who therefore must be able to deal with the complexity implied in the Interindividual stage. Such leaders will exhibit three important qualities: simplicity on the other side of complexity (Ricoeur's second naiveté); the ability to stand firmly, yet flexibly in one's own faith tradition so that one can affirm plurality and diversity; and openness to the stranger and explicit care for the common good. These leaders will need to help alter the environment of debate and name-calling fostered by a media addicted to sound bites and sensationalism, however much this environment suits many adults in the society at the present.[5]

Daloz, Keen, Keen, and Parks also examine the dilemma our culture poses, describing, as they do, the felt sense of dis-equilibrium many persons experience:

> Meaning does not exist by itself; we create it. A tree may flourish apart from us, but the meaning of that tree does not. Whether we see it as a source of shade, a complex biological system, inspiration for a poem, or as a provider of match sticks, depends in large measure on who we are. Each of us constructs the meaning of that tree differently. In that sense, we are inveterate meaning-makers.
>
> But the conditions of contemporary life assault our meaning-making capacity. The diversity of viewpoints and the complexity of contemporary conditions create an ambivalence that gnaws at the edges of our consciousness, eroding our conviction. Familiar ways of thinking no longer work. We try to understand, to make judgments, even to act. But when we do, ...we find ourselves confronted by a maze of experts, explanations, and countervailing evidence. Faced by competing perspectives and partial knowledge, we hesitate. We often feel removed from the roots of things and barred from the power to change them.[6]

The kinds of families and gathering places that have supported development and created communities of care have been transformed almost beyond recognition. Neighborhoods where everyone knew several generations of everyone else's family have yielded in large part to suburbs where neighbors never talk or to condominiums where the association impersonally enforces the covenant. Churches are increasingly empty, but individual psychotherapy is flourishing. Family meals have been replaced by restaurants and drive-though fast food. Ballparks have been replaced by video arcades, general stores by immense malls, and townhall meetings by chat groups on the internet. Daloz, Keen, Keen, and Parks want to look at a metaphor for the gathering place of the twenty-first century, which they call the "new commons," but more importantly, they want to suggest how we begin to build lives of commitment in a complex world.

What kind of capacities might we seek in order to prepare ourselves and our children to participate in the new commons? We might begin our search in the middle of this century. As the developmental strength of one stage appears in nascent form in an earlier stage, to come to fruition in its given time of ascendancy, so the developmental needs of one period may be modeled for us by exceptional individuals of an earlier period. Two such figures, each caught up in the Nazi tide, can point the way. The first, Etty Hillesum, was a young Jewish woman who died at Auschwitz in 1943. What is so striking about Etty is her clearsighted and unflinching choice to place herself squarely in harm's way in order to share completely the lot of her family and fellow Jews. She went to her death voluntarily, leaving with a friend eight closely penned journals recording her thoughts, feelings, experiences, and prayers for the express purpose of preserving a record to light the way for others. I concluded an earlier developmental study of Etty with the following:

> What...can we learn from Etty's short life? Perhaps these lessons:
>
> No circumstances are too grim to foreclose totally the transcendent possibilities in the human spirit. The transcendent possibility for a given individual human spirit is another matter altogether; far too many humans begin and end their life within such circumstances that their human potential is extinguished almost before it has begun to be realized.
>
> Etty arrived at her singular rendezvous with history with an already well-honed personality structure despite some rather pronounced neurotic tendencies. While it is not possible to engineer stage change in oneself or another, we can attend, with all the available resources, to creating developmentally useful environments especially for those most vulnerable and at risk among us. We can disconfirm rigid stereotypes of others not like us, we can expose ourselves and our children and youth to a broad expanse of the literature, arts and religious writings from various cultures throughout

the world. We can live in inclusive neighborhoods, rubbing shoulders with other racial-ethnic and religious communities. We can ask, and encourage others to ask, hard, impertinent questions about the way our society is structured to limit access to the world's material and spiritual goods to a tiny elite. We can pursue truth no matter what the personal cost. In other words, we can model for others, however our circumstances allow, what Etty models for us: living with radical difference, solidarity, flexibility, humor and refusal to blame or retaliate.[7]

That is, even under extreme circumstances, extreme challenges, extreme complexity, we can do simple things that allow us to better respond to our world. These actions, if sustained, make a difference in communities of care. These actions, then, can be understood as spiritual disciplines for the new century.

The second figure is Fritz Grabe, one of the "righteous Gentiles" who risked their own lives to save Jews from the Nazis. In a study of Grabe, Douglas Huneke isolated seven characteristics, which in turn point to ways we can develop the characteristics necessary to live in the new commons, or as I have called them, spiritual disciplines for out times. First, the ability to engage in *empathic imagination*, to place oneself in the actual situation or role of another person and to imagine the effect and long-term consequences of the situation or role. The rudiments of empathic imagination can be taught to even quite young children; any child capable of concrete operational thinking (typical of elementary school children) can be invited to engage in it. Churches offer numerous opportunities for empathic imagination through such varied activities as Bible study, mission trips, even sitting on the finance committee with people of very different values.[8]

Second, the ability to *take control of critical situations*. Fritz Grabe first learned this lesson as a young boy when his mother would engage him in the dilemmas of his neighborhood, asking "Fritz, what would you do?" Congregations and committees can continue to engage in collective brainstorming, and committee chairs can be supported in working out the dilemmas and crises that confront their committees without the pastoral staff's overriding their decisions. Moral and ethical reflection can be taught in education courses at varying levels, from at least middle school through adult, certainly with high school and young adult groups.

Third, acting in a *proactive and prosocial manner*. The significant adults who surround young children can model these traits for them. They can be practiced at developmentally appropriate levels by planning cooperative and responsible actions, by anticipating opportunities for having a positive and beneficial impact in the lives and circumstances of others and by actively promoting the well-being of others as well as oneself. Eastminster's Kitchen Ministry continues to offer to members of the congregation a variety of opportunities for proactive and prosocial behavior.

Fourth, the ability to *confront and manage one's prejudices*. This ability takes self-observation, but it also requires motivation to change. Communities that encourage their members to discard prejudicial behavior have the most hope of supporting this ability; however, it will require sufficient interiority that it becomes an integrated part of one's personality and conscious value system only after the Conformist stage.

Fifth, the development of *communities of compassion and support*. In the process of hiding and transporting Jews in Nazi-held territories, complex and dangerous rescues were seldom carried out alone; rescuers assembled networks of persons who both collaborated in the rescues at their own personal risk and sustained the people they were rescuing through times of extreme stress, fatigue, and depression. The likelihood of remaining faithful to any demanding commitment is significantly enhanced when shared in community. Eastminster's session became aware of this dynamic as they examined their own personal commitments to the housing issue at the end of the first year. From that experience, they realized they needed to create or broaden networks of investment in their unfolding attempts to house the homeless and subsequent Kitchen Ministry.

Sixth, the ability to *offer hospitality*. A steady stream of strangers welcomed into communities can dissipate a sense of the stranger as "other" to be feared; a variety of persons in the family or congregation on a regular basis can be experienced as normal. Dealing frequently and personally with otherness, however defined, eventually paces for the Interindividual stage, where interdependence is prized.[9]

These characteristics are strikingly similar to those uncovered by Daloz, Keen, Keen, and Parks as they investigated characteristics of ordinary people who have sustained long-term commitments to work on behalf of the common good, even in the face of global complexity, diversity, and ambiguity; that is, people whose lives illustrate the Interindividual stage. For example, in the chapter entitled "Conviction: Developing Critical Habits of Mind," Daloz and colleagues speak of six "habits of mind": *dialogue*, grounded in the understanding that meaning is constructed through an ongoing interaction between oneself and others; *interpersonal perspective-*

taking, the ability to see through the eyes and respond to the feelings and concerns of the other; *critical, systemic thought*, the capacity to identify parts and connections among them as coherent patterns and to reflect evaluatively on them; *dialectical thought*, the ability to recognize and work effectively with contradictions by resisting closure or by reframing one's response; and *holistic thought*, the ability to intuit life as an interconnected whole in a way that leads to *practical wisdom*.[10]

As Daloz, Keen, Keen, and Parks rightly point out, these practices are closely interrelated and developmentally sequential. Previous habits undergird each successive habit. As each evolves, the preceding ones are integrated, but not lost. Furthermore, these habits and their precursors are extremely effective in fostering structural development. They indicate the kind of virtues we will need for the twenty-first century.[11] Virtues, we might expect, are honed in collectivities organized around centers of value and power—that is, around spiritualities.

Can churches contribute to the needs of our times? Indeed they can. Insofar as churches can move toward becoming what James Fowler calls "public church" in spite of their limitations and their struggle to value the interdependence of all society's citizens, they may still be one of the most promising venues for creating thoughtful and prayerful dialogue about the social and moral dilemmas of our time.[12]

In *Weaving the New Creation*, Fowler offers seven characteristics of a public church. First, public church fosters a clear sense of Christian identity and commitment. Second, public church congregations manifest diversity in their membership. Third, public church consciously prepares and supports members for vocation and witness in a pluralistic society. Fourth, public church balances nurture and group solidarity with formation and vocational accountability in members' lives beyond the church walls. Fifth, public church involves a pattern of authority and governance that keeps pastoral and lay leadership initiatives in a fruitful balance. Sixth, public church offers its witness in publicly visible and publicly intelligible ways. Finally, public church shapes a pattern of *paideia* (practical wisdom based in practices) for children, youth, and adults that works toward the combining of Christian commitment with vocation in public.[13] We shall return to Eastminster Presbyterian Church, noticing as we do to what degree it embodies the characteristics of the new commons and public church.

Eastminster Revisited

Almost ten years have passed since Eastminster launched the process that resulted in its Kitchen Ministry, and even longer since the first stirring of concern about homelessness surfaced in its elders. Slow but steady changes have occurred in the neighborhood. The "white flight" lessened considerably, leaving the older generation of retired blue-collar families. More people of color with younger children began moving in; the boundaries of the neighborhood now include a noticeable percentage of African American and a smaller but still significant percentage of Cuban families. These three groups, however, have not managed to socialize together or to form coherent community groups to work for the welfare or restoration of the neighborhood beyond the Parent-Teacher Association at the local school. Even there, the activities are trimmed; most two-parent families find both spouses working, and the many one-parent families are consumed with getting food on the table and the kids to school. Several hours of after-school supervised study and sports are desperately needed, but do not yet exist. The infrastructure of the community reveals its aging too: more potholes dot the residential streets, more storefronts stand empty, and those remaining now sport bars over the windows. Repair from the recent tornadoes has been spotty; those parties with insurance have gradually repaired their homes and businesses, but the downed trees in the park have not been replaced, nor the washed-out baseball diamond.

Eastminster Presbyterian Church has also changed in the intervening years. Carol, the pastor under which the Kitchen Ministry began, now serves a church in a nearby city. The current pastor, Tim, has appreciated and supported the Kitchen Ministry, but recognizes that it is showing some of the same stresses as the neighborhood, aging and deteriorating infrastructure. The present chair of the Kitchen Ministry is tired and has indicated that he will resign at the end of September. It is not obvious who will take his place, though a search committee is at work on hiring his successor. The facilities, the best Eastminster could afford when it renovated the old building eight years ago, need some upgrading if the ministry is to continue serving six days per week. In fact, visitors to the Kitchen have increased and diversified in the past few years. Now Spanish-speaking women and children appear regularly, though not the more established Cubans. The newcomers are families of Mexican and Central American agricultural and day laborers. Those served also include a steadily-increasing number of African American women and children and retirees whose pensions do not quite stretch until the next

Social Security check, as well as the homeless for whom the Kitchen was originally established.

Tim recalled the last evaluation meeting by the session, now almost a year ago, when the elders and the chairpersons of the Kitchen Ministry's four subcommittees had begun talking about some tensions among those waiting in line for food, wondering how to stretch the human and material resources of the Kitchen a little farther to encompass these additional constituencies. He was not surprised to hear them say things like: "What we are doing is tremendous, but we are trying to push the water up the river. There are more and more hungry people, but the resources don't get bigger and bigger. Something has to give, or we have to get smarter about what we are already doing." But he *was* surprised when they decided to explore joining with other churches in a more extended ecumenical venture than they had heretofore imagined after someone observed, "Well, St. Peter's has got some ministry to Hispanics, and Wesley has a volunteer parish nurse. We've got food and a reasonably adequate building. Maybe we could expand if we combined our strengths."

To understand some of the ways Eastminster Presbyterian Church paces structural development in its members, encouraging in individuals the kinds of prosocial and proactive behaviors we saw in Fritz Grabe's and Etty Hillesum's lives, we need to look at a cross-section of the church life. We might, for example, overhear this exchange between Charlie, age six, and his Christian Education teacher last Sunday, just after their class:

"How come you hit Manuel, Charlie? I saw you hit him twice today and last week too."

"I don't like him, Mrs. Johnson."

"Why?"

"I dunno. I just don't. I don't have to if I don't want."

"Is it because he has a different name?"

"Nope."

"He doesn't look like you, does he? He's darker."

"Yea, and I can't understand him. He speaks funny. I don't like him."

"Actually, Manuel speaks a beautiful language called Spanish. That's what they speak where he was born, in Guatemala. His Mom and Dad speak it too. Next week I am going to bring a movie in Manuel's language (a cartoon in Spanish from the public library). Would you like to learn to speak some Spanish? Then you and Manuel could have a secret language. Or maybe we could all learn Spanish, and our class would have a secret language."

"Yea, that'd be neat, a secret language!"

"What's the first thing you want to learn to say? We'll get Manuel to teach it to us next week."

"Well, first we need a password, but that can't be in any language. We'll make it up special. Then, let's see,...we could learn 'We speak Spanish!'"

"Ok, that's what it will be. How about a song too? With drums?"

"Yea!"

Mrs. Johnson skillfully elicits one of the aspects of "otherness" that Charlie is reacting to, Manuel's still broken English, and devises a way for Manuel to show off his very real knowledge of language. If Charlie and Manuel can collaborate on a project of teaching their class a "secret language," Spanish, Manuel will become a valued member without looking and speaking just like everyone else. To do so, Mrs. Johnson relies on her knowledge of elementary age children's propensity for forming in-groups, but turns it to a more benevolent direction than it would have taken if the children were left to their own devices. If all goes well, in a few weeks the class can sing a Spanish hymn in the next children's worship, since "we can speak Spanish in our class!" After this exchange, Mrs. Johnson converses with Mary Beth (whom we met earlier in the book), who, since her graduation, has volunteered to become the head of the Christian Education program at her church, Eastminster. They agree to show the cartoon to grades 1–3 and devise a game for figuring out what is going on even though the children can't understand the language. If other classes seem to catch the spirit, they could also begin to learn the Spanish hymn, but not before Charlie's class gets to glory a while in being the class with the "secret language."

Mary Beth later checks in with her spiritual director, the same one she began with quite some years ago:

"Things are getting interesting at the church, now that some of the kids from the Kitchen Ministry have started coming on Sundays. Mrs. Johnson was really quick last Sunday and figured out a way to keep one of her kids from picking on the Guatemalan boy in her class. We are going to show a cartoon in Spanish, and the class is going to start learning a simple Spanish hymn, maybe "De Colores," to sing in the next children's worship. But, I have a feeling that everyone is not going to be happy to find out that the Guatemalan and Mexican kids from the Kitchen Ministry are starting to come to church school. My husband, for example. He sincerely thinks that the Mexicans are taking the local jobs. I can't convince him that the jobs they are taking are ones not even our teenagers want. But he really has come a long way since he was so negative about my going back to school.

"I remember that. It was just when you were beginning spiritual direction. You've come a long way since then too."

"Yea, I guess I have. Then I was really into not making any more waves than necessary at home, hoping everything would smooth out when the family got used to me being in school. But I remember that school really changed my way of thinking about life. I eventually decided it was ok to think my own thoughts, even if Pete didn't agree with me. Now we regularly disagree about such things as the Hispanics and jobs, and I know the world isn't going to end."

"I remember how scared you were about the images in your prayer. You wanted me to fix your prayer for you . . ."

"And now I'd be glad to have a bit of that passion and sexual imagery show up in my prayer again! It's been a good long while since that wonderful sense of intimacy and first love showed up, though either way it doesn't scare me like it did then."

"So what does God desire for you now, do you think?"

"Oh, there's that question again! You are always asking me that...Everyday faithfulness is what comes to my mind. And I want to figure out a way to head off the reaction to the kids in Sunday school, if I can, that is as gracious with the adults as Mrs. Johnson was with Charlie (smiles)..."

"Do you realize that you answered slightly differently than I asked?"

"What do you mean?

"Well, you answered 'What does God desire *of* you?' but I asked, 'What does God desire *for* you?'"

"Oh, so you did . . .Well . . .(slips into a few minutes of silence together with her spiritual director). What I seem to hear deep inside me is a longing for some of that passion again, the passion between me and God. I guess I have really missed it. I think I wondered if I had lost my first love—isn't that a phrase from Revelations?"

"Perhaps there is a relationship between this deep hunger—you know that God has likely planted that hunger in you, and desires that for you—and your earlier sense of everyday faithfulness. Does anything connect for you?"

"Well, yes, actually there does. I think it might have to do with being proactive with my husband and with the church as a whole about preparing a welcome for the Guatemalans in our midst. I don't know how to do it, or even if we should, but it came back in that silence too. I think I will bring it up at the staff meeting next week..."

Mary Beth has continued to solidify her Conscientious perspective in the intervening years, and now she is clearly indicating a move toward the complexity of the Interindividual stage in her willingness to face into complexity, her ability to live in process without closure, her increasing ability to look for God's call to her in her deep desires, her willingness to wade into a potentially controversial area in her ministry. But it is equally encouraging to notice Mary Beth's new hunger to extend the hospitality of Eastminster Presbyterian Church as a whole, and not just the ministry for which she has primary responsibility. She herself is planning prosocial actions to confront the latent prejudice in her family and the congregation, though she has not yet raised to her conscious attention her own complicity in the status quo.

A final vignette concerns the conversation begun a year ago between the Kitchen Ministry and the session. It has so far borne fruit in an interfaith advisory board for the Kitchen Ministry. As that advisory board grows into its potential, the session hopes that it will prepare the way for wider ecumenical and interfaith collaboration in the neighborhood. Its members include the pastor of the neighboring St. Peter's Catholic Church, Father Tom Z.; the Rabbi of the Reform Temple, Samuel Stein; the Unitarian minister, Sharon Jefferson; and Roger Q, minister of Wesley United Methodist Church, as well as Eastminister's pastor, Tim, and clerk of session, Audrey Campbell. We overhear the board interviewing a candidate for the director of the Kitchen Ministry.

The candidate presented to the board by the search committee is Katherine M., whom we also met earlier through her work with her spiritual director. She is dressed simply but professionally for this interview, wanting to signal solidarity with those served by the Kitchen Ministry and also the professional skills demanded by the position: personnel oversight, long-range planning, budgeting, staff meetings, fund-raising—the activities that engage any director of a church-based nonprofit. She greets each member of the ecumenical board as they are introduced to her, noting past connections. Tom Z. asks the leadoff question: "We have seen what you wrote on your application about why you are interested in heading up Eastminster's Kitchen Ministry, but will you please expand on it this evening?"

"Sitting here tonight is the result of a long journey," Katherine begins. "I suppose its roots lie at least fifteen years ago. One of the events that began to crystalize this direction—one that I can pinpoint anyhow—occurred when I was invited to go on an ecumenical fact-finding mission to Nicaragua, Guatemala, and Honduras. I was becoming increasingly interested in social justice, but this trip radicalized me profoundly. I began to experience for myself the discrepancy between the so-called 'haves' and 'have nots,' and it came home to me that this discrepancy was not simply inevitable, nor were the 'have-nots' somehow just lazy or indifferent. The differences were structural, and the structures were human-made. What we made—the 'we' here is the U.S.—we should be able to undo. As soon as I returned home, I began to work on two levels more or less simultaneously: to simplify my own life and to get at the structures that perpetuate the discrepancies. Neither one has been as simple as I thought at first. Ken, my husband, turned out to be my best reality check during those years as my struggles to make sense of this new call got worked out at the very practical levels of our life together. Now, these many years later, I'd just say that I have to use my education in a way that is both concrete—feeding real people every day—and structural at the same time. My question to you has to do with this second aspect: How do you see that the Kitchen Ministry is now or could be affecting the structures keeping the 'haves' and the 'have-nots' in their respective places?

"On another level, this position is the logical extension of my employment history. You know from my résumé that I began my professional life as an elementary teacher, then moved into social justice ministry on a volunteer basis. Finally, last year, this woman old enough to be a grandma finished her M.A. in Pastoral Care. I am looking for a church-based ministry which combines my passions. Perhaps I could say that I feel called to this position. I have been working with my spiritual director rather formally to discern where I should use my time and energy, and this position continually receives affirmation."

Speaking on behalf of the board, Sharon, its chair, notes: "Your question is a most interesting and fair one. I will make sure that we do respond to it before the evening concludes. Sam, however, has a question."

"You know, our congregation is across town, and I can't think of even one member who lives in the region served by the Kitchen Ministry. Why should we be involved? What might you tell the members of my congregation?"

"I think I might start by exploring the concept of *mitzvoth* with them, especially if there is a specific one dealing with feeding the hungry. As I see it, feeding the hungry is something we do without regard for what it will gain us, but simply because it needs to be done, and God commands us to do it. I would look for a member of the congregation who has been hungry himself or herself, or who can remember their parents' stories of being hungry. I would look for someone in the congregation whose life experience already deals with radical hunger and have these people involved with me for some time before I ever appear publicly in the congregation. I would also look for very concrete ways in which your congregation or segments of it could become directly involved with the Kitchen Ministry, and that can be done at a lot of points, including with the children. That personal involvement, Rabbi, would have to include you. Nothing would make a deeper impression on the congregation than to see you working directly in the ministry. If this were to become a truly interfaith ministry, I think the same thing would essentially have to occur in all your churches, and that would take a commitment of time from the director. So, with the board's involvement, I would want to rewrite the job description to increase the time for this kind of work among the collaborating congregations. In each case you, as the most senior and public of the congregation's leadership, would be important partners in bringing the issues of the Kitchen Ministry to your own congregations—you and your staffs, after all, know the people far better than I ever will."

"I can see a new commitment coming!" replies the Rabbi wryly.

"Yes, but think how it will bring honor to the God of the prophets, who could not abide the kind of economic slavery our system has created," Katherine returns, her eyes sparkling. "With your help, I want to find the people in your congregation who can't *not* do this. They will do the rest."

Roger inserts: "Changing the subject a bit, why would you, a Roman Catholic, want to work as a staff member in a Presbyterian Church? At least for now, that is how the position is structured."

"I've given that a good bit of thought, prayer, and discussion with my spiritual director. I have been concerned not to be running away from a rigidity I see in our own tradition right now with respect to women in ministry, but to be running toward a ministry in a positive sense. I think I can honestly say it is the latter. The stickiest point, I expect, will be worship, as I assume that I will need to appear at worship with some regularity in the church where I am employed. I think a solution might be to participate every Sunday in which Eucharist is not celebrated, but not participate when it is, and to explain my rationale regularly so people know both why I am there and not there. Not ideal, but workable. Of course I intend to continue to remain a member of my own parish and be at mass every week there. As far as staff meetings go, I expect that they are about the same all over. In the end, I think that both I and Eastminster will be enriched..."

From these short excerpts, we can see that Eastminster Presbyterian Church is growing towards Fowler's public church. Although there is much we have not seen in these vignettes, we do sense an openness to preparing its members for vocation and witness in a complex world. The session itself raised the issue of moving the Kitchen Ministry from an internal ministry to an interfaith one. It began taking the steps to move in that direction through establishing the interfaith board and potentially hiring a staff person from a different Christian church. The Kitchen Ministry serves a variety of clients, and the church itself is dealing practically with the issues of otherness and diversity that the ministry raises; in the incident we saw, it began with the children and is working outward toward more of the congregation. The governance structure for the Kitchen Ministry is opening to more voices; the ownership of the ministry is expanding to include a much wider base of support; and the leadership is moving to a professional lay person who will become an integral member of Eastminster's staff. Answering Katherine's question about how this position will relate to the underlying structural issues of poverty and homelessness will mean that these issues again become part of Eastminster's congregational consciousness, and potentially of the Kitchen Ministry's interfaith partners as well.

We have watched one of the church's ministers, a volunteer in the Christian Education program, in a deft and developmentally appropriate way, invite one of her students to greater empathic imagination and prosocial actions and to confront his prejudices at a developmentally appropriate level. She is acting to create in her classroom a community of greater compassion and support through offering hospitality to a newcomer in their midst.

The chair of the Christian Education program, Mary Beth, indicates a growing ability to unite contemplation with action, overcoming the all-too-frequent dichotomy that pits one against the other. She shows that she is increasingly willing to dialogue about difficult aspects of church life, to reflect critically and systematically on the relationship between her personal and family life and the call of the church, and to engage in the inevitable struggle that her insight about hospitality to the strangers in their midst will require if it is to become integrated into the life of the church.

Another of the church's potential public ministers, Katherine M., also exhibits the qualities of leadership in the public church. We saw in her the ability to stand clearly yet flexibly in her own faith tradition while affirming plurality and diversity. Her commitment to the common good has drawn her to the position, and she is committed to connecting the concrete action of feeding the hungry to the structures that provoke the hunger in the first place.

We have not, of course, seen all the day-to-day hard work behind each of the ministries. We have not struggled side by side with those parishioners who sincerely resist the presence of the Central Americans, whose construction of reality is threatened by these very different neighbors and community members. Nor have we struggled alongside the pastor as he blesses a family's departure from the church because "there's too much politics in this church," or as he buries Ida, the woman who instigated the regular time of prayer for congregational guidance almost ten years ago. Becoming a public church does not preserve the congregation or its members from the struggles inherent in any community's life together. But it does offer the possibility of creating a community that will nourish the spiritual disciplines necessary for the beginning of the new millennium.

Finally, what can we say about spiritual direction in this increasingly complex world? When all is said and done, simple things are still basic to this call:

In the end, God is in charge. The One who gave us the name, "I AM WHO CAUSES TO BE" dwells lovingly with all creation. Perhaps the very complexity we encounter in today's world is a grace that prevents us from quickly second-guessing this God and speaking as if we are the experts on what God desires for us, our directees, or the world.

In the end, our careful, empathic listening, our "connected knowing" is our deepest offering to those we accompany in spiritual direction. This contemplative listening brings us alongside our directees and parishioners in ways that can help them hear themselves and God's address to them. Developmentally helpful interventions, those geared to the developmental complexity of each person, remain one of the ways we may serve our directees, but only if we can resist the temptation to want to remake them in our developmental image and likeness. The temptation, as old as spiritual guidance, dogs us in the developmental realm too.

In the end, honoring God's action wherever we are able to recognize it, in creation, in ourselves, in our directees, and in our communities remains the essence of the spiritual director's task. To the degree that an understanding of human development uncovers the subtlety of God's creative life where before that creativity was hidden and to the degree that an understanding of human development allows us to join that creative activity more completely, to that degree understanding human development fosters our ministry of spiritual direction.

Select Bibliography

Ashley, Benedict. *Spiritual Direction in the Dominican Tradition*. New York: Paulist, 1995.

Au, Wilkie. *By Way of the Heart: Toward a Holistic Christian Spirituality*. New York: Paulist, 1989.

Ball, Peter. *Anglican Spiritual Direction*. Cambridge, MA: Cowley, 1999.

Barry, William and William Connolly. *The Practice of Spiritual Direction*. New York: Seabury, 1982.

Belenky, Mary, Blythe Clinchy, Nancy Goldberger, and Jill Tarule. *Women's Ways of Knowing: The Development of Self, Voice and Mind*. New York: Basic Books, 1986.

Bridges, William. *Transitions: Making Sense of Life's Changes*. Reading, MA: Addison-Wesley, 1980.

Brown, Lyn Mikel and Carol Gilligan. *Meeting at the Crossroads: Women's Psychology and Girls' Development*. New York: Ballantine, 1992.

Buckley, Michael. "Within the Holy Mystery," in *A World of Grace: An Introduction to the Themes and Foundations of Karl Rahner's Theology*. Edited by Leo O'Donovan, 31–49. New York: Seabury, 1980.

Carlsen, Mary Baird. *Meaning-Making: Therapeutic Processes in Adult Development*. New York: W. W. Norton, 1988.

Chamberlain, Gary L. *Fostering Faith: A Minister's Guide to Faith Development*. New York: Paulist, 1988.

Clinchy, Blythe McVicker. "Connected and Separate Knowing: Toward a Marriage of Two Minds," in *Knowledge, Difference and Power: Essays Inspired by Women's Ways of Knowing*. Edited by Nancy Goldberger, Jill Tarule, Blythe Clinchy, and Mary Belenky, 205–47. New York: Basic Books, 1996.

Conn, Joann Wolski. *Spirituality and Personal Maturity*. New York: Paulist, 1989.

Conn, Walter E. *The Desiring Self: Rooting Pastoral Counseling and Spiritual Direction in Self Transcendence*. New York: Paulist, 1998.

Conroy, Maureen. *The Discerning Heart: Discovering a Personal God*. Chicago: Loyola University Press, 1993.

Daloz, Laurent A. *Effective Teaching and Mentoring: Realizing the Transformational Power of Adult Learning Experiences*. San Francicsco: Jossey-Bass, 1986.

Daloz, Laurent, Cheryl Keen, James Keen, and Sharon Parks. *Common Fire: Lives of Commitment in a Complex World*. Boston: Beacon Press, 1996.

Dember, William. "The New Look in Motivation." *American Scientist* 53 (December 1965): 409–27.

Dougherty, Rose Mary. *Group Spiritual Direction: Community for Discernment*. New York: Paulist, 1995

Douglas, Julie M. *Handbook for Spiritual Directors*. New York: Paulist, 1998.

Duffy, Regis. *A Roman Catholic Theology of Pastoral Care*. Philadelphia: Fortress, 1983.

Dykstra, Craig and Sharon Parks. *Faith Development and Fowler*. Birmingham: Religious Education Press, 1986.

Empereur, James. *The Enneagram and Spiritual Direction: Nine Paths to Spiritual Guidance*. New York: Continuum, 1997.

————. *Spiritual Direction and the Gay Person*. New York: Continuum, 1998.

Erikson, Erik. *Childhood and Society*. 2nd. ed. New York: W. W. Norton, 1963.

————. *Insight and Responsibility*. New York: W. W. Norton, 1964.

Evoy, John. *A Psychological Handbook for Spiritual Directors*. Kansas City: Sheed and Ward, 1988.

Fischer, Kathleen. *Reclaiming the Connections: A Contemporary Spirituality*. Kansas City: Sheed and Ward, 1990.

————. *Women at the Well: Femininst Perspectives on Spiritual Direction*. New York: Paulist, 1989.

Fowler, James. *Faithful Change: The Personal and Public Challenges of Postmodern Life*. Nashville: Abingdon, 1996.

————. *Weaving the New Creation: Stages of Faith and the Public Church*. San Francisco: Harper San Francisco, 1991.

————. *Stages of Faith: The Psychology of Human Development and the Quest for Meaning*. San Francisco: Harper and Row, 1981.

Friedman, Edwin. *Generation to Generation: Family Process in Church and Synagogue*. New York: Guilford Press, 1985.

Gilligan, Carol. *In a Different Voice: Psychological Theory and Women's Development*. Cambridge, MA: Harvard University Press, 1982.

Goldberger, Nancy, Jill Tarule, Blythe Clinchy, and Mary Belenky. *Knowledge, Difference and Power: Essays Inspired by Women's Ways of Knowing*. New York: Basic Books, 1996.

Gratton, Carolyn. *The Art of Spiritual Guidance: A Contemporary Approach to Growing in the Spirit*. New York: Crossroad, 1993.

Groeschel, Benedict. *Spiritual Passages: The Psychology of Spiritual Development*. New York: Crossroad, 1984.

Guenther, Margaret. *Holy Listening: The Art of Spiritual Direction*. Cambridge, MA: Cowley, 1992.

Helminiak, Daniel. *Spiritual Development: An Interdisciplinary Study*. Chicago: Loyola University Press, 1987.

Hopewell, James. *Congregation: Stories and Structures*. Philadelphia: Fortress, 1987.

Houdek, Frank. *Guided by the Spirit: A Jesuit Perspective on Spiritual Direction*. Chicago: Loyola University Press, 1996.

Huneke, Douglas. *The Moses of Rovno*. Tiburon, CA: Compassion House, 1985.

Ignatius of Loyola. *The Spiritual Exercises of St. Ignatius*. Translated by Louis J. Puhl, S. J. Chicago: Loyola University Press, 1951.

Ivy, Steven. "The Structural-Developmental Theories of James Fowler and Robert Kegan as Resources for Pastoral Assessment." PhD diss., Southern Baptist Theological Seminary, 1985.

Johnson, Susanne. *Christian Spiritual Formation in the Church and Classroom.* Nashville: Abingdon, 1989.

Kegan, Robert. *In Over Our Heads: The Mental Demands of Modern Life.* Cambridge, MA: Harvard University Press, 1994.

_____. *The Evolving Self: Problem and Process in Human Development.* Cambridge, MA: Harvard University Press, 1982.

Kelsey, Morton. *Companions on the Inner Way: The Art of Spiritual Guidance.* New York: Crossroad, 1987.

Kohlberg, Lawrence. *The Psychology of Moral Development.* San Francisco: Harper and Row, 1984.

Leech, Kenneth. *Spirituality and Pastoral Care.* Cambridge, MA: Cowley, 1989.

Levinson, Daniel. *The Seasons of a Woman's Life.* New York: Knopf, 1996.

Liebert, Elizabeth. "The Thinking Heart: Developmental Dynamics in Etty Hillesum's Diaries." *Pastoral Psychology* 43 (July 1995): 393–409.

_____. "Seasons and Stages: Models and Metaphors of Human Development," in *In Her Own Time: Women and Development Issues in Pastoral Care.* Edited by Jeanne Stevenson Moessner. Minneapolis: Augsburg Fortress, forthcoming.

Loder, James. *The Logic of the Spirit: Human Development in Theological Perspective.* San Francisco: Jossey-Bass, 1996.

Loevinger, Jane. *Ego Development: Conceptions and Theories.* San Francisco: Jossey-Bass, 1976.

_____. "On the Self and Predicting Behavior," in *Personality and the Prediction of Behavior.* Edited by R. Zucker, R. Aronoff, and A. Rabin, 43–68. New York: Academic Press, 1984.

_____. "Theories of Ego Development," in *Clinical-Cognitive Psychology: Models and Integrations.* Edited by L. Breger, 83–135. Englewood Cliffs, NJ: Prentice-Hall, 1969.

Loevinger, Jane and Elizabeth Knoll. "Personality: Stages, Traits and the Self," *Annual Review of Psychology* 34 (1983): 195–222.

Loevinger, Jane and Ruth Wessler, *Measuring Ego Development 1: Construction and Use of a Sentence Completion Test.* San Francisco: Jossey-Bass, 1970.

Loevinger, Jane, Ruth Wessler and Carolyn Redmore. *Measuring Ego Development 2: Scoring Manual for Women and Girls.* San Francisco: Jossey-Bass, 1970.

Marstin, Ronald. *Beyond Our Tribal Gods: The Maturing of Faith.* Maryknoll, NY: Orbis, 1979.

Miller, Jean Baker. "The Development of Women's Sense of Self," *Work In Progress,* No. 12. Wellesley, MA: Stone Center for Developmental Services and Studies, 1984.

Miller, Wendy. *Learning to Listen: A Guide for Spiritual Friends.* Nashville: Upper Room, 1993.

Morgan, Elizabeth, et al. *Global Poverty and Personal Responsibility: Integrity through Commitment.* New York: Paulist, 1989.

Morneau, Robert F. *Spiritual Direction: Principles and Practice*. New York: Crossroad, 1992.

Ochs, Carol and Kerry M. Olitzsky. *Jewish Spiritual Guidance*. San Francisco: Jossey-Bass, 1997.

Parks, Sharon. *The Critical Years: The Young Adult Search for a Faith to Live By*. San Francisco: Harper and Row, 1986.

Perry, William. *Forms of Intellectual and Ethical Development in the College Years: A Scheme*. New York: Holt Rinehart & Winston, 1970.

Redmore, Carolyn, Jane Loevinger, R. Tamashiro, et al. *Measuring Ego Development: Scoring Manual for Men and Boys*. St. Louis: Washington University, 1978–1981.

Ricoeur, Paul. *Symbolism of Evil*. Boston: Beacon Press, 1978.

Saiving, Valerie. "The Human Situation: A Feminine View," in *Womanspirit Rising*. Edited by Carol Christ and Judith Plaskow, 25–42. San Francisco: Harper and Row, 1979.

Selman, Robert. *The Growth of Interpersonal Understanding: Developmental and Clinical Analysis*. New York: Academic Press, 1980.

Sheehan, Barbara. *Partners in Covenant: The Art of Spiritual Companionship*. Cleveland: Pilgrim Press, 1999.

Stanger, Frank Bateman. *Spiritual Formation in the Local Church*. Grand Rapids, MI: Francis Asbury, 1989.

Studzinski, Raymond. *Spiritual Direction and Midlife Development*. Chicago: Loyola University Press, 1985.

Surrey, Janet L. "Self-in-Relation: A Theory of Women's Development," *Work In Progress*, No. 13. Wellesley, MA: Stone Center for Developmental Services and Studies, 1985.

Watzlawick, Paul, John Weakland and Richard Fisch. *Change: Principles of Problem Formation and Problem Resolution*. New York: W. W. Norton, 1974.

Wilcox, Mary. *Developmental Journey: A Guide to the Development of Logical and Moral Reasoning and Social Perspective*. Nashville: Abingdon, 1979.

Wink, Walter. *Unmasking the Powers: The Invisible Forces That Determine Human Existence*. Philadelphia: Fortress, 1986.

Notes

Introduction

¹ For a survey of recent English-language materials on the *Spiritual Exercises* of Ignatius of Loyola see Paul Begheyn, S.J. and Kenneth Bogart, S.J., "A Bibliography on St. Ignatius' *Spiritual Exercises*," *Studies in the Spirituality of Jesuits* 23 (May 1991):1–68.

² All scripture citations follow the New Revised Standard Version.

Chapter I

¹ The first person whom I recall interpreting "direction" in this way is Sandra Schneiders, in "The Contemporary Ministry of Spiritual Direction," *Chicago Studies* 15 (Spring 1976):123.

² According to Edmund Hill, *ruach*, translated "spirit," means "vigorous life," transcending the humdrum limitations of the ordinary person's daily existence. *Being Human: A Biblical Perspective* (London: Geoffrey Chapman, 1984), p. 101.

³ As Hill, *Being Human*, p. 102, puts it: " 'Spirit' and 'spiritual' signify a divine quality of life, received as a gift from God . . . a share in his Spirit, which goes with a full active share in the body of Christ, with 'Christ living in me.' "

⁴ See Kathleen Fischer, *Reclaiming the Connections: A Contemporary Spirituality* (Kansas City: Sheed and Ward, 1990), especially Chapter 3, on God's will. Using biblical categories and process thought, Fischer seeks to reconcile this and other dualisms which have plagued spirituality in recent centuries.

⁵ *Spirituality and Pastoral Care* (Cambridge: Cowley, 1989), p. 64.

⁶ Fischer, *Reclaiming the Connections*, p. 13.

⁷ Dietrich Bonhoeffer, *Letters and Papers From Prison* (New York: Macmillan, 1972), pp. 360–61 and Abraham Heschel, *The Prophets* (New York: Harper and Row, 1962).

⁸ Fischer, *Reclaiming the Connections*, pp. 60–69.

⁹ *Christian Spiritual Formation in the Church and Classroom* (Nashville: Abingdon, 1989), p. 22.

¹⁰ The phrase originally rendered "Kingdom of God" is now also called "Reign of God," "Realm of God," "Commonwealth of Love," "Jesus' *basileia* vision" (E. Schüssler Fiorenza), all attempts to include women and other marginalized persons as full partners in this vision.

¹¹ Fischer, *Reclaiming the Connections*, p. 32.

[12] Joann Wolski Conn, *Spirituality and Personal Maturity* (New York: Paulist, 1989), p. 16.

[13] See, for example, Wilkie Au, *By Way of the Heart: Toward a Holistic Christian Spirituality* (New York: Paulist, 1989), pp. 4–6, 18–20; J. Conn, *Spirituality and Personal Maturity*, p. 3; S. Johnson, *Christian Spiritual Formation*, p. 112–16; and Frank Bateman Stanger, *Spiritual Formation in the Local Church* (Grand Rapids, MI: Francis Asbury, 1989), p. 17.

[14] One of the earliest proponents of this position was Valerie Saiving, "The Human Situation: A Feminine View," reprinted in *Womanspirit Rising*, ed. Carol Christ and Judith Plaskow (San Francisco: Harper and Row, 1979), pp. 25–42. Others who expanded her initial insight include Judith Plaskow, *Sex, Sin and Grace: Women's Experience in the Theologies of Reinhold Niebuhr and Paul Tillich* (Washington, D.C.: University Press of America, 1980) and Joann Wolski Conn, "Women's Spirituality: Restriction and Reconstruction," in *Women's Spirituality: Resources for Christian Development*, ed. Joann Wolski Conn (New York: Paulist, 1986), pp. 9–30.

[15] *In a Different Voice: Psychological Theory and Women's Development* (Cambridge: Harvard University Press, 1982).

[16] Clifford Swensen, "Ego Development and a General Model for Counseling and Psychotherapy," *The Personnel and Guidance Journal* 58 (January 1980):383.

[17] Craig Dykstra, "Faith Development and Religious Education," in *Faith Development and Fowler*, ed. Craig Dykstra and Sharon Parks (Birmingham, AL: Religious Education Press, 1986), pp. 257–8.

Chapter II

[1] 2nd ed., (New York: W. W. Norton, 1963), pp. 11 and 17.

[2] Some of the more prominent of these developmentalists include Harry Stack Sullivan, Daniel Levinson, Roger Gould, Gail Sheehey, Barbara Newman, Philip Newman, Robert Havighurst and Judith Viorst.

[3] See Benedict Groeschel, *Spiritual Passages: The Psychology of Spiritual Development* (New York: Crossroad, 1984); Raymond Studzinski, *Spiritual Direction and Midlife Development* (Chicago: Loyola University Press, 1985) and Morton T. Kelsey, *Companions on the Inner Way: The Art of Spiritual Guidance* (New York: Crossroad, 1987).

[4] Antoine de Saint Exupéry, *The Little Prince*, tr. by Katherine Woods (New York: Harcourt, Brace and World, 1943), pp. 10–19.

[5] "Social and Developmental Psychology: Trends Influencing the Future of Counseling," *The Personnel and Guidance Journal* 58 (January 1980):332.

[6] "Making the world better for other women's daughters and sons" is a phrase employed by Rosemary Curran Barciauskas and Debra Beery Hull in *Loving and Working: Reweaving Women's Public and Private Lives* (Bloomington: Meyer-Stone, 1989), Chapter 2.

[7] Robert Selman, *The Growth of Interpersonal Understanding: Developmental and Clinical Analysis* (New York: Academic Press, 1980) illustrates the process of self-conscious reflection on these three principles during the course of theory building and validation.

[8] Loevinger's major works include two coauthored volumes containing the Sentence Completion Test and its scoring manual: Jane Loevinger and Ruth Wessler, *Measuring Ego Development 1: Construction and Use of a Sentence Completion Test* and Jane Loevinger, Ruth Wessler and Carolyn Redmore, *Measuring Ego Development 2: Scoring Manual for Women and Girls* (both volumes San Francisco: Jossey-Bass, 1970), and a third theoretical volume, *Ego Development: Conceptions and Theories* (San Francisco: Jossey-Bass, 1976). Kegan's major work is *The Evolving Self: Problem and Process in Human Development* (Cambridge: Harvard University Press, 1982).

[9] This paper and pencil projective test consists of thirty-six sentence stems which can be completed in about thirty minutes. The self-teaching scoring manual is carefully designed so that even persons previously unacquainted with psychological testing can successfully administer and score the test with a high degree of inter-rater reliability and reproducibility. If spiritual directors so desired, they could accurately administer the Sentence Completion Test.

[10] Lawrence Kohlberg and Cheryl Armon, "Three Types of Stage Models Used in the Study of Adult Development" in *Beyond Formal Operations: Late Adolescent and Adult Cognitive Development* (New York: Praeger, 1984), pp. 383–94, distinguishes a "hard structural model," with all Piaget's formal stage properties, from a "soft structural model," which includes affective or reflective characteristics outside of a strict interpretation of the Piagetian

paradigm. Kohlberg's theory of moral development exemplifies "hard structuralism"; it attempts to define stages in terms of discrete operations of *reasoning*, and to explicate not only the inner logic of the stages but also the inner logic of the sequence from one stage to the next. Loevinger's theory of ego development exemplifies "soft structuralism." It explicates self-reflective meta-thinking; it does not lead, in itself, to a normative model; it assumes that developing to the higher stages is optional, not prescribed; and it does not claim that higher stages are more adequate.

Since spiritual direction is concerned with far more than how persons think/speak about issues, but with how whole persons respond to God, the flexibility of "soft structuralism" is more useful for spiritual guidance than the narrower focus of "hard structuralism." However, Loevinger's reticence about the inner logic of development creates a more difficult issue because it hampers our efforts to assess the direction to which behavior tends, as well as our ability to structure developmentally informed responses. Robert Kegan supplies these contributions.

[11] Daniel Helminiak treats the relationship of holiness to spiritual development in a philosophical analysis based on Bernard Lonergan's transcendental precepts. He concludes that holiness is human authenticity before God, and as an intensive quality, it does not follow a stage progression. Holiness will be manifested differently at the various stages: "The intensity of a person's authenticity at any stage is the gauge of holiness, and not the stage itself." See *Spiritual Development: An Interdisciplinary Study* (Chicago: Loyola University Press, 1987), pp. 143–56, quotation from p. 152.

[12] But, one might ask, can a scoring manual developed in the late 1960's still reflect accurately women's impulse control, interpersonal relationships, conscious preoccupations and cognitive style? Or, has the position of women in this society changed enough to date the scoring manual and even to vitiate the theory itself? Loevinger has replied that the *content* of the responses does not, by itself, determine ego level. The underlying *structure* does. It may certainly be the case that cultural changes encourage or discourage ego development among a large group of people, in this case, women. But this phenomenon does not affect the power of the theory itself, nor vitiate the scoring manual if it has been properly employed. See Elizabeth J. Nettles and Jane Loevinger, "Sex Role Expectations and Ego Level in Relation to Problem Marriages," *Journal of Personality and Social Psychology* 45 (September 1983):684.

[13] Loevinger does admit a possible bias in the opposite direction; interestingly, college-age women do score about a half level higher on Loevinger's test than do college-age men, while the reverse trend seems to be true for women and men taking Kohlberg's test. See Barbara Mary Gfellner, "Moral Development, Ego Development and Sex Differences in Adolescence" (Ph.D. dissertation, University of Manitoba, Canada, 1981). Loevinger and her colleagues recognize that men will respond in a skewed manner to incomplete sentence stems designed to appeal to women. Consequently, they designed separate forms for men and boys and prepared and validated a separate scoring manual for these forms: see C. Redmore, J. Loevinger, R. Tamashiro, et al. *Measuring Ego Development: Scoring Manual for Men and Boys* (St. Louis: Washington University, 1978-1981).

[14] Sometimes Loevinger or others explicitly acknowledge (or argue with) the correlations posited. For example, see Jane Loevinger, "On the Self and Predicting Behavior" in *Personality and the Prediction of Behavior,* ed. R. Zucker, R. Aronoff, and A. Rabin (New York: Academic Press, 1984), pp. 43-68; Jane Loevinger and Elizabeth Knoll, "Personality: Stages, Traits, and the Self," in *Annual Review of Psychology* 34 (1983):195-222; and Lawrence Kohlberg, *The Psychology of Moral Development* (San Francisco: Harper and Row, 1984). Frequently, however, such correlations are summarized by means of comparative charts. Examples include: Loevinger, *Ego Development,* especially Chapter 5; Robert Kegan, *The Evolving Self,* tables 6, 8-10; and Helminiak, *Spiritual Development,* pp. 72-73. Some of the proposed correlations have generated empirical research, as in the work of Barbara Gfellner, "Changes in Ego and Moral Development in Adolescents: A Longitudinal Study," *Journal of Adolescence* 9 (1986):281-302.

[15] Besides contributing to images of change, Robert Kegan also underscores the developmental significance of both affectivity and relationship, qualities with which spiritual guidance is intimately concerned. William Perry's pioneering and sensitive study of Harvard undergraduates, *Forms of Intellectual and Ethical Development in the College Years: A Scheme* (New York: Holt, Rinehart and Winston, 1970), brings home the struggle to move from dualistic thinking to relativity, to principled positions within relativity, a particularly crucial transition in moral thinking. In *The Growth of Interpersonal Understanding,* Robert Selman researches the development of interpersonal perspective taking. James Fowler brings together the work of Piaget, Selman and Kohlberg with his own

original contributions to a theory of faith development in *Stages of Faith: The Psychology of Human Development and the Quest for Meaning* (San Francisco: Harper and Row, 1981). Carol Gilligan, *In a Different Voice: Psychological Theory and Women's Development* (Cambridge: Harvard University Press, 1982), examines women's moral development as a unique and creative addition to our understanding of moral development of both women and men. Sharon Parks builds upon James Fowler's theory of faith development, concentrating particularly on young adults in *The Critical Years: The Young Adult Search for a Faith to Live By* (San Francisco: Harper and Row, 1986). Mary Baird Carlsen's *Meaning-Making: Therapeutic Processes in Adult Development* (New York: W. W. Norton, 1988) returns to Robert Kegan's work and moves it forward to a theory of therapy, contributing to our understanding of the potential and process of developmental change. Mary Belenky, Blythe Clinchy, Nancy Goldberger and Jill Tarule's coauthored study, *Women's Ways of Knowing: The Development of Self, Voice, and Mind* (New York: Basic Books, 1986), while not claiming to be a structural theory, elaborates with women, both inside and outside formal educational institutions, what William Perry illustrated with male collegians. Two contributions to pastoral practice come from works based on structural developmental theories: Steven Ivy develops resources for pastoral assessment based on Fowler and Kegan in *The Structural-Developmental Theories of James Fowler and Robert Kegan as Resources for Pastoral Assessment* (Ph.D. dissertation, Southern Baptist Theological Seminary, 1985). Gary L. Chamberlain illustrates how Fowler's faith development theory can enhance a variety of ministries within the parish context in *Fostering Faith: A Minister's Guide to Faith Development* (New York: Paulist, 1988).

[16] William Perry, *The Forms of Intellectual and Ethical Development*, provides poignant illustrations of the failure of dualistic thinking, its gradual replacement with relativistic thinking, and still later with what could be called "contextual" thinking.

[17] Since Jane Loevinger's Sentence Completion Test lends itself to comparative developmental research, including large-scale studies which are prohibitively time-consuming for research methods based on in-depth interviews, the conclusions which follow are based primarily on Loevinger's theory. See especially Robert Holt, "Loevinger's Measure of Ego Development: Reliability and National Norms for Male and Female Short Forms," *Journal of Personality and Social Psychology* 39 (November 1980):909–20.

[18] Loevinger, *Ego Development*, p. 19.

[19] See Craig Dykstra, "Faith Development and Religious Education," in *Faith Development and Fowler* ed. Craig Dykstra and Sharon Parks (Birmingham, AL: Religious Education Press, 1986), pp. 251–71, for a description of how this dynamic has, in fact, occurred in religious education. Gary Chamberlain also addresses the appropriate uses of Fowler's faith development theory in pastoral situations in *Fostering Faith*, pp. 183–84.

[20] Janet L. Surrey ("Self-in-Relation: A Theory of Women's Development," *Work in Progress* No. 13 [Wellesley, MA: Stone Center for Developmental Services and Studies, 1985], p. 3) provides a description of accurate empathy:

> Accurate empathy involves balancing of affective arousal and cognitive structuring. It requires an ability to build on the experience of identification with the other person to form a cognitive assimilation of this experience as a basis for response. Such capacities imply highly developed emotional and cognitive operations requiring practice, modeling, and feedback in relationships.

Accurate empathy clearly requires a relatively strong developmental base. It therefore raises the question of the developmental prerequisite necessary for becoming an effective spiritual director, since all potential spiritual directors will not be developmentally able to respond with accurate empathy.

Chapter III

[1] See William Barry and William Connolly, *The Practice of Spiritual Direction* (New York: Seabury, 1982), pp. 65–79 for a more extended discussion on "noticing key interior facts." These authors do not, however, discuss the possibility that the inability to notice and express interior movements may be an indicator of or influenced by developmental level.

[2] I am indebted for the nucleus of these cases to Vie Thorgren. I have altered the details for their inclusion here.

Chapter IV

[1] Paul Watzlawick, John Weakland, and Richard Fisch, *Change: Principles of Problem Formation and Problem Resolution* (New York: W. W. Norton, 1974), pp. 82–83. See also p. 110 for their four-step therapeutic procedure.

[2] Jane Loevinger, "Theories of Ego Development," in *Clinical-Cognitive Psychology: Models and Integrations*, ed. L. Breger (Englewood Cliffs, N.J.: Prentice-Hall, 1969), p. 85.

[3] This phrase is Robert Kegan's colorful description of equilibration.

[4] Loevinger, *Ego Development*, p. 199.

[5] Selman, *The Growth of Interpersonal Understanding*, pp. 175–82.

[6] *The Evolving Self*, p. 256.

[7] *The Evolving Self*, pp. 119–20, 184–254.

[8] Carlsen, *Meaning-Making*, p. 71.

[9] William Dember, "The New Look in Motivation," *American Scientist* 53 (December 1965):409–27.

[10] Loevinger, *Ego Development*, p. 309.

[11] *Stages of Faith*, p. 299.

[12] James Fowler's extended case study of "Mary" illustrates the power of culture and interpersonal relationships to foster arrest. *Stages of Faith*, pp. 217–91.

[13] See Laurent A. Daloz, *Effective Teaching and Mentoring: Realizing the Transformational Power of Adult Learning Experiences* (San Francisco: Jossey-Bass, 1986), for a cogent description of mentoring and its role in promoting developmental transition. I was particularly struck by the similarity between his description of the mentor's role and my understanding of the spiritual director's role:

> *Mentors are guides.* They lead us along the journey of our lives. We trust them because they have been there before. They embody our hopes, cast light on the way ahead, interpret arcane signs, warn us of lurking dangers, and point out unexpected delights along the way (p. 17).

[14] Jean Baker Miller, "The Development of Women's Sense of Self," *Work in Progress*, No. 12. (Wellesley, MA: Stone Center for Developmental Services and Studies, 1984), pp. 6–7.

[15] *Ego Development*, pp. 409–10.

[16] Michael Buckley, "Within the Holy Mystery," in *A World of Grace: An Introduction to the Themes and Foundations of Karl Rahner's Theology*, ed. Leo O'Donovan (New York: Seabury, 1980), pp. 31–49.

[17] Selman, *The Growth of Interpersonal Understanding*, p. 311.

[18] Steven Ivy, *The Structural-Developmental Theories of James Fowler and Robert Kegan as Resources for Pastoral Assessment*, (Ph.D. dissertation, Southern Baptist Theological Seminary, 1985), pp. 144–49.

Chapter V

[1] William Bridges, *Transitions: Making Sense of Life's Changes* (Reading, MA: Addison-Wesley, 1980) describes in depth the experience of transition.

[2] As Selman says in *Growth of Interpersonal Understanding*, p. 310:

> It also is misleading to state "This child *first thinks* at Stage x and *then acts* according to this stage about this event." It may be more reasonable to state, "This child has *acted* in certain consistent (or inconsistent) ways across a number of observed social interactions; from these we can infer that he or she is *capable* of structuring his or her social interactions in ways best characterized by Stage x."

[3] Loevinger, *Ego Development*, p. 15.

[4] Kegan, *The Evolving Self*, pp. 113–14.

[5] Kegan, *The Evolving Self*, p. 31.

[6] Janet Surrey, "Self-in-Relation," critiques differentiation as a norm for human development unless it is understood that self makes sense only within the relationships which frame and constitute it. Therefore, differentiation appropriately refers to the "process which encompasses increasing levels of complexity, choice, fluidity and articulation within the context of human relationship" (p. 8). Precisely because "differentiation" is so seldom understood within a relational context, I generally avoid it in favor of the phrase "increasing complexity."

[7] Kegan, *The Evolving Self*, pp. 81–82.

[8] Kegan, *The Evolving Self*, p. 45.

[9] These stage descriptions appear in the following sources: Loevinger, *Ego Development*, p. 16; Jane Loevinger, "The Relation of Adjustment to Ego Development," in *The Definition and Measurement of Mental Health*, ed. Saul B. Sells (Washington, D.C.: U.S. Department of Health, Education and Welfare, Public Health Service, 1968), p. 166; Pauline Young-Eisendrath, "Ego Development: Inferring the Client's Frame of Reference," *Social Casework: The Journal of Contemporary Social Work* 63 (June 1982):328;

Clifford Swensen, "Ego Development and a General Model for Counseling and Psychotherapy," *The Personnel and Guidance Journal* 58 (January 1980):384; Robert Selman, *The Growth of Interpersonal Understanding: Developmental and Clinical Analyses* (New York: Academic Press, 1980), pp. 132 and 147; Fowler, *Stages of Faith*, pp. 133–34; Gilligan, *In a Different Voice*, p. 74.

[10] Whether this next developmental construction is a full-blown stage or merely a transitional level is a matter of discussion among developmentalists, but this theoretical issue need not detain us here. For our purposes, I shall treat this construction as a stage, but adopt the name which Loevinger gives to her transitional level because of its descriptive value.

[11] Remember that this behavior is part of the typical developmental progression and therefore, "normal" in children up to a certain age. When used in reference to children, such terms as "exploitative" and "manipulative" are not moral judgments, but simply descriptive of children's present level of relationship compared to adults.

[12] Treatments of this stage appear in Loevinger, *Ego Development*, pp. 16–17; "The Relation of Adjustment," pp. 166–67; Loevinger and Wessler, *Measuring Ego Development 1*, pp. 4, 59; Young-Eisendrath, "Ego Development," p. 328; Swensen, "Ego Development," p. 384; Kegan, *The Evolving Self*, p. 88; Selman, *The Growth of Interpersonal Understanding*, pp. 138–40, 144–45; Fowler, *Stages of Faith*, pp. 135–50; and Perry, *Intellectual and Ethical Development*, pp. 60–71.

[13] This could occur in situations where spiritual direction is required, such as in the formation programs of religious congregations, dioceses, or other church judicatories. John Evoy recalls an instance where a woman who did not seem to be making much progress in spiritual direction finally remarked that it wasn't really her idea. Going for spiritual direction had become the "in thing" in her group of friends. She wanted to be able to say, when asked who her spiritual director was, that it was none of their business! See *A Psychological Handbook for Spiritual Directors* (Kansas City: Sheed and Ward, 1988), p. xi.

[14] Treatments of this stage appear in the following: Loevinger, *Ego Development*, pp. 17–19; "The Relation of Adjustment," p. 167; Loevinger and Wessler, *Measuring Ego Development 1*, pp. 4–5; Young-Eisendrath, "Ego Development," pp. 328–29; Swensen, "Ego Development," p. 384; Selman, *The Growth of Interper-*

sonal Understanding, pp. 134, 140, 145, 146; Kegan, *The Evolving Self,* pp. 184–220; and Fowler, *Stages of Faith,* pp. 151–73.

[15] See Arthur W. Chickering, "Developmental Change as a Major Outcome," in *Experiential Learning,* ed. Morris T. Keeton (San Francisco: Jossey-Bass, 1976), p. 73 for a correlation between Loevinger's dimension of cognitive style, Piaget's theory of intellectual development and Perry's transformations of epistemological styles.

[16] A caution is in order here. Before one interprets this phenomenon developmentally as characteristic of the Conformist stage, one ought also to observe aspects of that stage (or any other stage, for that matter) across the other dimensions. Ego level as a concept involves the interpenetration of all dimensions. Flat affect may also occur for reasons as diverse as cultural or familial rewards for controlling emotions, organic and chemical side-effects, or affective disorders.

[17] Reba E. Roebuck, "The Relationship between Level of Ego Development and Dogmatism in Women" (Ph.D. dissertation, Boston College, 1981), concluded that almost all Self-Protective and Conformist persons will be highly dogmatic, but that the converse does not hold. That is, a subject must be high in dogmatism to test at Self-Protective or Conformist, but that closed-mindedness, as she measured it, works against, but does not preclude, the attainment of higher ego levels.

[18] See Richard L. Gorsuch and Daniel Aleshire, "Christian Faith and Ethnic Prejudice: A Review and Interpretation of Research," *Journal for the Scientific Study of Religion* 13 (June 1974):281–307. The authors note that people who are extrinsic in their orientation and accept stereotyped Christian beliefs are the most prejudiced subgroups (p. 284). These findings imply that to the extent that a particular style of denominational leadership, doctrinal interpretation, and closed society encourages Conformity as the average expected level of development among large numbers of its members, prejudicial, negative or rigid attitudes toward groups perceived as different, bad or wrong may also periodically surface.

[19] Loevinger, "Measuring Personality Patterns of Women," *Genetic Psychology Monographs* 65 (1962), p. 113. Loevinger attributes to Adorno the suggestion about extending one's view of family to God.

[20] *Stages of Faith,* p. 275, italics his. Despite Fowler's assertion

of the value of each stage, he leaves open the possibility that stages may have outlived their usefulness. The pastor or spiritual director may have a privileged opportunity to ally with an emergent self, just as a therapist may have the same opportunity in another context.

[21] In Ignatius of Loyola's usage, "desolation" includes "darkness of soul, turmoil of spirit, inclination to what is low and earthly, restlessness rising from many disturbances and temptations which lead to want of faith, want of hope, want of love." *The Spiritual Exercises of St. Ignatius*, 317, trans. Louis J. Puhl, S.J. (Chicago: Loyola University Press, 1951), p. 142.

Chapter VI

[1] Depending on the source, Loevinger also names the Self-Aware level "Conscientious-Conformist," highlighting its position as a transition between the Conformist and Conscientious stages. The "Self-Aware" nomenclature, used throughout this book, highlights the central developmental gain rather than the order of progression. As with the Self-Protective level/stage, the discussion about whether this position is a stage or a transition need not concern us; we will briefly summarize its gains and focus more deeply on the Conscientious stage.

[2] Sources for this stage description include Loevinger, *Ego Development*, pp. 19–20; Young-Eisendrath, "Ego Development," p. 329; and Swensen, "Ego Development," p. 384.

[3] Parks, *The Critical Years*, pp. 73–106.

[4] Belenky, et al., *Women's Ways of Knowing*, pp. 52–86.

[5] Belenky, et al., *Women's Ways of Knowing*, pp. 55 and 84.

[6] *Forms of Intellectual and Ethical Development*, p. 88.

[7] Perry, *Forms of Intellectual and Ethical Development*, p. 200. Parks, *The Critical Years*, pp. 133–205, discusses at some length the notion of mentoring which is so helpful to a person at this position on the developmental continuum. Much of what she says can apply to pastors and spiritual directors as well.

[8] To be reflexive is to be conscious of the self as a constructor of identity and of meaning categories. See Riv-Ellen Prell, "The Double Frame of Life History in the Work of Barbara Myerhoff, in *Interpreting Women's Lives: Feminist Theory and Personal Narratives*, ed. Personal Narratives Group (Bloomington: Indiana University Press, 1989), pp. 250–54.

[9] Treatments of this stage occur in Loevinger, *Ego Development*, pp. 20–22; Loevinger and Wessler, *Measuring Ego Develop-*

ment 1, pp. 5–6; Young-Eisendrath, "Ego Development," pp. 329–30; Selman, *The Growth of Interpersonal Understanding*, pp. 135, 141, 146–47; and Kegan, *The Evolving Self*, pp. 221–54.

[10] Erika Wick, "Lost in No-Man's-Land Between Psyche and Soul," in *Psychotherapy and the Religiously Committed Patient*, ed. E. Mark Stern (New York: Haworth Press, 1985), pp. 13–24, calls this phenomenon "transnomia." It can occur as part of a normal developmental transition between stages of moral development, brought on by shifts in psychosocial reference systems. Spiritual direction may be at least as appropriate a context as therapy for dealing with such value-disorientation.

[11] *Forms of Intellectual and Ethical Development*, especially pp. 109–52. Loevinger's own correlation of her theory with that of Perry places relativism squarely in the Conscientious framing of reality. See *Ego Development*, p. 109.

[12] *Forms of Intellectual and Ethical Development*, pp. 182–89.

[13] *Forms of Intellectual and Ethical Development*, p. 131. Italics Perry's.

[14] *Forms of Intellectual and Ethical Development*, p. 191.

[15] Dan P. McAdams, Laura Booth and Richard Selvik, "Religious Identity Among Students at a Private College: Social Motives, Ego Stage and Development," *Merrill-Palmer Quarterly* 27 (July 1981):230–31. This study indicates that subjects scoring at Conscientious and above on the Sentence Completion Test tended to report identity crises in which a concerted questioning of fundamental religious beliefs had taken place, whereas subjects at Self-Aware or lower reported little questioning or no crisis.

[16] Laurent Daloz, *Effective Teaching and Mentoring*, pp. 97–106, describes the poignancy of a stalemated relationship between Betty, a returning student in her early forties and Ken, her academic advisor and teacher; such stalemated relationships can happen in spiritual direction as well.

[17] The use of the term in this context is James Fowler's, *Stages of Faith*, p. 180.

[18] This level of development opens up a new degree of critical analysis, but it is not necessarily a turn to "thinking" as the mode of that analysis. The processes of evaluation and critique may occur through the presence or absence of an intuitive "fit" with one's newly clarified and clarifying sense of "right-for-me."

[19] Gilligan, *In a Different Voice*, describes the particular difficulty that caring for others at the expense of caring for oneself can be for women. Sharon Parks, *The Critical Years*, pp. 57–58, places

the resolution of this dilemma earlier than I do, at her equivalent to the Conscientious Stage. My experience suggests, however, that women who have been strongly socialized toward the "virtues" of humility and selflessness, also have imbibed a particularly strong bias against care for self that makes it seem selfish. Perhaps women who have not internalized such a deep proscription against selfishness, can, in fact, resolve this dilemma earlier. Or, perhaps the discrepancy between Parks and me on this point is more one of initial versus habitual resolution of this dilemma. I favor the thesis that there are several styles of resolving this dilemma, the most complete occurring at the Interindividual stage or the transition into it. See Loevinger, *Ego Development*, p. 23.

[20] *The Spiritual Exercises of St. Ignatius*, #333, trans. Puhl, p. 148.

Chapter VII

[1] Loevinger, *Ego Development*, pp. 22–23; Young-Eisendrath, "Ego Development," p. 330.

[2] Martin H. Rock, "Self-Reflection and Ego Development" (Ph.D. dissertation, New York University, 1975).

[3] Nancy J. Richardson, "Developmental Shifts in Constructions of Success: The Relationships among Ego Stages, Social Motives, and Women's Life Patterns." (Ph.D. dissertation, Harvard University, 1981).

[4] *Spirituality and Personal Maturity*, p. 56.

[5] Loevinger, *Ego Development*, pp. 23–26; "The Relation of Adjustment," pp. 167–68; Loevinger and Wessler, *Measuring Ego Development 1*, p. 6; Young-Eisendrath, "Ego Development," p. 330; and Fowler, *Stages of Faith*, pp. 184–97.

[6] Parks, *The Critical Years*, p. 60.

[7] Wolfgang Edelstein and Gil Noam, "Regulatory Structures of the Self and 'Postformal' Stages in Adulthood," *Human Development* 25 (November–December 1982):414.

[8] *Stages of Faith*, p. 185.

[9] *The Spiritual Exercises of St. Ignatius*, 15, trans. Puhl, p. 6:

The director of the Exercises ought not to urge the exercitant more to poverty or any promise than to the contrary, nor to one state of life or way of living more than another. . . . Therefore, the director of the Exercises, as a balance at equilibrium, without leaning to one side or the other, should permit the Creator to deal directly with the creature, and the creature directly with his Creator and Lord.

¹⁰ Paul Ricoeur, *Symbolism of Evil* (Boston: Beacon Press, 1978), pp. 36–58. It was Fowler's reference to "second naivete" in *Stages of Faith*, p. 187, which alerted me to reflect on this dynamic of reclaiming and simultaneously being claimed by that which grants ultimate meaning.

¹¹ *In a Different Voice*, p. 74.

¹² Gilligan, *In a Different Voice*, p. 63.

¹³ Loevinger, *Ego Development*, p. 26; "The Relation of Adjustment," p. 168; Young-Eisendrath, "Ego Development," p. 330.

¹⁴ Fowler, *Stages of Faith*, pp. 199–211.

¹⁵ Helminiak, *Spiritual Development*, pp. 87–89.

¹⁶ See Bridges, *Transitions*, especially Ch. 4.

¹⁷ Joann Wolski Conn and Walter Conn, "Developmental Psychology: From Moral Theology to Spirituality," in *Proceedings of the Fortieth Annual Convention*, ed. George Gilcourse (San Francisco: The Catholic Theological Society of America, 1985), p. 171, note that Kegan's theory is especially useful regarding the tension between autonomy and self-emptying because it traces successive poles of emphasis which find their ultimate reconciliation at the Interindividual stage.

¹⁸ *The Spiritual Exercises*, 335, trans. Puhl, p. 149:

In souls that are progressing to greater perfection, the action of the good angel is delicate, gentle, delightful. It may be compared to a drop of water penetrating a sponge.

The action of the evil spirit upon such souls is violent, noisy, and disturbing. It may be compared to a drop of water falling upon a stone.

¹⁹ An emotional triangle can be formed of any three persons or issues. See Edwin Friedman, *Generation to Generation: Family Process in Church and Synagogue* (New York: Guilford Press, 1985), pp. 35–36:

The basic law of emotional triangles is that when any two parts of a system become uncomfortable with one another, they will 'triangle in' or focus upon a third person, or issue, as a way of stabilizing their own relationship with one another. A person may be said to be 'triangled' if he or she

gets caught in the middle as the focus of such an unresolved issue. Conversely, when individuals try to change
the relationship of two others (two people or a person and
his or her symptom or belief), they 'triangle' themselves
into that relationship (and often stabilize the very situation they are trying to change).

Chapter VIII

[1] The Stephen Ministry is a group of lay persons trained and
supervised to offer ministries of pastoral presence, accompaniment
and care to other members of the congregation.

[2] James Hopewell, *Congregation: Stories and Structures*, (Philadelphia: Fortress, 1987), pp. 12–13, defines a congregation as "a
group that possesses a special name and recognized members who
assemble regularly to celebrate a more universally practiced worship but who communicate with each other sufficiently to develop
intrinsic patterns of conduct, outlook, and story." Following
Hopewell, I shall also use "congregation," "local church" and
"parish" synonymously, but unlike him, I intend that congregations serve as exemplars of other concrete forms of Christian community. Hopewell's symbolic style of congregational analysis and
his comments on narrative are useful for our purposes.

[3] In recent years, the image of pastor as spiritual guide for the
congregation and its members has faded. Although a narrow and
rigid interpretation of the pastor's role as spiritual guide can result
in stifling individual spiritual liberty and undermining the place of
the laity as providers of spiritual guidance and direction, to dismiss
completely the image and practice of pastoral spiritual guidance is
also to jettison a long tradition within pastoral care. If we were to
take the image of pastor as spiritual guide seriously, we would then
need to examine the qualifications for the office of pastor, and
include among them the aptitude, desire and ability to enter into
spiritual guidance.

[4] Susanne Johnson, *Christian Spiritual Formation*, discusses
the church as the ecology of Christian care and formation.

[5] Hopewell, *Congregation*, especially Chapters 1 and 7. Walter
Wink discusses this phenomenon as "the angel of the church" in
*Unmasking the Powers: The Invisible Forces that Determine Hu-
man Existence* (Philadelphia: Fortress, 1986).

[6] Gary Chamberlain, *Fostering Faith*, pp. 23–26, identifies
these three factors as essential components of all transitions from
one faith stage to the next.

[7] Hopewell, *Congregation*, pp. 113–14, holds that biblical stories *contend with* congregational self-characterizations. The kerygma does not void the alternate myths by which societies characterize themselves; rather it "gives them radical, critical, and finally redemptive meaning."

[8] Chamberlain, *Fostering Faith*, p. 24.

[9] Regis Duffy, *A Roman Catholic Theology of Pastoral Care* (Philadelphia: Fortress, 1983).

[10] The whole force of Belenky, et al., *Women's Ways of Knowing* illustrates the fate of women when deprived of their own voice.

[11] Loevinger, *Ego Development*, pp. 27–28.

[12] These categories imply Kohlberg's stages of moral decision-making as well as the more general issues of ego development. See Elizabeth Morgan with Van Weigel and Eric DeBaufre, *Global Poverty and Personal Responsibility: Integrity through Commitment* (New York: Paulist, 1989), pp. 7–21, for a discussion of these categories and further examples.

[13] Morgan, et al., *Global Poverty and Personal Responsibility*, p. 14.

[14] Mary Wilcox, *Developmental Journey: A Guide to the Development of Logical and Moral Reasoning and Social Perspective* (Nashville: Abingdon, 1979), pp. 221–23.

[15] Although James Hopewell analyzes congregational narratives in explicitly non-hierarchical and non-developmental categories, the *methods* he proposes, participant observation, guided interviews and carefully chosen tests and surveys, lend themselves to developmental interpretation. See *Congregation*, Ch. 6.

[16] Chamberlain, *Fostering Faith*, contains numerous suggestions for developmentally sensitive ministries.

[17] Synod of Bishops, "Justice in the World," 1971, in *Renewing the Earth*, ed. David J. O'Brien and Thomas A. Shannon (New York: Image Books, 1977), p. 391.

[18] Ronald Marstin, *Beyond Our Tribal Gods: The Maturing of Faith* (Maryknoll, N.Y.: Orbis, 1979), p. 110.

[19] Chamberlain, *Fostering Faith*, p. 172.

Chapter IX

[1] Erik Erikson made a similar claim from within a different conception of development in *Childhood and Society*.

[2] The boundaries for acceptable intimacies differ, depending upon the kind of relationship and the spoken and unspoken covenants in operation. However, in every case, the responsibility for

maintaining appropriate boundaries rests with the party which has the most power or authority in the relationship: parent, pastor, spiritual director. It is never ethically permissible to abdicate that responsibility to the other party.

[3] Belenky, et al., *Women's Ways of Knowing*, pp. 155–57.

[4] Belenky, et al., *Women's Ways of Knowing*, pp. 190–229.

[5] Belenky, et al., *Women's Ways of Knowing*, p. 226. Hopewell, *Congregation*, pp. 87–90 and the resources in note 4, p. 99, describes participant-observation methodology.

[6] See *Insight and Responsibility*, (New York: W. W. Norton, 1964), pp. 47–80.

[7] Belenky, et al., p. 194, attribute this phrase to Jerome Brunner in *The Process of Education* (Cambridge, MA: Harvard University Press, 1963), p. 52.

Chapter X

[1] See, for example, Lyn Mikel Brown and Carol Gilligan, *Meeting at the Crossroads: Women's Psychology and Girls' Development* (New York: Ballantine, 1992); James Fowler, *Weaving the New Creation: Stages of Faith and the Public Church* (San Francisco: Harper, 1991) and *Faithful Change: The Personal and Public Challenges of Postmodern Life* (Nashville: Abingdon, 1996); Nancy Goldberger, Jill Tarule, Blythe Clinchy and Mary Belenky, *Knowledge, Difference, and Power: Essays Inspired by Women's Ways of Knowing* (New York: Basic Books, 1996); Robert Kegan, *In Over Our Heads: The Mental Demands of Modern Life* (Cambridge: Harvard University Press, 1994); and Laurent Daloz, Cheryl Keen, James Keen and Sharon Parks, *Common Fire: Lives of Commitment in a Complex World* (Boston: Beacon Press, 1996). In addition, a significant theological work on human development has also appeared during this period: James Loder, *The Logic of the Spirit: Human Development in Theological Perspective* (San Francisco: Jossey-Bass, 1996). Daniel Levinson balanced his work on men's development with *Seasons of a Woman's Life* (New York: Knopf, 1996) during this period as well.

[2] Because this work primarily concerns human development as it impacts spiritual development, I did not attempt to review the literature on spiritual direction in the first edition, citing only those materials involving the definition and the theological grounding of my understanding of spiritual direction. However, for the second edition, I note major full-length treatments of spiritual direction that have appeared since the first edition was published. These include: Benedict Ashley, *Spiritual Direction in the Dominican Tradition*

(New York: Paulist, 1995); Peter Ball, *Anglican Spiritual Direction* (Cambridge: Cowley, 1999); Walter E. Conn, *The Desiring Self: Rooting Pastoral Counseling and Spiritual Direction in Self-Transcendence* (New York: Paulist, 1998); Maureen Conroy, *The Discerning Heart: Discovering a Personal God* (Chicago: Loyola University Press, 1993); Rose Mary Dougherty, *Group Spiritual Direction: Community for Discernment* (New York: Paulist, 1995); Julie M. Douglas, *Handbook for Spiritual Directors* (New York: Paulist, 1998); James Empereur, *The Enneagram and Spiritual Direction: Nine Paths to Spiritual Guidance* (New York: Continuum, 1997); James Empereur, *Spiritual Direction and the Gay Person* (New York: Continuum, 1998); Carolyn Gratton, *The Art of Spiritual Guidance: A Contemporary Approach to Growing in the Spirit* (New York: Crossroad, 1993); Margaret Guenther, *Holy Listening: The Art of Spiritual Direction* (Cambridge: Cowley, 1992); Frank Houdek, *Guided by the Spirit: A Jesuit Perspective on Spiritual Direction* (Chicago: Loyola Press, 1996); Wendy Miller, *Learning to Listen: A Guide for Spiritual Friends* (Nashville: Upper Room); Robert Morneau, *Spiritual Direction: Principles and Practice* (New York: Crossroad, 1992); Carol Ochs and Kerry M. Olitzsky, *Jewish Spiritual Guidance* (San Francisco: Jossey-Bass, 1997); and Barbara Sheehan, *Partners in Covenant: Art of Spiritual Companionship* (Cleveland: Pilgrim Press, 1999).

[3] Kegan, *In Over Our Heads*, pp. 1–11.

[4] Fowler, *Faithful Change*, p. 164.

[5] Fowler, *Weaving the New Creation*, pp. 151–62.

[6] Daloz, Keen, Keen and Parks, *Common Fire*, p. 107.

[7] Elizabeth Liebert, "The Thinking Heart: Developmental Dynamics in Etty Hillesum's Diaries," *Pastoral Psychology* 43 (July 1995): 393–409. See Etty Hillesum, *An Interrupted Life: The Diaries of Etty Hillesum, 1941-1943.* Ed and intro by J. G. Garlandt, trans by Arno Pomerans (New York: Pantheon Books, 1983).

[8] For further discussion of empathic imagination see Blythe McVicker Clinchy, "Connected and Separate Knowing: Toward a Marriage of Two Minds" in *Knowledge, Difference, and Power: Essays Inspired by Women's Ways of Knowing*, ed. Nancy Goldberger, Jill Tarule, Blythe Clinchy, and Mary Belenky (New York: Basic Books, 1996), pp. 205–247. "Connected knowing," as the authors of *Women's Ways of Knowing* call one of the epistemologies they noticed as they listened to women talk about the ways they "know," is in fact a form of empathic imagination. It is a respectful, compassionate and interested inquiry into other's experiences. See also other essays in *Knowledge, Difference and Power* on connected knowing.

[9] Douglas Huneke, *The Moses of Rovno* (Tiburon, CA: Compassion House, 1985), pp. 177–87.

[10] Daloz, Keen, Keen and Parks, p. 108.

[11] Elizabeth Liebert, "Seasons and Stages: Models and Metaphors of Human Development," in *In Her Own Time: Women and Development Issues in Pastoral Care*, ed. Jeanne Stevenson Moessner (Minneapolis: Augsburg Fortress, forthcoming).

[12] Fowler, *Faithful Change*, pp. 177–78.

[13] Fowler, *Weaving the New Creation*, pp. 151–62.

Appendix

List of Tables

Table 1: Approximate Correlations between Structural Developmental Theories

"Imaginary Planet"	Liebert, Changing Life Patterns	Loevinger, Ego Development	Kegan, Evolving Self
POE (Port of Entry)	Impulsive	Impulsive I–2	Impulsive
RAR (Rough and Ready)	Self-Protective	Self-Protective	Imperial
CON (Community of Neighbors)	Conformist	Confirmist I–3	Interpersonal
	Self-Aware	Conscientious-Conformist I–3/4	
SAG (Self as Guide)	Conscientious	Conscientious I–4	Institutional
	Individualistic	Individualistic I–4/5	
HOT (Help Others Too)	Interindividual	Autonomous I–5	Interindividual
BAT (Balance All Things)	Integrated	Integrated I–6	

Table 2: Some Milestones of Ego Development

Stage	Code	Impulse Control, Character Development	Interpersonal Style	Conscious Preoccupations	Cognitive Style
Presocial			Autistic		
Symbiotic			Symbiotic	Self vs. nonself	
Impulsive	I-1	Impulsive, fear of retaliation	Receiving, dependent, exploitative	Bodily feelings, especially sexual and aggressive	Stereotyping, conceptual confusion
Self-Protective	Δ	Fear of being caught, externalizing blame, opportunistic	Wary, manipulative, exploitative	Self-protection, trouble, wishes, things, advantage, control	
Conformist	I-3	Conformity to external rules, shame, guilt for breaking rules	Belonging, superficial niceness	Appearance, social acceptability, banal feelings, behavior	Conceptual simplicity, stereotypes, cliches
Conscientious-Conformist*	I-3/4	Differentiation of norms, goals	Aware of self in relation to group, helping	Adjustment, problems, reasons, opportunities (vague)	Multiplicity
Conscientious	I-4	Self-evaluated standards, self-criticism, guilt for consequences, long-term goals and ideals	Intensive, responsible, mutual, concern for communication	Differentiated feelings, motives for behavior, self-respect, achievements, traits, expression	Conceptual complexity, idea of patterning
Individualistic	I-4/5	Add: Respect for individuality	Add: Dependence as an emotional problem	Add: Development, social problems, differentiation of inner life from outer	Add: Distinction of process and outcome

(continued)

213

Table 2: Some Milestones of Ego Development (*Continued*)

Stage	Code	*Impulse Control, Character Development*	*Interpersonal Style*	*Conscious Preoccupations*	*Cognitive Style*
Autonomous	I-5	*Add:* Coping with conflicting inner needs, toleration	*Add:* Respect for autonomy, interdependence	Vividly conveyed feelings, integration of physiological and psychological, psychological causation of behavior, role conception, self-fulfillment, self in social context	Increased conceptual complexity, complex patterns, toleration for ambiguity, broad scope, objectivity
Integrated	I-6	*Add:* Reconciling inner conflicts, renunciation of unattainable	*Add:* Cherishing of individuality	*Add:* Identity	

NOTE: "*Add*" means in addition to the description applying to the previous level.
From: Loevinger, Jane. *Ego Development*, pp. 24–25. San Francisco, Jossey-Bass, 1976.
*Also called Self-Aware Level.

214

Table 3: Balances of Subject and Object as the Common Ground of Several Developmental Theories

	Stage 0 Incorporative	Stage 1 Impulsive	Stage 2 Imperial	Stage 3 Interpersonal	Stage 4 Institutional	Stage 5 Interindividual
Underlying structure (subject vs. object)	S–Reflexes, (sensing, moving) O–None	S–Impulses, perceptions O–Reflexes (sensing, moving)	S–Needs, interests, wishes O–Impulses, perceptions	S–The interpersonal, mutuality O–Needs, interests, wishes	S–Authorship, identity, psychic administration, ideology O–The interpersonal, mutuality	S–Interindividuality, interpenetrability of self-systems O–Authorship, identity, psychic administration, ideology
Piaget	Sensorimotor	Preoperational	Concrete operational	Early formal operational	Full formal operational	Post-formal Dialectical?
Kohlberg	—	Punishment and obedience orientation	Instrumental orientation	Interpersonal concordance orientation	Societal orientation	Principled orientation
Loevinger	Pre-social	Impulsive	Opportunistic*	Conformist	Conscientious	Autonomous
Maslow	Physiological survival orientation	Physiological satisfaction orientation	Safety orientation	Love, affection, belongingness orientation	Esteem and self-esteem orientation	Self-actualization
Erikson	—	Initiative vs. guilt	Industry vs. inferiority	Affiliation vs. abandonment?	Identity vs. identity diffusion	—

* In Loevinger's later work, this level is called Self-Protective.
Adapted from: Kegan, Robert. *The Evolving Self*, pp. 86–87. Cambridge, MA: Harvard University Press, 1982.

Table 4: Forms and Functions of Embeddedness Cultures

Evolutionary balance and psychological embeddedness	Culture of embeddedness	Function 1: Confirmation (holding on)	Function 2: Contradiction (letting go)	Function 3: Continuity (staying put for reintegration)	Some common natural transitional "subject-objects" (bridges)[a]
(0) INCORPORATIVE Embedded in: reflexes, sensing, and moving.	Mothering one(s) or primary caretaker(s). *Mothering culture.*	Literal holding: close physical presence, comfort and protecting. Eye contact. Recognizing the infant. Dependence upon and merger with oneself.	Recognizes and promotes toddler's emergence from embeddedness. Does not meet child's every need, stops nursing, reduces carrying, acknowledges displays of independence and willful refusal.	Permits self to become part of bigger culture, i.e., the family. High risk: prolonged separation from infant during transition period (6 mos.–2 yrs.).	Medium of 0–1 transition: *blankie, teddy,* etc. A soft, comforting, nurturant representative of undifferentiated subjectivity, at once evoking that state and "objectifying" it.
(1) IMPULSIVE Embedded in: impulse and perception.	Typically, the family triangle. *Parenting culture.*	Acknowledges and cultures exercises of fantasy, intense attachments, and rivalries.	Recognizes and promotes child's emergence from egocentric embeddedness in fantasy and impulse. Holds child responsible for his or her	Couple permits itself to become part of bigger culture, including school and peer relations. High risk: dissolution of marriage or	Medium of 1–2 transition: *imaginary friend.* A repository for impulses which before *were me,* and which eventually will be part of me, but

(2) IMPERIAL Embedded in: enduring disposition, needs, interests, wishes.	Role recognizing culture. School and family as institutions of authority and role differentiation. Peer gang which requires role-taking.	Acknowledges and cultures displays of self-sufficiency, competence, and role differentiation.	feelings, excludes from marriage, from parents' bed, from home during school day, recognizes child's self-sufficiency and asserts own "other sufficiency." Recognizes and promotes preadolescent's (or adolescent's) emergence from embeddedness in self-sufficiency. Denies the validity of only taking one's own interests into account, demands mutuality, that the person hold up his/her end of relationship. Expects trustworthiness.	family unit during transition period (roughly 5–7 yrs.). Family and school permit themselves to become secondary to relationships of shared internal experiences. High risk: family relocation during transition period (roughly early adolescence, 12–16).	here a little of each. E.g., only I can see it, but it is not me. Medium of 2–3 transition: chum. Another who is identical to me and real but whose needs and self-system are exactly like needs which before were me, eventually a part of me, but now something between.

(continued)

217

Table 4: Forms and Functions of Embeddedness Cultures (Continued)

Evolutionary balance and psychological embeddedness	Culture of embeddedness	Function 1: Confirmation (holding on)	Function 2: Contradiction (letting go)	Function 3: Continuity (staying put for reintegration)	Some common natural transitional "subject-objects" (bridges)[a]
(3) INTERPERSONAL Embedded in: mutuality, interpersonal concordance.	Mutually reciprocal one-to-one relationships. Culture of mutuality.	Acknowledges and cultures capacity for collaborative self-sacrifice in mutually attuned interpersonal relationships. Orients to internal state, shared subjective experience, "feelings," mood.	Recognizes and promotes late adolescent's or adult's emergence from embeddedness in interpersonalism. Person or context that will not be fused with but still seeks, and is interested in, association. Demands the person assume responsibility for own initiatives and preferences. Asserts the other's independence.	Interpersonal partners permit relationship to be relativized or placed in bigger context of ideology and psychological self-definition. High risk: interpersonal partners leave at very time one is emerging from embeddedness. (No easily supplied age norms.)	Medium for 3–4 transition: going away to college, a temporary job, the military. Opportunities for provisional identity which both leave the interpersonalist context behind and preserve it, intact, for return; a time-limited participation in institutional life (e.g. 4 years of college, a service hitch).

218

	Culture of (confirmation)	Acknowledges (contradiction)	Recognizes/promotes (continuity)	Medium of 4–5 transition
(4) INSTITUTIONAL Embedded in: personal autonomy, self-system identity.	*Culture of identity or self-authorship* (in love or work). Typically: group involvement in career, admission to public arena.	Acknowledges and cultures capacity for independence; self-definition; assumption of authority; exercise of personal enhancement, ambition or achievement; "career" rather than "job," "life partner" rather than "help-mate," etc.	Recognizes and promotes adult's emergence from embeddedness in independent self-definition. Will not accept mediated, non-intimate, form-subordinated relationship.	Ideological forms permit themselves to be relativized on behalf of the play between forms. High risk: ideological supports vanish (e.g., job loss) at very time one is separating from this embeddedness. (No easily supplied age norms.)	Medium of 4–5 transition: *ideological self-surrender (religious or political); love affairs protected by unavailability of the partner. At once a surrender of the identification with the form while preserving the form.*
(5) INTER-INDIVIDUAL Embedded in: interpenetration of systems.	*Culture of intimacy* (in domain of love and work). Typically: genuinely adult love relationship.	Acknowledges and cultures capacity for interdependence, for self-surrender and intimacy, for interdependent self-definition.		

a. In the construction of this column I am indebted to the thinking of Mauricia Alvarez.
From: Kegan, Robert. *The Evolving Self*, pp. 118–120. Cambridge, MA: Harvard University Press, 1982.

Table 5: Pastoral Assessment of Symbolic Communication

Stage of Ego Development (Liebert)	Spiritual Consciousness (Ivy)	Characteristic Criteria
PRESOCIAL	Stage 0:	Affective communication dominates. No narrative experience. Embedded consciousness in word of affect and image.
IMPULSIVE	Stage 1:	Magic, fantasy, and non-reflective affect. Little capacity for narrative. Consistency and comprehensiveness are irrelevant.
SELF-PROTECTIVE	Stage 2:	Predictability and non-reflective orthodoxy. Dramatic narratives in which identification with heroic images is primary. One-dimensional, literal consciousness with rigid requirements for consistency.
CONFORMIST	Stage 3:	Evocative symbols embedded in conventional, tacitly held meaning-systems. Authoritative narratives communicate existential values through limited abstraction and critical reflection. Conventional, multi-dimensional, undifferentiated consciousness with more attention to consistency.
SELF-AWARE	Stage 3–4:	Ideal translation of symbols to thought with powerful affective content. Narratives are critically measured by explicit values which are "over-against" the previous, tacit values. Idealizing, differentiated consciousness with focus on consistency with the ideal.
CONSCIENTIOUS	Stage 4:	Ideology and pragmatism within explicit meaning systems. Symbols are reduced to their ideational content. Narratives are critically measured by explicit, self-conscious experiences and values.

(continued)

Table 5: Pastoral Assessment of
Symbolic Communication (*Continued*)

Stage of Ego Development (Liebert)	Spiritual Consciousness (Ivy)	Characteristic Criteria
		Dialectical, multi-dimensional consciousness with focus on consistency.
INTERINDIVIDUAL	Stage 5:	Paradoxical joining of opposites (affect-cognition, symbol-idea) which allows multisystemic mediation.
		Narratives maintain tensions of self, groups and ultimate while relatively representing the ultimate.
		Multisystemic, paradoxical consciousness in which symbols evoke deeper reality of self and world.
		Comprehensiveness valued more than consistency.
INTEGRATED	Stage 6:	Unity beyond paradox joins symbols, self, and ultimate reality into a complex system.
		Narratives hold the tension and interpenetration between mundane and ultimate realities.
		Unifying consciousness in which direct awareness of and participation in "Oneness" transcends consistency and comprehensiveness.

Adapted from: Ivy, Steven. *The Structural-Developmental Theories of James Fowler and Robert Kegan as Resources for Pastoral Assessment*, pp. 147–48, Ph.D. dissertation, Southern Baptist Theological Seminary, 1985.

Table 6: Pastoral Assessment of Self-Other Perspective

Stage of Ego Development (Liebert)	Spiritual Consciousness (Ivy)	Characteristic Criteria
PRESOCIAL	Stage 0:	Mothering culture. Attachment with little differentiation. Affective embeddedness within family.
IMPULSIVE	Stage 1:	Parenting and family culture. Attachment with growing sense of will. Unreflective identity with visible signs of power and family; e.g., sex, ethnic, size, impulses.
SELF-PROTECTIVE	Stage 2:	Peer culture; those like me. Autonomy, role differentiation, and competence. Personal relatedness, cooperation, and stereotypical images. Traditional meanings.
CONFORMIST	Stage 3:	Mutual, interpersonal, tacitly valued groups and persons. Attachment and belonging with those whose commitments are similar. A derived identity of subjectively shared experiences and feelings. Leads to hierarchy of compartmentalizing of values.
SELF-AWARE	Stage 3–4:	Mutual, interpersonal, explicitly valued groups and persons. Attachment and belonging with those whose commitments are similar. A derived identity of shared ideals in which authoritative

(continued)

Table 6: Pastoral Assessment of Self-Other Perspective (*Continued*)

Stage of Ego Development *(Liebert)*	Spiritual Consciousness *(Ivy)*	Characteristic Criteria
		leaders are validated by the individual.
CONSCIENTIOUS	Stage 4:	Self-authorship and self-selected culture.
		Autonomy yet shares intimacy with those who share norms.
		Internalized identity and authority with encouragement for achievement and choice that is self-congruent.
INTERINDIVIDUAL	Stage 5:	Intimacy within interdependent and complex cultures.
		Attachment and autonomy dialectically joined for interdependent self-definition.
		Paradoxical quality which joins personal experience and reflection on others' experiences in search for love and justice.
INTEGRATED	Stage 6:	Intimacy with universal community of persons and Being.
		Attachment and autonomy transended for sense of at-one-ness.
		Compassionate identification with universal principles linked through purified ego and disciplined intuition with ultimate ground of being.

Adapted from: Ivy, Steven. *The Structural-Developmental Theories of James Fowler and Robert Kegan as Resources for Pastoral Assessment*, pp. 150–51. Ph.D. dissertation, Southern Baptist Theological Seminary, 1985.

Table 7: Delineation of Stage Specific Pastoral Care

Stage of Ego Development (Liebert)	Spiritual Consciousness (Ivy)	Adaptive Pastoral Care
PRESOCIAL	Pleasure	Support and encourage investment and dedication on part of parents. Provide predictability, comfort, and pleasurable involvement when in presence.
IMPULSIVE	Magical	Support and encourage family to provide tolerant yet firm boundaries for autonomy and will. Provide symbols and fantasy experiences which help organize diverse action and feeling levels in light of real limits. Use stories to externalize both fear and trust in such a way as to decrease sense of vulnerability.
SELF-PROTECTIVE	Literalizing	Support assertiveness and competence in peer culture. Tell and provide dramatic stories in which heroes demonstrate difference between good and evil. Gospel is presented as a trustable promise. Expect traditional responses, nurture sense of fairness, and provide emotional intimacy.
CONFORMIST	Interpersonal	Support engagement in peer groups and attachment with those who are similar to the person. Provide authoritative, multi-dimensional perspective with affirmation of tacit acceptance of values. Because of other-directedness of expectations and tacit quality of belief, independent answers are unlikely. Watch for dichotomizing between authorities. Gospel as acceptance and guide.

224

Table 7: Delineation of Stage Specific Pastoral Care (*Continued*)

Stage of Ego Development (Liebert)	Spiritual Consciousness (Ivy)	Adaptive Pastoral Care
SELF-AWARE	Idealizing	Support development of self-identity. Use idealization of critically accepted values. Provide clear statement of ideals with possibility of rejection. Engage in critical consideration of previous tacit values in context of those who share values. Attend to dynamics or marital and vocational choices. Challenge too easy acceptance of dominant myths.
CONSCIENTIOUS	Reflective	Support explicit, self-conscious reflection on values and self in relation to self-authority and ultimate meaning. Balance ideal and pragmatic in support of self-definition. Evaluate direction of marriage and vocation. Articulate acceptance of personal myth and reflection upon adaptive involvements.
INTERINDIVIDUAL	Integrative	Support both coping with inner needs and toleration of needs of others. Evaluate and interpret previous ideology. Examine deeper and more holistic ways of knowing. Encourage search for love and justice through self-surrender. Support complex, multi-systemic self-definition.
INTEGRATIVE	Unitive	Support mediation of master myths with commitment to present fulfillment. Nurture dreaming and prospective symbols which give the future living meaning in the present. Allow relativization of ideology and support universal compassion.

Adapted from: Ivy, Steven. *The Structural-Developmental Theories of James Fowler and Robert Kegan as Resources for Pastoral Assessment*, pp. 161–62. Ph.D. dissertation, Southern Baptist Theological Seminary, 1985.

225